DReam
WISDom

DReam WISDOM

Uncovering Life's Answers in Your Dreams

Alan B. Siegel, Ph.D.

ceLestiaL aRts
BeRkeLey/toRonto

First published as *Dreams That Can Change Your Life,* in 1990, by Jeremy P. Tarcher, Inc., Los Angeles, California.

Celestial Arts
P.O. Box 7123
Berkeley, California 94707
www.tenspeed.com

Distributed in Australia by Simon and Schuster Australia, in Canada by Ten Speed Press Canada, in New Zealand by Southern Publishers Group, in South Africa by Real Books, in Southeast Asia by Berkeley Books, and in the United Kingdom and Europe by Airlift Book Company.

Cover design by Toni Tajima
Book design by Betsy Stromberg

Library of Congress Cataloging-in-Publication Data

Siegel, Alan B.
    Dream wisdom: uncovering life's answers in your dreams/Alan B. Siegel.
      p. cm.
    ISBN 1-58761-158-9
    1. Dreams. 2. Dream interpretation. I. Title.

  BF1091 S.555 2003
  154.6'3—dc21

                                                          2002074122

First printing, 2002
Printed in the United States of America

1 2 3 4 5 6 7 8 9 10 — 06 05 04 03 02

contents

foreword

Since time immemorial, the great cultural myths of native people have served several functions. They have explained the world's creation and the workings of nature. They have forged a connection between a community of human beings and the realm of spirits. They also have provided a society's framework for work, play, and human relationships, establishing behavior patterns based on age, gender, and social class. Cultural mythologies have also assisted community members during times of developmental passage—birth, coming of age, marriage, having children, coping with illness and death.

For example, there are three wedding ceremonies among the Filipino Bisayasi. In the first, the future groom announces his intentions; in the second, the extended family gives its blessings at a wedding feast; in the third, vows are exchanged. There are mythic antecedents for each of these events.

In West Africa, a father raises his newborn child into the air so the universe can take note of its newest inhabitant. In many Native American tribal groups, adolescents embark on "vision quests" to discover their secret name, totem animal, or curing song. Among some mountain tribes of Southeast Asia, older community members are given the responsibility of initiating young people into the joys of sexuality.

Voodoo devotees in Haiti worship Baron Samedi, the lord of sex and death, portraying his skull-like countenance in paintings, dances, and carved masks. Elaborate funeral rituals characterize the Tanya Toraja tribe of Indonesia. The tribe provides a special home for the corpse while the family raises the money for a proper funeral—a task that might take years. Until then, the deceased individual is not considered "dead," only "sleeping"; children take turns keeping the corpse company until the rituals can be observed.

Among hunting and gathering groups, shamans were the custodians of tribal myths. They took this role seriously, as they sang, danced, and acted out the tales and legends of gods and goddesses, heroes and villains, lovers and warriors. Shamanic practitioners were allowed considerable latitude to be creative, especially when treating illnesses, locating game, protecting the tribe from danger, or interpreting dreams.

Today, in our technological age, various mythologies have competed for individual and group allegiances. Some individuals, bewildered by the plethora of beliefs, doctrines, and admonitions that exist in their societies, simply withdraw from the fray, allowing whim or habit to govern their moral choices or to settle internal conflicts when critical life decisions need to be made. Others fall back on the faith of their ancestors or jump on the band-wagon of the most charismatic cult leader who passes their way.

Nevertheless, another option is available. Each of us has what my colleague David Feinstein and I refer to as an "inner shaman," who is able to create a personal mythology that represents the most profound wisdom we are capable of mustering for dealing with the turning points of our exis-tence. Myths, both cultural and personal, are imaginal statements or stories that address the core issues of our lives, influencing our daily behavior and decision making. Personal myths reflect what we have learned from our bodies, our cultures, our interpersonal encounters, and our spiritual experi-ences. Sometimes these myths are dysfunctional (as when we mutter, "I can never do anything right" or "Everyone is against me"), but they can also empower us (as when we tell ourselves, "I will put my best effort into this task" or "I cannot expect perfection from myself or from those I love"). Largely unconscious, these mythic statements and stories have filled the gap created by the disintegration of the monolithic cultural mythologies that gave direction to social groups for millennia—and that still affect the behavior of the few native societies that attempt to maintain their traditions in isolated areas throughout the globe.

Our dreams can give us the most direct access to our much-needed personal myths. Four, five, or six times each night, our lower brains initiate a random firing of nerve cells, probably in an attempt to provide some sort of neurological equilibrium during sleep. These nerve cells stimulate the higher brain, or cortex, evoking images and memories—most of them visual or kinesthetic. To make sense of these images, the brain weaves them together into a narrative, and in many cases, this narrative is one of the ready-made myths that have gradually coalesced in our unconscious over the years. When the randomly evoked images trigger a mythic framework that begins to integrate them into a meaningful narrative, that particular myth usually is reinforced and bolstered. And when we recall a dream of this nature, it can yield a valuable insight into the inner working of our minds. It can, for example, point out how a personal myth has outlived its usefulness. It can portray how current myths can help us solve problems. And it can assist our detection of emerging myths that might serve us in the future.

Alan Siegel has worked with these narrative types of dreams for many years, finding them a critically important personal resource. He has been able to decode the metaphors and symbols in these dreams, discovering that they were not necessarily disguises but a remarkably cogent way to represent life's conflicts and possible solutions. By respecting a dream's narrative quality, Dr. Siegel has been able to elucidate a dream's content and message. Dr. Siegel has also read widely about cultural myths and about Native American vision quests, integrating this material into his dream workshops and classes.

Although Freudian and Jungian approaches to dreams differ, Dr. Siegel has been instructed by both of these great psychoanalytic pioneers, both of whom read widely on the topic of cultural myths, the results of which can be found in the essence of their work. However, Dr. Siegel departs from the psychoanalysts in a vital way: he endorses carefully focused do-it-yourself dream work as well as leaderless dream groups, which rely on mutual respect and common sense to illuminate dreams.

This book is unique in that it focuses on "turning point" dreams, those dreams with life-changing potential. Unlike native cultures, modern societies have few meaningful rites of passage. However, according to eminent mythologist Joseph Campbell, facilitating developmental transitions is a key function of cultural mythologies, as can be seen in the three-stage wedding ceremonies of the Bisayasi.

Like the instructions given in the books of the dead common in many cultures, this is a "book for the living," describing ways in which mythic dreams can identify turning points in one's life, such as midlife "crises," menopause, and fears of death. Dr. Siegel shows how these dreams can galvanize one's personal potentials in coping with misfortune and taking advantage of opportunity. And just as cultural myths once provided the template for courtship and marriage, personal myths—as revealed by Dr. Siegel's dreamers—show how our feelings regarding intimate relationships can emerge from dreams, guiding the interpersonal transition at hand.

Each cultural mythology had its unique interpretation of conception, pregnancy, and childbirth; personal myths about these events also differ dramatically, as illustrated by Dr. Siegel. Yet each set of dreams paints a vivid portrait of the dreamer, just as each set of myths bears the stamp of the tribe that lived out its dictates. To assign a dead body to its own room would be laughed at in a society where space is at a premium.

Cultural mythologies assist—and often mandate—vocational pathways; dysfunctional personal myths can be just as inflexible as the caste system that assigns "untouchables" and their descendants to menial work. These dictatorial myths can bind people to inappropriate careers or to unsatisfying jobs because "Your family has always put its life into this business" or "You have a family to support and cannot risk failure." But breakthrough dreams can reveal alternative myths and job choices that are more appropriate to the dreamer. Dr. Siegel's detailed suggestions on exploring and even "incubating" career dreams will be both revelatory and practical for many readers. Working with a series of dreams rather than only a solitary dream can be especially pertinent in exploring our relationships with employers, employees, or with a job itself.

Some neuroscientists and psychotherapists still take the position that dream content is without significant meaning or that dream material is better forgotten. These debunkers should read the stirring accounts of how nightmares often reflect posttraumatic stress, and how, if skillfully explored and worked through, they can help resolve trauma.

I suspect that dreams often help us rehearse future behavior, sort out our day-by-day memories, and make sense of our ongoing experiences, whether we recall them or not. I believe that dreams can be even more effective if we give them the attention that they deserve. In *Dream Wisdom,* Dr. Siegel has provided an excellent guide for those who are able to accept this challenge.

I have a final, quite personal reaction to this brilliantly conceived book. Dr. Siegel gives credit to the late Gordon Tappan of Sonoma State University for stimulating and mentoring his original work with dream rituals. Professor Tappan was one of our first doctoral students at Saybrook Institute; his decision to complete his doctoral work with us helped give our neophyte graduate school valuable support and credibility during its early years. Professor Tappan touched the lives of many students, profoundly affecting the course of their development. In many ways, this book is a tribute to his sensitivity and his genius.

Stanley Krippner, Ph.D.
Alan Watts Professor of Psychology, Saybrook Institute

acknowLeDgments

First and foremost, my gratitude goes to the many adults and children who contributed their time and dreams. Their stories were a continuing source of inspiration.

The consummate editorial skills of Alan Rinzler were crucial to the completion of the first edition of this book. Peter Beren helped me launch the book and develop my concepts and assisted in this revised and updated edition. The guidance of Windy Ferges was invaluable to me in completing *Dream Wisdom*.

I want to offer a special note of thanks to my colleagues who generously shared their research and clinical expertise with me: Adrienne Aron on the dreams of Central American political refugees, Barbara Baer and Karen Muller for collaboration on the Oakland Firestorm nightmare research, Kelly Bulkeley for his collaboration and insights on children's dreams, Kuuipo Ordway for the dreams of the survivors of the World Trade Center, Jane Hawes on earthquake victims, John Prendergast on the dreams of people with serious illness and those facing death, and Dale Westbrook on premarital dreams. Thanks also go to experts in the field of dream studies who inspired my thinking and whose work I drew heavily upon. These include Deirdre Barrett, Rosalind Cartwright, Bill Domhoff, Harry Fiss, Patricia Garfield, Ernest Hartmann, Stan Krippner, Gordon Tappan, Jeremy Taylor, Montague Ullman, and Harry Wilmer.

For their editorial assistance on this edition, I want to thank Saul Rosenberg; Rosemary McBride; Rae Oser; and Bob, Perle, and Jerry Siegel. For other contributions and consultation, thanks also go to David Donner, Adam Duhan, Mary Ford, Patrick Gannon, Robert Lewis, Bart Ostro, and Gary Stolzoff.

I want to thank my colleagues and friends from the Association for the Study of Dreams who have provided mentorship and intellectual inspiration, encouragement for my writing and teaching, friendship and personal support, and an international family of dream explorers.

Finally I want to thank my family for their love and encouragement: my mother and father, Perle and Jerry Siegel; my mother-in-law and father-in-law, Mae and Sam Green; and my daughters, Zoe and Sophia, for giving my life a wonderful new dimension. And a special thanks to Masako Davenport for her continuing help and support to my family. Most of all, I want to thank my wife, Tracy, for editorial and emotional support beyond the call of duty and for dreaming with me through all our important turning points.

INTRODUCTION

This book will show you how to use dreams to resolve crucial turning points in your life. It's based on the ways I've used dreams in my life, during twenty-five years of experience using dreams as a psychotherapist and dream researcher, and in personal and professional dream workshops and courses I have taught for thousands of people of all ages and backgrounds.

Inspired by undergraduate courses on Freud and Jung at Johns Hopkins University, I began a daily dream journal in 1971. After some time I noticed remarkable patterns in the symbolism of my dreams. Without any conscious attempt to control or shape them, I experienced recurring images of certain people, places, and events.

During the first year of keeping my dream journal, I had repetitive vivid dreams about the two houses I had lived in as a child. Almost every week I made a dream pilgrimage back to my old neighborhood, to my family's home and the room I shared with my brother before I was ten years old. Sometimes the house would be remodeled. Other times I would see the old carpet and furniture and wait for the wind to cool me as it did on hot Florida nights in the mid-1950s.

Having these nostalgic dreams about my childhood home while I was in my sophomore year of college showed me that I was more connected to my parents than I had imagined in my nineteen-year-old fantasies of being an independent adult. The dreams made me more aware of the difficulty I was having in striking off on my own. Being able to acknowledge the strength of my lingering emotional ties helped me to be more realistic in my quest to develop my own adult identity. Decades later I still have Childhood Home dreams which occur when issues related to my family or growing up are triggered by events and relationships in my current life.

During the early period of keeping my dream journal, I also had a puzzling dream series involving plane crashes. In these Plane Crash dreams I would see an airplane and know that it was about to crash. I would watch helplessly as the plane lost altitude and went down in flames. These dreams were so vivid and recurred so many times that I was tempted to take them literally. I wondered whether the dreams were an omen that I should give up flying. For a while, I even became convinced that I would witness a real plane crash.

I began to document many associations to these dreams in my journal. I had suffered from a mild fear of flying in the past. My father and uncle had both been fascinated by planes and were pilots when I was a child. I had read voraciously about the early development of the space program. When I was seventeen, I'd been on a plane that was hijacked to Cuba and then quickly returned.

This dream series had more than one meaning for me. As I documented my life events surrounding the plane crash dreams, it became clear that they were not literally about planes. They were a metaphor for stressful events and periods in my life. They occurred when I was becoming too frantic, working too hard, or making too many commitments. Linking the plane crash dreams with upsetting times in my life helped me see that the dreams were warning me of an emotional imbalance. They were telling me that I was "flying too high"—that if I didn't slow down, I was risking a fiery crash back to earth.

In the ensuing years, my plane crash dreams became much more infrequent. Even after the horrific hijackings and plane crashes on September 11, 2001, these dreams did not return as many of my related issues have been resolved or expressed through other dream metaphors. However, for many people worldwide, Plane Crash dreams have become more common. They represent actual fears about terrorism and flying as well as metaphors that may reflect periods of emotional distress in our world and in our families and cultures.

How I Learned to Use My Turning-Point Dreams

As more of my dream journals filled my shelf, I began to observe themes and symbols that were closely related to disturbing events and personal crises in my life. Shortly after moving into my first off-campus apartment as a sophomore in college, I came home to discover that I had been robbed. I had been warned that the neighborhood was not safe, but I had ignored the warnings. That night I had a terrible dream.

SNAKE IN PARADISE

I am near my hometown in Florida, walking near a citrus grove. I see a lawyer reading a book called *Lawyer Talk*. I assume there are law offices nearby. I go over to a tree, pick some oranges, but I get tangled in the branches and stuck by thorns. I can't get untangled. I fall down. There is a thin green rope next to me. I think it's a snake but assume it's harmless. The lawyer somehow communicates to me that the snakes in that area are extremely dangerous. Terrified, I try frantically to untangle myself. The rope now looks like an arrow-headed poisonous snake. I toss violently as I wake up.

I sketched the snake and the clutching arms of the thorny orange tree. The image of the snake fascinated and terrified me. In my journal, I spent a considerable amount of time writing down feelings and memories that were inspired by the dream.

As I pictured the snake, I realized that this was not my first Snake dream. The very first dream I can remember was a nightmare I had several times when I was four and five years old.

PLEASING THE SNAKE

I am submerged and swimming peacefully in sea vegetation. A water snake begins to stalk me, and I am scared to death. Panic-stricken, I try to flee, but I am trapped and forced to face the vicious snake. My panic grows to hysterical proportions. I think, "How can it do this to me?" I will do anything to escape death. Suddenly I try to win it over and offer to be friends. I will do what it wants if it will spare me.[1]

The serpents in my dream were terrifying. For me, Snake dreams seemed to represent a primal sense of danger and vulnerability, a powerful force that could threaten or destroy me. I knew from my studies that threatening animals, monsters, and creatures are especially common in children's dreams[2] (a more extended discussion of creature threat dreams is in chapter 2). But why were my dreams choosing the snake as a symbol for the dangerous or vulnerable times in my life? Like the Plane Crash dreams, the Snake dreams responded directly to events in my life. Observing the clear linkages helped me understand the threatening snakes in my dreams. They were alerting me to vulnerable feelings in a particular situation or relationship. I continued to have Snake dreams periodically: after a car accident, and during stressful periods in my life. They continue to serve as a warning from my unconscious when I am facing an impasse in resolving a turning point.

Dreams also helped me come to terms with feelings of grief over the loss of my grandfather. Immediately following his death, I had a series of dreams that portrayed the stages of my mourning. In the first dreams, he appeared just as I remembered him before his death from stomach cancer: gaunt and obviously mortally ill. In these dreams, I was worried about him and tried to talk with him. Either he would not be very communicative or the dream would end before I could talk to him. The painful quality of these dreams made me realize that I still had strong feelings of loss that were unresolved, and reflecting on the dreams helped me to clarify important aspects of my relationship with my grandfather. As I worked through my grief, those dreams became less frequent.

About a year after my grandfather's death, I had a Grief Resolution dream (see chapter 10 for more details on grief dreams) that made it clear to me that I'd reached a breakthrough in my grieving.

IN THE ORANGE GROVE WITH MY GRANDFATHER

I am walking in an orange grove and talking to my grandfather. There are many ripe oranges on the trees, and the grass and trees seem very green. My grandfather is talking with me and giving me some advice about my career, encouraging me to finish school or to pursue something. He seems rotund and healthy, and I am surprised that he is alive, but somehow it makes sense.

In this fertile orange grove, my grandfather was acting like a mentor, giving me advice and encouragement as he did when he was alive. He'd been restored to a healthy appearance and no longer appeared gaunt or cancer-stricken. This image was devoid of the upsetting feelings of loss that had plagued me consciously and in my earlier dreams. This Inner Mentor dream and others like it allowed me to see that I had reached a stage where the most painful mourning was over. I was no longer preoccupied with his illness and death and was more focused on remembering the positive qualities that he gave to me while he was alive. Inner Mentor dreams portray characters such as doctors, clergy, respected elders, shamans, and healers that offer advice, guidance, or a reassuring presence. They also represent the inner wisdom of the dreamer, which we draw from our own experiences and ideals as well as from wisdom we have gained from mentors in our life.

Twenty-five years after his death, I still have occasional dreams with images of my grandfather, and of my grandmother who died in the 1990s. These dreams are no longer painful and often stimulate positive memories of key aspects of my relationships with them. Observing and exploring grief dreams has helped me and my psychotherapy patients recover from painful losses and progress to a point where the continuing dreams allow us to cherish memories of those we love.

How I Used My Dreams to Resolve a Career Turning Point

In my early twenties, I searched for explanations that would clarify the striking patterns in the dreams I had at turning points. Through undergraduate course work, I encountered the writings of the renowned Swiss psychiatrist Carl Jung. Jung had observed that critical turning points often were accompanied by exceptionally vivid dreams that seemed to have universal themes. He called these Archetypal or Big dreams.[3] Inspired also by mythologist Joseph Campbell,[4] and religious studies scholar Mircea Eliade,[5] I studied how shamans and healers in other cultures utilized dreams and visions at turning points in the life cycle. I discovered that throughout recorded history, dreams have been a part of spiritual and healing practices and have been viewed as critically important during life transitions.

I became eager to use my own dreams to resolve a major life dilemma of my early twenties: the choice of a career. I was in a graduate program in psychology and working in a psychiatric halfway house, but I wasn't sure that I wanted to embark on the arduous training involved in a doctoral program in psychology. I longed for a career vision that would inspire me. With my professor and graduate advisor, the late Gordon Tappan, as my guide, I created a dream ritual based upon healing ceremonies practiced in hundreds of dream incubation temples in ancient Greece.[6] I also drew inspiration from the vision quest of the Plains Indians of North America, who sent their teenage sons into the wilderness to seek a dream that would give them a path in life.[7] Such Career Vision dreams often defined a young man's adult role in the tribe as a hunter, warrior, healer, or leader.[8]

Sleeping alone in a grove of redwoods in the California coastal hills, I had a series of dreams that announced a significant turning point in my life. In the dreams, I faced my self-doubt and fears of growing up, of making adult commitments. From the depths of my fearful dreams of failure and emptiness came a vivid dream of tall, carved totem poles.

SACRED TOTEM POLES

There is a foolish man working for my guide. I wake up in the dream, and suddenly the man has carved the redwoods into intricate lattice designs that stretched upward to an unreachable height. I am amazed. Previously my guide didn't think this man was competent, yet now he has done this beautiful work. I think I can do the same. My guide leaves, and I fall back to sleep and envision each post as a totem pole. The one closest to me has especially vivid-colored faces.

Exploring this and other Career Vision dreams that I had in the redwoods helped me find a reservoir of confidence and decisiveness to counter my self-doubt. I began to gain a clearer picture of what I wanted to offer others in my career as a psychologist and teacher. In the Sacred Totem Poles dream, my guide had doubted that the foolish man was capable of creating those beautiful poles, just as in my life, I had imagined others were judging me as incapable of carving out my own artistic and professional vision.[9]

These dreams didn't erase my self-doubt, but they did help me move more decisively forward in my career and resolve long-standing tendencies toward harsh self-judgment. (See chapter 6 for more examples and discussion of Career Vision dreams.)

How I Helped Others Learn to Use Their Turning-Point Dreams

Since beginning my work as a psychotherapist in 1974, I have observed unique patterns in my clients' turning-point dreams. As clinical director of a psychiatric halfway house, I heard reports from schizophrenic clients about their terrifying nightmares just prior to their descent into psychosis.[10] While working with underprivileged urban teens, I observed that those who had suffered abuse had repetitive and excruciating Creature Threat nightmares of monsters chasing them. Being fluent in Spanish, I worked with immigrants from Latin America and learned of their recurring Journey dreams of returning to their homeland and their roots, reflecting their struggle to adjust in a new and bewildering culture.

I began to conduct dream-sharing groups. In addition, I taught courses and workshops on dreams through community colleges and privately.[11] Many of the individuals who took my courses and workshops were undergoing life transitions and were troubled as well as inspired by vivid dreams and nightmares. Because of my interest in dreams, many colleagues and friends also shared with me important dreams that they experienced during life passages.

As I became aware of the amazing patterns in the dreams of people undergoing life transitions, I focused my courses on the healing power of dreams and their potential for resolving the emotional dilemmas of life passages and crises. I experimented with different specialized dream groups, including groups for expectant parents and groups for teens with learning and behavior problems.

In the expectant parents groups, almost every participant had Anticipatory Anxiety dreams about their baby having birth defects, about the sex of their baby, and about birthing kittens, puppies, or other furry mammals, and they had dreams in which their baby could precociously walk and talk. Many had dreams about neglecting to feed or care for their babies. Surprisingly, quite a few men had as many or more pregnancy-related dreams as their wives.

Discussing these Anticipatory Anxiety dreams during pregnancy allowed the expectant parents to acknowledge their fears and to feel more secure in the knowledge that their anxieties were shared by couples experiencing a similar transition. Anticipatory Anxiety dreams exaggerate and distort our fears and doubts and thus prepare us for important life changes by rehearsing worst-case scenarios and keeping us vigilant. Exploring the symbolism of the dreams was somehow safer and more rewarding than directly discussing a troubling issue, such as their doubts about whether they would be competent or nurturing parents. The exciting response of the expectant parents dream groups led me to initiate the first formal research on the dreams of expectant fathers. For many more details on the dreams of expectant mothers and fathers, see chapter 4.

In the 1970s I began a series of wilderness therapy workshops, which I called Dream Quests, inspired by my own use of dream incubation to resolve an impasse at an important life passage. Dream incubation is a modern version of an ancient Greek medical practice that sought to induce dreams that would heal physical or emotional ailments or find solutions to life problems. The workshops I designed combined individual and group dream exploration techniques with a structured wilderness backpacking journey. On different trips, I took inner city youth, psychiatric halfway-house patients, and community college students from Vista College in Berkeley, California.

In 1984, I presented my work on the Dream Quest workshops at the first international conference of the Association for the Study of Dreams (ASD).[12] Eventually, I became more involved with ASD and served as editor-in-chief of the ASD Magazine, *Dream Time,* for nine years and as president of ASD in 1999. My active participation with ASD has allowed me to get to know the principal researchers, authors, and teachers in the field of dream studies as well as teachers, artists, anthropologists, and people from all over the world who share a passionate interest in dreams and belong to ASD.

On my fortieth birthday in 1991, while returning home from a morning picnic at the ocean, I saw a huge inferno engulfing the Berkeley and Oakland hills. In the aftermath of the Oakland Firestorm, which killed twenty-five and displaced five thousand people, I initiated research on the dreams and nightmares of the survivors.[13] Using two-week dream journals, in-depth interviews, and scientific analysis of the dream content, we found that those who lost their homes and those who nearly lost homes suffered devastating nightmares. The nightmares dealt with their emotional trauma and financial losses in the fire, but many also had dreams that evoked troubling emotional wounds from the past such as grief, divorce, abuse, and other traumatic memories. The firestorm survivors reported that keeping a journal and sharing their dreams helped unburden the pain from their nightmares and gave them both insight and hope in the dark days after the fire. The dream experiences of these Firestorm survivors are described in chapter 8.

Over the last ten years, I have evaluated and treated many children with emotional, learning, and attention problems. In addition, I have explored dreams with my own daughters and their friends and schoolmates and have looked more systematically at the patterns and potential of children's dreams. I led dream workshops for children of all ages from preschool through college and saw many patterns similar to the turning-point dreams of adults.

Children of divorce dreamed of being left out or abandoned—themes very similar to adults' divorce dreams. Like adults, children's Left-Out dreams went through an evolution. Gradually, they appeared to master or overcome metaphors for their distress in a series of less and less disturbing dreams. My work with children's turning-point dreams is described in chapter 2 and in my subsequent book, *Dreamcatching: Every Parent's Guide to Exploring and Understanding Children's Dreams and Nightmares,* which was coauthored with my colleague, Kelly Bulkeley, Ph.D.[14]

In the aftermath of the events of September 11, 2001, we witnessed an epidemic of nightmares as people in the United States and other parts of the world were traumatized by the tragic attacks, which were accompanied by incessant replaying of footage of the planes colliding with the World Trade Center buildings, people jumping, and the collapsing of the buildings into rubble. Not just in lower Manhattan, but all over the world, people were deeply troubled by recurring nightmares related to the attacks and the ensuing war. As part of the international effort to heal the wounds of trauma, I worked with my colleagues at the Association for the Study of Dreams, where we created a nightmare education page (www.asdreams.org/nightmares.htm), a nightmare hotline, and special track for our 2002 international dreaming conference in Boston.[15] Because of my expertise on turning-point dreams and nightmares, I was interviewed extensively by the media to provide information and reassurance on the nature of posttraumatic nightmares. Viewers from all over the world emailed nightmares about planes crashing and being trapped in buildings. Many of the nightmares seemed to tap general insecurities and past traumas that were coming to the surface. I describe nightmares related to September 11 and other crises and disasters in chapter 8.

For over twenty years, I have conducted professional training seminars for psychotherapists, health professionals, and graduate students in psychology on how to employ dreams to help clients resolve the emotional dilemmas of life transitions and on general techniques for using dreams in psychotherapy and healing. I served for many years as continuing education chair for the Association for the Study of Dreams and have sponsored research on dreams and life transitions by serving on dissertation committees of graduate students at Alliant University's California School of Professional Psychology.

Throughout my work, the most effective means for insight and understanding has proved to be an individual's in-depth exploration of his or her own dreams. It is a continual source of professional inspiration to see my clients, students, and colleagues learn how to explore and derive deeper meaning from their dreams.

Dreams in Psychotherapy and Personal Growth

This book is a guide to the healing power of dreams as a source of inner guidance and creative change during turning points. Its perspective is complementary to the pioneering insights of Sigmund Freud and C. G. Jung and to more contemporary research and clinical theories and techniques for exploring the meaning and creative potential of dreams.

Freud emphasized the distinction between the manifest content and the latent content of dreams. According to Freud, the manifest or apparent content was a sophisticated camouflage for deeper instincts or wishes that caused anxiety or conflict and thus had to be disguised.[16] Although Freud emphasized sexual or aggressive wishes, contemporary proponents of psychoanalysis have embraced the importance of a dream's manifest content and have questioned the idea that dreams have one specific latent content or bottom-line interpretation. Rather, there are numerous latent or hidden meanings—a collage of possibilities that can only be helpful when explored in a relationship with a psychotherapist trained in working with dreams.[17]

Contemporary schools of psychotherapy have built on the breakthroughs of Freud and Jung and have branched out in many fruitful directions. Existential and humanistic psychotherapists have reminded us of the importance of working with the experience of the dream and the personal growth potential of dreams for integrating our personalities. Transpersonal and Jungian theories promote the use of dreams to connect the dreamer with mystical and spiritual awareness, and the universal themes in dreams. Cultural and anthropological approaches have underscored the value of using dreams to understand identity and acculturation issues and the differences in how cultures value and interpret dream symbolism. Cognitive strategies for dream interpretation have emphasized the need to resolve nightmares and use dreams to gain insights and make practical life changes.

From the fertile ground of the developing humanistic and transpersonal psychology movements in the late 1960s and 1970s came the blossoming of interest in individual and group exploration of dreams as an adjunct to psychotherapy and as a self-directed quest for meaning and inspiration. Self-help books on dreams by Patricia Garfield,[18] Ann Faraday,[19] and others became best-sellers, and artists, educators, clergy, and those seeking self-awareness began to experiment with exploring dreams through keeping journals, creative writing, and the expressive arts. Innovative techniques such as dream groups, dream incubation, experiential techniques, and lucid dreaming gained prominence in the 1980s and 1990s. Educators, scientists, and businesspeople have used dreams for problem solving and inspiration.[20]

Using Dreams to Resolve Your Own Turning Points

A turning point or period of stress is an ideal time to develop experience and confidence in exploring your dreams. The manifest content and underlying meanings are usually closely related to the emotional challenges you are facing. For example, in the weeks before marriage or the birth of a baby, or in the weeks after a serious injury or illness, your dreams will nearly always be focused on important conflicts related to the turning point that you're trying to resolve.

In each chapter, I have identified common dream themes that are capitalized in the text and listed in the dream theme index at the end of the book. Many of the themes are universal and are experienced frequently across cultures, ages, gender, and class distinctions. The majority of the dream themes are identified because of their relevance to a particular life event or turning point, such as the fact that expectant mothers have Animal Birth dream themes; such dreams often portray women giving birth to furry mammals, which symbolize aspects of the mother's relationship to her growing fetus. Another example is the tendency of those grieving a loss to dream about the person close to them who has died. These dreams may begin soon after the death and continue for months or years afterward.

Identifying, naming, and describing narrative themes in dreams can help you understand underlying issues and conflicts in your emotional life and identify specific psychological reactions during life transitions. Although the dream theme index is provided to make it easier to recall dream patterns and to identify universal tendencies in dreams, your dreams are unique and may differ from the featured themes. It is important not to view the dream theme index as a cookbook or dream dictionary where you can look up prepackaged recipes for dream interpretation. The names and narrative description of themes should be used as anchor points that will give you ideas and inspiration to discover the unique meaning of your own dream themes. For that reason, chapter 12 provides you with instructions for creating your personal dream theme index which may include some covered in this book as well as themes that are unique to your dream life.

This book seeks to empower and guide you to develop a sense of confidence and expertise in working with your own dreams. It builds upon your current experiences of important life events, and your unique ideas and hunches, rather than trying to fit your dreams, themes, or feelings into a rigid theoretical framework. *Dream Wisdom* emphasizes the value of using our dreams as a launching pad for active exploration of our feelings and memories. Through examples, suggestions, and exercises, you will learn how you can search for emotional linkages between turning points you are experiencing and the people, places, activities, and feelings in your dreams This book also illustrates how turning-point dreams can help you access important memories and conflicts from your past. These linkages to the past can provide vital clues to resolving emotional stumbling blocks in the present.

How to Use This Book

In the following chapters, we'll explore the extraordinary patterns of dreams that occur at specific life passages: growing up, falling in love, forming a committed relationship, pregnancy and birth, separation and divorce, career transitions, midlife crisis, traumatic incidents, injury and illness, and loss. From early childhood through the end of the life cycle, we'll see how dreams provide an accurate emotional gauge that can offer us insights, creative solutions, and hope that will nurture our spirits during troubling times.

Some chapters may relate to a transition you are going through or have encountered in the past. As you read about turning points that you have already experienced, use them as an opportunity to review the inner changes you experienced at the time. Reading about the dreams and fantasies, terrors and joys of a person preparing for marriage may recall memories of your own period of courtship, engagement, and adjustment to marriage. As you read about turning points you haven't yet experienced, imagine how you might react when you arrive at a midlife crisis or experience the death of a parent or close friend.

The 150 or so dreams you'll read about are reported exactly as told to me by the dreamers. The names and biographical details, however, have been altered to protect the confidentiality of the dreamers. The dreams were selected from those reported to me by my patients, students, friends, colleagues, workshop participants, research subjects, and people whom I interviewed while collecting material for this book. Some dreams are drawn from other sources and are so noted in the notes at the back of the book.

Don't be concerned if your dream themes are less obvious or differ some-what from the patterns described in this book. These examples have been selected for their vividness and clarity. Also don't be deceived by explana-tions that may seem obvious or simplistic. Even the greatest dream experts may be blind to obvious symbolism in their own dreams, and many of the explanations that appear simple and straightforward are a distillation of extensive exploration and discussion.

In order to discover the vital connections between the emotional chal-lenges of a turning point and the bewildering images of our dreams, we need to devote special time and attention to our dreams and inner feelings. Many of us are intrigued or frightened by a vivid dream. Often a flash of insight will lead us to an explanation of the dream that feels satisfying. In this book, I will stress the value of persevering beyond that first flash of insight and discovering deeper layers of meaning in a dream. Continuing the process of exploring the many levels of meaning will be more valuable than finding a specific bottom-line interpretation.

Keep in mind that your own impressions about the unique images, feel-ings, and memories of your dreams are more important than what an expert says about their meaning. Even if your dreams are different from those described in this book, the process of comparing your own dreams with those in this book may trigger vital insights and help you grasp key psycho-logical issues at each turning point. Seeing how others confront and resolve an emotional impasse will help you understand crucial patterns in the way you face similar turning points.

Before we embark on our dream journey through life's turning points, I recommend the following steps to enhance your appreciation of your own dreams as you read this book.

Dream Journal

Keep a journal by your bed while you read this book. Write down your dreams and the feelings and ideas that accompany them. *Consider every dream as important, even if it seems confused, fragmentary, trivial, or nonsensical.* Many dreams that don't seem "worthwhile" in the morning may bear rich treasures later in the day. For children or adults, purchase or create a dream journal that you can decorate with art or a collage of your dream symbols or with photos of frequent dream characters and settings.

Dream Recall

Reserve a few quiet moments in the morning, preferably while still in bed, to gather and mentally review your dreams. Jot some notes or write down dreams soon after waking or at breakfast if possible. Record dreams in their raw form without censoring or editing. Don't be disappointed if a dream is illogical or fragmentary; every dream is worthy and filled with possibilities for self-understanding.

Dream Sharing

Share and exchange one or more of your dreams with your spouse or partner or with a trusted friend. Dream sharing can be informal, such as in bed with your partner, at the breakfast table with family and children, during a coffee break, or via phone or email. Sharing dreams can also be done in more formal settings, such as with a psychotherapist or in a special dream-sharing group or workshop. Tell your dream in the present tense and be aware of feelings and ideas you experience as you relate it. Also listen to your friends' dreams. Try not to analyze or interpret each other's dreams. Instead, take a supportive stance. Empathize with the feelings and marvel at the images.

The Family That Dreams Together

Children who are encouraged to recall and talk about their dreams will have a lifetime of access to the healing and creative powers of the dreaming mind. Keep a dream journal for your children or for the whole family. The most fruitful techniques for helping children appreciate and explore their dreamworld revolve around simple expressive-arts projects. Have your children draw, paint, act out, or dance their dreams. Welcome their dreams, and praise their creativity and originality. Reassure them if they are having nightmares. Keep a family gallery of dream-inspired art and writings.

Dream Wisdom Journal

If you're eager to learn or review more detailed guidelines for remembering your dreams and creating a dream wisdom journal, turn to chapter 12, "A Practical Guide to Exploring Your Dreams and Nightmares."

Chapter 12 also provides you with a cornucopia of well-tested do-it-yourself techniques I have discovered for creatively exploring the meaning of your dreams. The emphasis is on empowering the dreamer with tools to explore his or her own dreams through creative writing, visual and expressive arts techniques, and self-directed analysis and categorization of personal dream and nightmare symbolism. In addition, innovative techniques for exploring children's dreams will be described to help parents, as well as educators and psychotherapists, enhance communication, resolve nightmares, and unlock the creative potential of dreams.

As you read this book, or complete the creative exercises in the dream wisdom journal featured in chapter 12, you may notice a heightened receptivity to remembering your dreams. This frequently occurs for people who participate in dream classes or workshops or read books about dreams. So use the period while you are reading this book as a special time for paying attention to your dreams. Your efforts will be rewarded with insight, inspiration, and a closer sense of alignment with your own inner dream wisdom.

1. THE WISDOM OF DREAMS at Life's transitions

Have you ever wished for a source of guidance during times of crisis or critical change, such as the formation or breakup of a relationship, a career transition, an illness, or the loss of someone close? Have you ever hoped for a voice from within that could express your deepest feelings and needs?

Our dreams offer a source of wisdom that can guide and inspire us in unique and profound ways at times of crisis. Dreams give us access to hidden feelings and unexpressed needs. They highlight issues we need to work on and point to creative solutions to emotional roadblocks we are facing. If we remember and explore our dreams, we can acquire wisdom that will enhance our ability to resolve the unique challenges that confront us at life's turning points.

Throughout our lives, we face an inevitable series of profound changes. Many of these are predictable life passages, like leaving home, forming a relationship, having a family, changing jobs, reaching midlife, or retiring. Others are unexpected or traumatic, such as contracting a serious illness, getting divorced, having a car accident, being the victim of a crime, or enduring the death of a loved one.

Life's turning points can pave the way for dramatic personal growth. Our stable pattern of life is shattered, and we are confronted with a sense of urgency. In this emotionally raw state, we are more open to taking risks and making significant changes than we would be during more stable times.

Life passages present emotional hazards as well as opportunities for growth. We may feel out of control or confused. We may say or do things that are uncharacteristic of our usual responses. During these sensitive times, we are also more likely to suffer from emotional distress, self-defeating behaviors, and even physical ailments.

The choice of how to experience these occasions is ours. If we don't resolve the unique emotional challenges that confront us, we may reach an impasse that prolongs or even paralyzes our ability to make healthy choices. On the other hand, by throwing us off-balance, crises and transitions paradoxically offer an opportunity to heal old emotional wounds and achieve new levels of fulfillment in love and work.

When you remember your dreams, you remember your hidden wounds, fears, desires, and joys. When you explore your dreams, you begin to make yourself whole by reclaiming the powerful feelings of grief, rage, and love that you've denied or avoided. When you share your dreams, you offer deeply personal feelings that create bonds of intimacy that open you to the love and support needed to heal and grow during times of change.

The following example illustrates how turning-point dreams can be viewed as an X ray of our inner life. Rose was a woman in her late forties who had three grown daughters. She had recently made a decision that would profoundly affect the course of her life. After twenty-eight years of marriage, Rose had separated from her husband. She had wrestled with the decision to leave him for over five years and was still plagued with doubts about whether she had done the right thing. She had the following dream after visiting her husband for the first time in five months.

RIDING a UNICYCLe

I dream that I am riding along in a group of bicycles. All of a sudden I realize that everyone's attention is focused on the fact that I am riding a unicycle and not a regular two-wheeler bike. In the dream, I am thinking this is weird because I've never ridden a unicycle before. I'm feeling very self-conscious. I begin to ride away from the group, and somehow I'm able to keep riding. I am incredibly happy that I can actually ride the unicycle.

At the time of the dream, Rose was pondering whether to follow through with the divorce and had met with her husband to try to make a final decision. As she discussed her dream with me, she realized that despite all of the distracting attention, she was able to ride the unicycle. For Rose, riding the unicycle instead of the conventional two-wheeler bike symbolized her struggle to do things on her own for the first time in her life. Her dream talents at unicycle riding were unexpected and confirmed her emotional ability to make it on her own.

Exploring this Unexpected Talents dream gave Rose a renewed sense of certainty. Pondering the striking image of the unicycle helped her maintain her newly emerging sense of independence. She realized that being single felt like being a unicycle in a world of married two-wheelers. Despite the fact that she felt stigmatized by her new status, Rose was able to take pride in her unique new way of getting around. Discussing this dream and others helped bolster her confidence that she could thrive on her own. This surprising insight helped to crystallize her decision to follow through with the divorce and to pursue graduate training for a career in business. Rose did not regret her dream-inspired decision. In the years following her divorce, she developed her own successful business and found fulfillment within a web of new personal and professional connections, something that she had never explored while she was married. (For more information on Rose's dreams and on separation and divorce dreams, see chapter 5.)

The Healing Power of Turning-Point Dreams

Dreaming is a crucial part of how we recover from events that upset the sense of balance and security in our lives. When we are off-balance, the conscious mind may feel overwhelmed and out of control. Simultaneously, the unconscious, dreaming mind becomes more active, producing compelling images, fantasies, and nightmares that respond to the emotional challenges we are facing.

There is a dramatic upsurge in the number and intensity of dreams at life crises and transitions. Even the physiological experience of dreaming undergoes a transformation. Normally the first of the four to six rapid eye movement (REM) periods begins after about ninety minutes of sleep[1]. During periods of upheaval such as a divorce or other crisis, we enter the first REM period much sooner in the sleep cycle, and our periods of intense dreaming lengthen and involve different patterns of brain activity.[2]

Some of the biologically restorative and emotional-healing powers of dreams occur whether we remember them or not. However, as soon as we begin to focus on our dreams or keep a written record of them, we activate their therapeutic potential. Ideas and creative inspirations connected to a dream may occur to us spontaneously, and we may perceive insights and solutions to personal problems by the mere act of recalling and documenting a dream.[3] The full range of benefits of our dreams can be tapped only if we devote sufficient time and attention to experiencing, interpreting, and understanding the messages our dreams are sending us.

Following the wisdom of our dreams may take many forms. At times it may mean working through feelings that we have repressed. At other times it may lead to dramatic insights that we can test in important relationships. Dreams can even inspire us to consider making significant changes in our job situation, close relationships, habits, or behavior patterns. For example, renowned sleep researcher William Dement gave up smoking immediately after a dream warned him of the deadly health consequences of the habit.[4]

In this book we'll demonstrate the many ways that dreams can help us navigate a smoother course through the emotional turbulence of life's turning points. In particular we will look at how the wisdom of dreams can guide us to successfully resolve the challenges of life transitions by:

* allowing us to identify and reclaim powerful hidden feelings that undermine our ability to move forward

* warning us about emotional conflicts and self-defeating behaviors that are blocking our ability to cope with change

* helping us to see the importance of reaching out to others for emotional support at times of change

* alerting us to wounds from the past that have reemerged to plague us in the present

* allowing us to perceive solutions to conflicts in our close relationships

* getting us in touch with new sources of creativity and inspiring new directions and projects

* restoring a sense of meaning and instilling the hope that we can make it through troubling times

The Seasons of Life

As we walk the journey of life, we pass through many stages. Erik Erikson's work[5] extended Freud's emphasis on the importance of early psychological development to include the entire life cycle. According to Erikson, our personalities are shaped by events and relationships in early childhood. However, psychological development does not stop there. We continue to evolve psychologically through adulthood, middle age, old age, and even as we approach death.[6]

Contemporary journalists such as Gail Sheehy—in her books, *Passages*[7] and *New Passages*[8]—have popularized the importance of dealing with the emotional stumbling blocks and opportunities presented by life transitions such as leaving home, establishing committed relationships, reaching midlife, enduring separations and losses, and growing older.

It is clear that our personalities continue to change during adulthood. Critical periods can lead to increased personal growth or alternatively to psychological stagnation. Just growing older does not guarantee wisdom. We must remain open to the unique challenges posed by life's events and observant of the growth and maturation of our body, mind, and spirit.

Near the age of two, the process of individuating and establishing separateness from our primary caretaking parent begins. In adolescence, we identify with peers and become more self-reliant and test the limits of our emerging autonomy. Moving away from our parents and entering adulthood is a time of experimentation, career development, and developing mature friendships and love relationships. Forming a committed relationship and having children alter our identities and relationships with our family of origin.

In his influential book *The Seasons of a Man's Life,* Daniel Levinson, Ph.D.,[9] emphasized that reaching certain crucial age brackets, especially around the ages of forty and fifty, provokes intense reevaluation and changes in almost all aspects of life. (For more on midlife dreams, see chapter 7.)

Later in their forties and fifties, women go through menopause, and child-bearing is no longer possible. Men go through a male "menopause" with emotional and some biological changes. In later adulthood, we experience some of our physical powers waning and greater vulnerability to the afflictions of aging. These physical and mental changes begin to alter our identity. In this era there are also many losses to bear, including the deaths of our parents and eventually some of our friends and peers. Despite these losses, the era of late adult life can be a time of growth. We can continue to grow and learn, as well as teach others. Age may bring wisdom and the opportunities to mentor others.

Stages of a Crisis or Turning Point

In his book *Transitions,* William Bridges emphasizes that all turning points have three stages: an ending, a period of disorientation, and finally a resolution or new beginning.[10] Every turning point begins with an ending: the end of being a single person, the end of a job or a marriage, the death of a loved one. The ending stage disrupts our sense of security and stability. At the same time, the disruption prepares us to accept new circumstances. It is important not to skip over the sense of loss that emerges in the beginning stage of a turning point.

The second stage of a transition is often a period of disorientation. During this middle stage, old familiar ways of being have been jarred loose, but a new solution has not emerged. For example, a physically active person who becomes disabled with a chronic back injury may experience an extended period of depression or anger. A woman whose husband abandoned her with two children may be so filled with resentment that she is unable to begin the arduous work of rebuilding her life.

People in this stage may not be ready to let go of the way things were. Nor can they face their grief for what's been lost or their fear of the unknown circumstances ahead. They may succumb to the instinctive human tendency to cling to the old way of being and of doing things even when it's no longer appropriate for the current situation. For example, the teenager who demanded independence at college may have secretly longed for the protected security of the parental nest. A man or woman who enters marriage joyfully may secretly grieve over their loss of independence as a single person. People may choose divorce, yet regret the loss of some features of their former married life. Those who are unable to accept what the writer Judith Viorst calls "necessary losses" may linger in emotional limbo, unable to move forward and accept the change facing them.[11]

In the final stage of a transition, painful feelings and confusion begin to subside. There has been a metamorphosis. Our identities, the roles we play in relation to others, and our feelings have all changed. In this stage, a divorcing woman may begin to feel pride in her independence and accomplishments. She may be much more hopeful about life's prospects and willing to risk forming a new love relationship. New friendships and new career directions may seem more feasible.

The final stage of a transition may lead a person back to their previous level of adjustment or allow them to reach a new level of fulfillment in love and work. When we reemerge from the stages of a turning point, we often enter a new period of stability that lasts until the next transition or destabilizing event arrives.

The Signs of a Turning-Point Impasse

An impasse results when you are unable to progress through the stages of a turning point and begin to suffer from persistent signs of emotional or physical distress. There may be pronounced avoidance of the very issues that need to be resolved. In addition to dreams and nightmares, a variety of symptoms of distress may signal that you have reached a turning-point impasse. For example, during a life transition or after a stressful or traumatic event, you may find yourself:

* withdrawing from or sabotaging important relationships
* denying your needs and feelings

* increasing your use or abuse of alcohol and drugs
* engaging in reckless or self-destructive behaviors
* less able to concentrate and be productive at work
* feeling sad, hopeless, or otherwise sinking into depression
* increasingly irritable, angry, and blaming others
* behaving compulsively by overworking
* using food or sex in a compulsive or self-destructive way
* having increased physical symptoms and illnesses

It is not unusual to experience mild flare-ups of one or two of these signs at any turning point. When several of these signs appear in a more pronounced form, however, it's important to take steps to resolve the impasse. When you are alert to these signs in yourself or in people close to you, you can minimize the potentially destructive effects of a turning-point impasse by paying attention to turning-point dreams. The dreaming mind has an uncanny ability to shine a spotlight on the emotional issues that are most challenging to us. We cannot shield ourselves from life's inevitable changes, but our dreams offer a way to overcome the hidden barriers of life's passages. They are direct signals from the unconscious about what's really going on inside us, including upsetting issues that we may not be acknowledging consciously.

Resolving Turning Points

Be patient. There is no way to rush through the emotional stages of a turning point. The emotional effects of changing careers, facing the death of a parent, or watching your last child leave for college do not disappear after a few weeks. They come and go in waves. The cycle may continue for months as you overcome your resistance to change and gradually gather strength to confront the core of your feelings.

Even so-called positive turning points that please us consciously, such as having a child, getting married, or receiving a promotion, are filled with hidden stresses. Because we feel we are supposed to show a happy face during these times, it is hard to admit to any worries.

Many people feel deeply ashamed that they're still troubled by feelings left over from an unresolved turning point. They feel that they should have worked out all the changes and gotten back to normal. However, long after friends and family members stop inquiring about their distress, they may have lingering feelings of grief, anger, or doubt.

Different kinds of turning points will be more devastating to one person than to another. After a divorce one person may be well on the road to recovery after a few weeks. A year or more later, another person may still be seriously depressed and showing signs of an impasse. If your thoughts and feelings and dreams continue to be dominated by a transition, you probably need more time and some assistance to get through it.

Ask for help. The best antidote to the hazards of a turning point is to seek extra emotional support from others. At times when they need help the most, many people withdraw from others or neglect valuable sources of support in their life. At these critical times, supportive friends and family members may be your best medicine. It's important to set aside the shame or doubts you may feel and reach out to others at a moment of need. Seeking support often triggers other constructive actions that will move you in the direction of a healthy resolution. If you are experiencing the signs of an impasse at a critical juncture in your life, you may also want to consider professional help from a psychotherapist, support group, or clergy person.

Try not to judge the nature of your emotional reactions or measure the timetable of your recovery. Keep in mind that we all resist changes and that our mind protects us from feelings that are too uncomfortable to bear by using psychological defenses such as denial and repression—for example, denying the emotional impact of a loss or banishing a painful memory from our awareness. These defenses are adaptive. They protect us from overwhelming emotions. However, when our defenses become too powerful, and block the emotions we need to experience more fully to get over painful losses, we need to learn to bypass our defenses so we can get through our grief and continue to grow emotionally.

Remember that our defensiveness and slow response time at turning points are not evidence of moral weakness or laziness. They reflect our struggle to deal with profoundly upsetting changes in our identity, relationships, and life circumstances.

Use your dreams. They offer a sensitive gauge of conflicts that may be bogging you down. By tapping into your inner reservoir, you can navigate the emotional perils of a turning point and chart a new, healthier life course.

Dramatic Dream Patterns at Life Passages

In the last decades of the twentieth century, a growing body of research established the presence of dramatic patterns in the content of turning-point dreams. Research has included studies of expectant mothers' and fathers' dreams;[12] dreams around the time of marriage and divorce; dreams while coping with cancer, HIV,[13] and other serious illnesses; dreams of elderly people and those facing imminent death;[14] dreams of depressed and suicidal individuals;[15] and dreams of people recovering from traumatic accidents and from the devastating impact of violent crime, terrorism, and war.[16]

This research has helped us understand recurrent dream themes that are common to most individuals who undergo similar transitions. For example, brides-to-be and grooms-to-be often dream about disastrous events at their weddings, liaisons with old lovers, or their new partner suddenly showing ghastly characteristics that were previously concealed. Recent widows or widowers may dream that they are visited by images of their departed spouses beckoning to them or disappearing and abandoning them. People with grave illnesses may dream about time running out and clocks breaking. Immigrants often have recurrent Journey dreams about returning to their homeland. Survivors of the destruction of the World Trade Center Towers have experienced frequent apocalyptic nightmares of cataclysmic forces threatening to destroy them.

Pregnancy is a turning point that is fertile for dreams. Pregnant women may dream about birth defects, nurturing furry puppies and sea otters, and whether the baby will be a boy or girl. Expectant fathers are also prolific dreamers. An especially common turning-point dream for them is what I call Fetal Identification dreams.[17] In these dreams, the father-to-be unconsciously expresses the power of his prenatal bond with his child by taking on a role that is directly parallel to the experience of the fetus in the womb. Late in pregnancy, it is not uncommon for men to dream of popping out of caves or emerging from underwater bubbles.[18]

Daniel, age thirty-two, who worked in public relations, had a classic Fetal Identification dream. Daniel was enthusiastic about the birth of his child. Prior to telling me his dream, he expressed strong views about the decision that he and his wife had made to have a home birth attended by a midwife and labor coach. The dream he related to me went as follows.

WINNING the Race

I was in a swimming pool, and there was going to be a race. I was swimming very fast. Our labor coach was on the side of the pool cheering me on. I was winning the race, but it felt like I was swimming downhill. Suddenly I am in the locker room. It seems like I won the race, and I am being wrapped in a towel by a woman, maybe our midwife.[19]

Despite the transparent symbolism of identification with the fetus traveling and emerging from the waters of the birth canal, when I asked Daniel what feelings or ideas occurred to him, he indicated that the only thing he could get from the dream was that perhaps he should swim more. He said he hadn't been getting much exercise recently and needed to get back into his swimming routine. When I pointed out the dream's possible connection to the birthing process, he was a little embarrassed but very excited, as if something he had been searching for but couldn't quite grasp had been confirmed.

Prior to exploring this dream, he had felt uncertain about his role in the pregnancy and nervous about his impending fatherhood. Discussing his dream helped Daniel understand the strength of his psychological identification with his child.

For men, awareness of dreaming about their partner's pregnancy and their child-to-be provides a visual, sensory, and emotional connection to their baby. Remembering and discussing his dreams can help a man more fully acknowledge the magnitude of his emotional response to pregnancy and the importance of taking a collaborative role in the preparation for parenting. (For further details on the dreamworld of expectant parents, see chapter 4.)

This book draws upon our growing knowledge about the special wisdom of the dreaming mind. As we embark on a guided tour of the passages and crises of adulthood, you'll see a theme emerging. During each turning point, our dreams tell the inner story of our deepest feelings. These include hidden feelings of grief, confusion, anger, even joy and fulfillment—feelings that we are unaware of, not ready to face, or that we fear may leave us devastated.

Nightmares: Toxic or Healing?

Nightmares are fearful dreams that overwhelm us and often cause us to awaken. Psychoanalyst and eminent nightmare researcher Ernest Hartmann, M.D., defines a nightmare as "something from inside that awakens a person with a scared feeling."[20] Because nightmares awaken us and waking up is necessary for remembering dreams, we recall a larger proportion of our nightmares. Especially during crises, it may seem that the world of dreams is a realm of nightmares. As painful as nightmares feel, they are one of the most direct sources of self-knowledge. They give us a raw, uncensored view of the very issues that are most upsetting to us.

Nightmares are more frequent and more vivid at turning points than during periods of stability. They are indications of the inner turmoil that accompanies momentous passages, even supposedly positive ones such as marriage, pregnancy, and graduation.

Just when you're most vulnerable and really need those precious hours of sleep, nightmares may invade your psyche like terrifying marauders that torture you and leave you shaken. There are many variations on the basic nightmare theme of being overwhelmed by powerful forces. You may have Mortal Threat dreams that you're being chased by homicidal terrorists with bombs strapped to them, or that your car is going out of control but your foot is paralyzed so you can't hit the brakes, or that a giant earthquake destroys your home and you don't know if your family was inside. Such nightmares occur intermittently during stable times in our lives but may be more frequent during times of upheaval and instability.

Nightmares often involve profound anxiety and a threat to our physical safety or survival. In our nightmares, we commit, witness, or are threatened by acts of violence and immorality. The most common themes include being chased, paralyzed, violently attacked, abandoned or rejected, imprisoned or kidnapped, and subject to disasters such as tidal waves, earthquakes, fire, terrorism, or life-threatening diseases.

Nightmares are the reason that many people prefer to forget their dreams. Like a child who can't distinguish dream from reality, the awesome emotional power of a nightmare may leave us in a state of confusion. Will we be arrested for the murder we committed in a nightmare? Will our spouse file for divorce after that flagrant affair we had in our sexual dream?

It is important to be aware of the potentially toxic impact of nightmares and to recognize when they are contributing to a worsening of our mental health. For people who have experienced extreme trauma, or who are suffering significant depression or a posttraumatic reaction to crisis, nightmares can rub salt in your emotional wounds.

For survivors of disasters, accidents, or violent attacks, each nightmare can be a painful reexperiencing of the horror the dreamer has lived through. During waking hours, we can try to avoid or deny troubling thoughts, but during a nightmare we feel greater vulnerability and more acute terror because we cannot protect ourselves. We wish we could dismiss it as "just a dream," but the nightmare feels more terrifying than waking memories and thoughts.

What are the signs that your nightmares have become toxic? If they have the following characteristics, it may be a sign that you are suffering depression or an acute reaction that could lead to posttraumatic stress disorder. Toxic nightmares may:

* portray extremely graphic violence, mortal threats, and helpless victims
* show little or no struggle to fight back against dream adversaries or resolve overwhelming conflicts
* force a reliving of traumatic events that are still too painful to tolerate

* contain terrifying, repetitive themes and symbols

* leave a residue of emotional disturbance that can trigger massive
  waking anxiety and depression and significantly impact the ability
  to function during the day

* reinforce significant fears of sleeping and dreaming and cause
  insomnia or worsen existing sleep disorders

If your nightmares have one or more of the above characteristics, they may
have become toxic; you may need emotional support to resolve them. In
addition, if your nightmares cause significant and persistent emotional distress
or impact your relationships or capacity to function during the day, you
may need assistance from a mental health professional.

Breaking the Spell of Nightmares

In nightmares, traumatic memories bubble to the surface. Our emotional
Achilles heel is exposed. We can see the deepest layers of our fears and insecurities from both the present crisis and from past emotional wounds and
losses. How can such painful experiences help us to resolve the emotional
challenges of a life passage? If we can learn to break the painful spell of our
nightmares, we can begin to decode the vital messages they bring us.

To break that spell, it is important to understand that nightmares increase
during crises as well as during expected transitions such as leaving home,
pregnancy, or midlife. Nightmares exaggerate our deepest fears, but if
we begin to explore their themes and symbols, searching for patterns, their
terrifying grip will loosen. As soon as we remember, write down, share, or
explore a nightmare, we are beginning to break its spell. When that happens,
we can see our nightmares as a source of awareness rather than as a nightly
stint in a torture chamber.

For example, a series of nightmares about being pursued by homicidal
terrorists becomes less daunting when you realize that the leader reminds
you of your verbally abusive boss and the dreams are being triggered by your
reactions to unfair demands that he's imposing. The aftermath of a nightmare is less upsetting if you can understand how it relates to unresolved
issues in your life.

Nightmares are not necessarily a sign of pathology. Although they feel
emotionally toxic, most nightmares have the potential to be a vaccine and
not a poison.[21] Vaccines prevent severe illness by infecting us with a small
dosage of a dreaded disease, such as smallpox. In response, we produce antibodies that allow us to develop immunity.

The function of nightmares in human evolution may be thought of in a similar way. They are a warning and a stimulus to our emotional antibodies when we are facing stress or a transition. In a study of pregnant women, those who remembered more dreams with threatening and hostile themes actually had shorter labors and fewer complications.[22] This may seem illogical at first blush, but the women who could tolerate the recall of their nightmares were more open to the normal anxieties of pregnancy and were more ready to let go—emotionally and physically—when the moment of birth arrived.

Pioneering dream researcher Rosalind Cartwright, Ph.D., has identified a related dynamic in her extensive research on the dreams of divorcing women. Those women who were able to remember dreams and nightmares with content directly related to their divorce were adjusting and coping better a year later when compared to those who had little recall of divorce-related dreams and nightmares.[23]

Thus, having a moderate number of nightmares, even if some are distressing, may indicate that we are beginning to deal with the challenges of a turning point. Having no dreams during a crisis may suggest that we are in denial and are not actively coping with our conflicts and are not ready to give birth to a solution.

Nightmares prepare us to face the next day and the next emotional challenge by exaggerating the issues from which we are recovering. The man facing elective leg surgery dreams that he is being carved up by a butcher's knife in a meat shop.[24] This is a grotesque exaggeration but may help the dreamer understand his fears.

The divorcee who dreams that she is totally alone exaggerates how desolate she really is but this may be an accurate description of the emotional emptiness of the early stages of a divorce. This nightmare of abandonment is painful. However, under the best of circumstances, it forces the divorcing person to be more acutely aware of her need for companionship and emotional support. In this way the terror of our Left-Out nightmares stimulates us to become aware and inspires us to take actions in waking life to overcome our most daunting emotional challenges. By bringing our hidden fears into the light of day, nightmares can clarify exactly what's troubling us and open up opportunities for growth.

Painful as they are, nightmares provide important advantages for furthering self-awareness and facing challenges in love or work. Unlike most dreams, we remember nightmares vividly and are motivated to soothe the distress they induce and make sense out of what they are telling us. In addition, through the symbolism and metaphor of the tales told by our nightmares, current life stresses are connected and mixed with emotionally parallel conflicts from our past. Through their amazingly creative condensation or connection function,[25] dreams and nightmares search for emotional solutions that were tested and learned from past experiences.[26]

Remembered or not, dreams and nightmares function to assimilate or process everything we encounter in waking life that requires new learning, and they stimulate coping when we are stressed by threats to our physical or psychological well-being. Remembered or not, the intense nightly dramas in our dreams help maintain psychological balance by soothing our moods[27] and restoring our identity and sense of connection to those we love and count on.

When we pay attention to the messages of our nightmares, windows of awareness open. With reassurance and a playful attitude of exploration, we can change the dead-end metaphors of our nightmares, detoxify their emotional poison, and discover clues as to how to work through challenges to our sense of security. With a magic wand from the Hogwart school, we can rescript the endings of our worst nightmares and transform their poison into a healing potion of insight, emotional catharsis, and creative inspiration. (For more information on remedies for nightmares, see chapter 12.)

A Lifetime of Dreaming

We dream every night of our lives, and have dreams throughout the night. According to Hartmann, the most memorable dreams are during four to six episodes of REM, sleep occurring about every ninety minutes.[28] These REM periods are storms of brain activity accompanied by rapid eye movements, sexual arousal, and a paralysis of most muscles to prevent us from acting out our dreams. Each REM period gets longer and longer as the night progresses, which is why we are most likely to remember a dream in the morning.[29]

In a normal life span, we may experience over 150,000 episodes of REM, or four or more solid years of dreaming. Any activity that is so physiologically and psychologically intense and requires so much of our time must have a crucial role in the evolution of our species as well as in shaping the stories of our individual lives.

We dream at every season and storm in our life. If we listen to the wisdom of our dreams and nightmares, they can help us navigate life's passages and crises. Let us begin the journey through the life cycle of dreaming. We will see the patterns and common themes in dreams, starting with childhood, entering the prime of adulthood, passing through midlife and aging, and ending with dreams that prepare for and precede death.

2. first Dreams
HOW CHILDREN'S DREAMS INSPIRE CREATIVITY, INSIGHT, AND COMMUNICATION

Dreaming begins in the womb. Fetal monitoring has demonstrated that the nightly cycles of rapid eye movement (REM) sleep that are associated with vivid dreams are clearly detectable in utero. Swimming within the protective amniotic waters, what do fetuses dream? The substance of their dream experience may be shaped by the rhythmic pulse of their mother's heart, the muffled sounds of their mother's voice, or the conversations of their father and siblings. Are there sublime, blissful dreams of perfect comfort? Are there nightmares after the mother undergoes an intrusive ultrasound or amniocentesis test? We can only speculate about the nature of fetal dreaming.

Newborns are no longer floating in the womb, but for the first few weeks and months of life, they are swimming in dreams. Fifty percent of sleep in normal newborns and up to 80 percent of sleep in premature infants is devoted to REM dreaming. This is by far the peak of dreaming in the human life cycle. Older children enter this dream-rich phase of the night during about 25 percent of their sleep time. Every ninety minutes, adults enter the REM state for a total of about 20 percent of the time they are sleeping.[1]

Preverbal Dreams

The overwhelming presence of REM dreaming in the first months of life corresponds to an explosive phase of cognitive development. The brain is maturing and beginning to exercise seemingly miraculous powers that lead to understanding language, gaining mobility, and becoming aware of one's existence. This early storm of preverbal dreams also parallels the most critical early period of forming emotional attachments with parents.

Researchers strongly suspect that the infants' extended journeys into the realm of dreams supports the theory that dreaming has a crucial function in evolution. More specifically, the physiological and ultimately psychological experience of infants' and toddlers' dreaming is integral to developing the brain and maintaining emotional balance. This is consistent with research that asserts that dreaming is an inner laboratory where new behaviors and key information needed for physical and emotional survival are rehearsed and new metaphors for problem solving are generated.[2]

Until language emerges, infants can't tell us about their myriad daily and nightly dreams. Perhaps they are dreaming of sweet, health-giving breast milk or of the pangs of hunger and the pain of separation from their mother. Many of the frequent sleep disturbances during the first year of life may well be caused by nightmares. Alfred Adler and other twentieth-century theorists have emphasized the traumatic impact of birth. Are the nocturnal shrieks of our babies caused by posttraumatic nightmares related to birth trauma, or are they perhaps related to a neurological overload from processing and organizing each massive new experience and rehearsing responses for the next day's challenges? In keeping with the life cycle focus of *Dream Wisdom*, this chapter explores the evolution of awareness of childhood dreaming from the first reported dreams of toddlers, through entry in the world of school, the coming of age in adolescence and the inner challenges of leaving the security of home to enter into the world of adulthood. We will look at common childhood dreams such as the Creature Threat dreams which afflict virtually all young children, dreams related to stressful events such as divorce, dreams related to the dawning of sexuality, and the performance anxieties of becoming an adolescent and young adult and children's Career Vision dreams. We will also examine the fascinating and very meaningful dreams that adults remember from their childhood. Although most adults only remember one or two childhood dreams, exploring their content can open up important and often unresolved memories. Additional examples of children's turning-point dreams related to divorce, accidents and other traumas, grief, and illness can be found in subsequent chapters.

First Reported Dreams

When toddlers first connect words and create rudimentary sentences, they can begin to reveal the outlines and silhouettes of their dream experiences. Between eighteen and thirty months of age, toddlers' receptive language skills are blossoming. At some time during this period, their expressive language makes the quantum leap into the realm of simple two- and three-word sentences. With gentle encouragement from parents, children can begin to describe their first dreams.

Sigmund Freud reported the following vivid and very oral first dream of his nineteen-month-old daughter, Anna, who had been deprived of food to quiet her stomach after an episode of vomiting. In the middle of the night she called out.

LittLe aNNa's first DReam

Anna Fweud, strawbewwies, wild strawbewwies, omblet, pudden!

This dream[3] may have been embellished in Dr. Freud's recall or translation. What is accurate is the fact that highly verbal toddlers can report dreams and nightmares around the age of two. In addition, precocious reporting of dreams may bode well for future interest in dreaming and the unconscious. Anna Freud went on to be a pioneer in the field of child psychoanalysis. Her writings on children's dreams emphasized the need to approach children's dreams gently, appealing to their creativity and using the dream as a lush artistic palette for free associations. The moral of this vignette may be that if you teach your children the art of dreaming, they may enjoy a lifetime of remembering, valuing, and using their dreams (having Sigmund Freud as her father was obviously a significant influence on Anna).

Creature Threat nightmares symbolize a wide variety of early childhood fears and insecurities. They can occur during family stresses and even during events that may confuse a young child such as a parent's business trip or a change in babysitter or family routines.

For toddlers and preschoolers the most common dream characters are animals and the most frequent nightmare theme is being chased or threatened by an animal, monster, or imaginary creature.

Around the time my younger daughter, Sophia, turned two, she woke up, pointed to the window, and shouted, "Bird fly away." She appeared to be referring to a dream. She had heard her older sister talking about dreams and seemed to covet the power that her sister possessed. A few weeks after her first dream, she woke up in tears, pleading.

SOPHIA'S SPIDER DREAM

Pider on Sophia's leg. Pider bite Sophia!

She continued to sob, saying, "Sophia scared." I reassured her that "Daddy will protect you from spiders. I am going to teach you how to get those bad spiders away from Sophia." She listened with wide eyes. "When you see those spiders, tell them, 'Go away bad spiders! Get out of Sophia's bed and don't come back!'" After I repeated my anti-spider anthem three times, little Sophia smiled a slightly mischievous smile. "Go way piders." She said this tentatively and then repeated it twice and smiled while waving her hands as if to motion the spiders away. She was significantly calmed and after a bit of rocking and a short story, she fell back to sleep easily.

When Sophia woke the next morning, I asked, "Did you have any more dreams?" She flashed a playful smile and said "Piders!" and laughed. For two more days, she grinned and said "piders" when she woke. These subsequent dream reports were probably fabricated, judging by the mischievous look on her face. However, within a few days she began to report other dreams, mostly involving animals, some threatening and some friendly. Sophia's dream spiders were more terrifying to her than anything in her waking reality. I took the dream spiders seriously by talking to them directly and offering Sophia reassurance (both physical and emotional), a concrete strategy for facing the dream creatures and a follow-up to reinforce her ability to break the spell of the attacking dream spiders.

For those who remember childhood dreams, the symbols and themes may recur at crucial points of transition. We each have our own catalog of stress-related nightmare themes that may repeat intermittently for decades. My own snake and serpent dreams recurred for years at times of crisis. Sophia's spider dreams continued to crop up intermittently at times of stress for her. With a strong interest in science and the natural world, she now finds spiders to be fascinating creatures as long as they don't turn up in her bedroom or in her nightmares.

What is the function of these Creature Threat dreams? If we defer discussion on the rich meaning of spider imagery, we can speculate that many young children's monster and creature dreams are generic symbols of anxieties in their waking and dreaming world. These dreams present exaggerated versions of the core vulnerabilities of being human, including fears of abandonment, injury to self and others, threats to their esteem, and disruptions in the emotional bonds with close family members on whom they depend.

The Menacing Unicorn—
A Kindergartner's Nightmare

The preparatory or rehearsal function of dreams is evident prior to anticipated turning points in life. For a preschooler, the birth of a sibling, moving to a new home, or entering kindergarten are events that are accompanied by a flurry of dreams.[4]

Ariel was a bright five-year-old and a star in her gymnastics class. All summer, she and her parents were abuzz with conversations and preparations for her first day of kindergarten. After three years at a very nurturing preschool called the Unicorn School, she proudly proclaimed that she felt more grown-up and ready for something new. As the big day approached, she began to have recurring nightmares that disturbed her sleep and left her anxious during the day. On the second day of kindergarten, she dreamed the following.

the menacing UNICORN

I am walking to school, and all of a sudden, a huge unicorn with a really mean face starts chasing me. He looks like he wants to hurt me, and I start running into the hills behind my school, trying to climb a tree. I just make it up a tree, and he tries to bite me, but he can't reach me.

Beneath Ariel's conscious excitement lurked unseen emotional fears. She had to make many adjustments—a new teacher, unfamiliar kids, and a longer school day with a new after-school program. The Unicorn School had been a secure nest in which Ariel had flourished. Now the good unicorn had been replaced by her evil twin, and Ariel was experiencing school as something treacherous.

At turning points, dreams rehearse us for new roles and relationships by exaggerating the dangers of new and unfamiliar situations, relationships, and tasks. Ariel's Creature Threat dream emphasizes both the dangers and her modestly successful attempts to cope. Although the dream unicorn appears deadly, Ariel summons her considerable gymnastics ability to survive the menace, but not without a residue of waking anxiety.

Understanding the meaning of the unicorn image reassured Ariel's parents. Without further explanation from Ariel, the dream revealed that her excitement was tempered with normal fears, which she was trying to suppress. Once her fears were more visible to her parents, they could offer more guidance about how to fend off evil unicorns and how to make friends and adjust to kindergarten.

At times of transition, children's Creature Threat nightmares shine a spotlight on the issues that are most upsetting, yet inexpressible for them. To a parent whose ears and heart are open, listening to your child's nightmares is like hearing their unconscious speak directly to you, delivering a special call for help.

Adults Remember Childhood Dreams

Most adults only remember one or two dreams from childhood. These long-remembered childhood dreams are like amber—preserving memories embedded in the psyche, dormant, but ready to be activated by the recall or telling.

One of the best ways to understand children's dreams is to recollect your own childhood dreams from memory. If you don't recall a childhood dream you may want to consult your parents who might remember repetitive dreams or nightmares that you suffered. Parents or older siblings may also be able to provide background information that will give you a context for understanding your childhood dream.

Those one or two preserved dreams or nightmares are often linked to traumatic childhood issues or events. They are like a Rorschach inkblot response laden with unconscious themes mapping some important issue in your childhood.

When I teach my graduate and postgraduate courses on the clinical uses of dreams, I invite my students to recall their first dreams as a warm-up for working clinically with children's dreams. Mara, an enthusiastic thirty-year-old psychology doctoral candidate, was the first in one class to blurt out a repetitive childhood dream that she remembered taking place when she about nine years old. The dream was vivid, but she felt vexed about its significance.

TRAPPED BETWEEN THE GIANT FINGERS

There were always two giant fingers, strange and much larger than life. There was a little child trapped between the huge fingers. It might have been me. I was frightened and always woke up crying.

When I asked Mara if any upsetting events had occurred during that time frame, she blushed slightly and indicated that her parents had divorced that year and described the impact of the long, acrimonious custody battled that unfolded during that year and the next.

While Mara had not repressed the dream or that terrible year, the emotions of the dream had been repressed. By connecting the vivid image of the giant fingers to her emotional memories, Mara (and her classmates) was better able to comprehend how dreams symbolize unresolved trauma.

Children's dreams with two imposing figures, monsters, animals, or other threatening entities may represent the child's images of the power of their own parents, which in the exaggerated symbolism of the dream state is the power to rescue and heal or alternately to terrorize.

What is the function of Mara's repetitive nightmare? When she was nine, it was an unresolved posttraumatic dream—a distress signal from a terrified child unable to cope with being at the center of her parents' vicious verbal conflicts. As an adolescent and adult, recalling this dream without the emotions and context helped preserve the part of the memory that was bearable until she could get enough distance from her childhood to resolve the conflict. Training to be a child psychologist, Mara will certainly be a wounded healer in touch with the pain that children of divorce suffer.

Coming-of-Age Dreams

In many religious traditions, there are special rituals aimed at introducing children to the adult community of believers. As children prepare for these ceremonies, their dreams often turn to imagining what the rites of passage will bring and how their new status as church or synagogue members will change their lives. A few days before his bar mitzvah, twelve-year-old Brad had these two dreams.[5]

I am Late for my bar mitzvah

I'm driving in a Porsche (our family actually has a minivan) to my synagogue. We are running late, and somehow I know that there is a three- or four-year-old kid there trying to cover for me until I arrive. I read my portion from the Torah but forget to read my own speech. At first, no one notices. Finally, people realize I have forgotten my speech; for some reason it's too late for me to give it now, and the congregation gets mad and starts throwing tomatoes at me.

I forget BARUCH

I forget how to pronounce the Hebrew word *Baruch,* which is the first word in most of the Jewish prayers and is also my Hebrew name.

In addition to the celebration of his own bar mitzvah in just a couple of days, Brad had several other things he was worrying about on the night he had the dreams: homework, student council meetings, the state spelling-bee finals, and the school play in which he had the lead role. The day before the dreams, Brad had been talking with a friend during class about Porsche sports cars, and their teacher had sternly reprimanded the boys for not paying enough attention to their lessons. Brad's two dreams weave all these stressful elements into an upsetting vision of inadequacy and public scorn. While dreams about performance anxiety are quite common, dreams like Brad's point to the special worries that a child's religious rite of passage may generate. Usually such dreams do more than simply mirror a child's anxieties; they also point to possible sources of strength and resilience. In this case, the key dream element is the Hebrew word *Baruch,* which means "blessed" or "praised." It is both Brad's Hebrew name and the first word in many of the prayers recited at a bar mitzvah. By highlighting the significance of that word, the dream is reminding Brad that he does belong in the Jewish tradition, and that despite his worries he is truly an important member of his religious community.

Bob had an unusually strong awareness of his dreams during his childhood. He had recurring nightmares about ghosts terrifying him, which eventually resolved when some issues in his relationship with his father improved. When he was an early teen entering puberty, he had a Coming of Age dream that both expressed and stimulated his sexual curiosity. He was at the early stage of forming a relationship with his first girlfriend. He was thrilled, but also very insecure; he didn't really know how to behave with her. Soon he had the following dream.

SEEING my GIRLfRIEND's PRIVATE PARTS

I'm with my girlfriend, and we're being very romantic with each other, hugging and kissing and things like that, and then somehow she took off her clothes, and I looked at the area of her private parts—and what I see are patterns of spirals, squares, and circles of rainbow color, and I'm fascinated and excited by how beautiful they are.

Bob was reassured and intrigued by the psychedelic beauty of his fantasy of how his girlfriend would look naked. The dream amused him and helped quell his anxiety and uncertainty about his sexual longings.

As a parent you may not be privy to hearing about your adolescent's first erotic dream. Nevertheless, if your teenager is very open and shares a dream with a sexual theme, it can be a good time to reassure them about the normalcy of sexual dreams and of their sexual development. Reassurance and some information may be especially important for adolescent boys, whose nocturnal emissions or "wet dreams" may bewilder them and remind them of bed-wetting. Girls who are experiencing the onset of menstruation, on the average at about eleven and a half, may also have dreams that are upsetting and reflect what they may think of as a shameful or disgusting occurrence. Girls are more likely to talk about dreams in general, and when they do have dreams suggesting images of menstruation or early erotic or sexual feelings, information and reassurance that they are normal can be beneficial.

The most common contents of adolescent Coming of Age dreams revolve around interactions with friends, siblings, parents, and teachers. In these dreams, adolescents reflect on their waking-life efforts to form mature personal relationships of various kinds. Because these life events are so often filled with tension and conflict, adolescents' dreams frequently have an anxious, frightening quality.

Leaving Home Dreams

Teenagers on the verge of leaving home are often convinced that they are fully equipped to handle any problem and all the responsibilities of young adulthood. When they get their college acceptance or go through the exciting high school graduation parties and rituals, they may have exhilarating dreams of flying, finding money, or playing star roles in movies or performances. These are not just adolescent dreams but occur during peak experiences and positive life passages throughout adulthood. They may symbolize a sense of creative power and the joy of accomplishment and new maturity.

When the moment of departure grows near, the adolescent may still deny any anxiety, but the steps he or she will take reverberate deeply. As clearly as anything else, this is the end of childhood, the end of being able to depend fully on parents, and the beginning of what for many is a more rocky road into early adulthood than they anticipated in their fantasies about independence.

For the young adult who is open to his or her feelings, there is a mixture of excitement about the new horizons of independence, and simultaneously there is grief about leaving the safety of their parents' home and maybe even a bit of terror about the responsibilities ahead of them.

When eighteen-year-old Edward was ready to go across the country to college, he had the following Apocalyptic nightmare.[6]

I'm standing on a hill overlooking my town. It's like it's World War III, and everything is about to be blown up by nuclear bombs. I think that maybe I should try to find a market and get some food so I can survive.

This Apocalyptic dream showed Edward the dark side of the journey ahead. He is looking back at his town, so in his dream he already is beginning to see himself as separate from his childhood residence and family. However, this future as an adult was not looking too promising. Dreams often exaggerate our fears. That is certainly true of Edward's dream. It is doubtful that his leaving home would be as bad emotionally as a nuclear disaster. Nevertheless, he would have to survive on his own, away from his family. Like many dream symbols, going to the market appears to have many levels of meaning. He will need to nurture himself physically and emotionally, and he will someday have to enter the job market and earn money to buy his own food when his parents no longer support him.

Although Edward was initially frightened by the dream, the extreme level of exaggeration ultimately allowed him to acknowledge his anxiety about leaving home. He found the apocalyptic nature of the dream so outrageous that he was able to laugh at his worries. Talking about the dream allowed him to see both sides of his feelings about leaving home and to gain a more realistic perspective on what going away to college meant to him.

Learning from Childhood Dreams

From the twenty-five thousand or so dreams we have during childhood, most of us only remember one or two as an adult. We don't recognize this invaluable resource that is accessible every night. In fact, most of us are taught that dreams are unimportant or unintelligible. When we have a nightmare, the experience is dismissed as "just a dream." It is important that we value the dreams and the inner experiences of our children and of our own childhood and take advantage of the emotional and creative awareness they inspire.

When children are not encouraged to remember their dreams, they are more likely to remember the occasional nightmares that wake them up during stressful times. This sets up an association of dreaming with terrifying experiences and may teach children not to remember dreams and even to develop sleep disorders. This can also reinforce fears and even phobias as the residue from nightmares generalizes into more broad fears of the dark, of sleep, and of dreams.

When dreams are taken seriously and discussed in the family, children will remember more dreams, often throughout their lives, and will recall a mixture of both upsetting and positive dreams. Sharing dreams helps to increase a child's emotional IQ by helping them identify and express important issues. Family dream sharing can also promote quality time by giving both parents and children a focus for talking about their feelings.

At life passages and times of stress, repetitive nightmares are a clear signal that some deeper conflict has not been resolved. For young children and those who are not emotionally expressive, they may not have the words to communicate their confusion about the birth of a sibling, changing schools, or the death of a grandparent. Telling dreams to a parent or teacher or mental health professional may provide the child with a vehicle for expressing unresolved feelings that they have no other way to talk about.

Dreams are an incredible source of creativity, and they provide unique opportunities for parents to raise their children's self-esteem by praising the originality that every dream possesses. When the interesting images and stories of their dreams are paid attention to and encouraged, children feel proud of their creative powers.

In addition to having nightmares during life passages, children may also have profound dreams with visionary qualities. In two instances, I have worked with adults who had childhood Career Vision dreams that helped shape their careers, one as a doctor and one as a physicist. In another instance, a child's dreams of golden bicycles coupled with a childhood passion for biking led him to become a bicycle designer as an adult.[7] See chapter 6 for more examples of adult Career Vision dreams.

As a four-year-old, Carl Jung had a profound and disturbing dream that stayed with him his entire life.[8] In the dream, he entered a hole in the ground, descended a stone staircase, and finally arrived at a throne where a terrifying man-eating cyclops was sitting. Although he awoke in terror and kept the dream secret for many years, Jung attributed this vivid nightmare with awakening his interest in dreams and other mystical experiences.

As a child, novelist Stephen King reportedly had joyful dreams of flying. He also had vivid nightmares, including a ghoulish nightmare that haunted him well into adulthood.[9] In the dream, he had a horrific vision of a man hanged on the gallows. The hangman was still present, and there were birds flying all around him. Even as a child, King respected the power of his dreams and kept the memory of his nightmare alive. Ultimately, he transformed his childhood fear into the best-selling novel *Salem's Lot*, which incorporated all the elements of his childhood dream.

Rather than treating them as "just a dream," we should recognize our childrens' dreams and nightmares as a source of many emotional, creative, and spiritual benefits. Encouraging discussion and exploration of dreams during periods of stress can help parents understand what is bothering their child, help them communicate about the issues in a new way, and help them discover creative solutions together with their child.

For additional creative and practical strategies for encouraging the recall and exploration of childhood dreams, see chapter 12, which includes details on many strategies that parents, teachers, and psychotherapists can use to guide children in the creative exploration of their dreams as well as techniques for adults to explore their first dreams from childhood.

3. Relationship Dreams working out fears of commitment before marriage

Three months before her wedding, Sarah, a thirty-six-year-old woman who was marrying for the first time, had a series of nightmares that seemed to suggest that the wedding ceremony might turn out to be a disaster.

Forgetting the Ring

It's the middle of the wedding ceremony, and when the minister says it's time to exchange rings, I realize that I have forgotten to buy one. I feel stunned and deeply ashamed.

Your Wedding Dress Is Not Going to Be Ready

I'm at the bridal shop to pick up my wedding dress. I am told that it is not going to be ready on time. I plead with the woman to put a rush order on it, but she is adamant. She's screaming at me: "You didn't come in early enough! You knew it wasn't going to be ready!"

Sarah's Ceremonial Disaster dreams portrayed her as a delinquent bride. She had awakened with a painful feeling of being unprepared. And yet there was no objective truth to the dreams, since Sarah was ahead of schedule in arranging the wedding's practical details. In fact, both the rings and the wedding dress had already been purchased. Was her unconscious telling her that she should call off the wedding? Sarah *was* unprepared—emotionally. It was hard for her to admit to herself or anyone else that she was intensely ashamed about being uncertain as she approached her wedding. Until she faced the fears that were causing her uncertainty about the marriage, Sarah's nightmares continued. In the section of this chapter titled "Dreams of Losing Valuables," I will present one more of Sarah's nightmares and describe how exploring her dreams helped her to acknowledge her ambivalence about marriage and take constructive steps to resolve her anxieties.

Dreams Reveal the Agony and Ecstasy of Preparing for Marriage

At each stage of the courtship process and with each successive level of emotional commitment, new themes emerge in our dreams. And after we decide to tie the proverbial knot, wedding-related themes dominate our dreams during the last three months before marriage.[1]

The tears of joy often shed by a bride or groom on their wedding day may express the profound emotional commitment that they are publicly declaring. But this apparent bliss shouldn't give the illusion that getting ready for marriage is easy. In reality, like other major turning points, such as having a first child or beginning a planned retirement, marriage requires extensive and often stressful preparations.

After the marriage plans are set and deposits for the caterer, florist, photographer, and dress are paid, a claustrophobic feeling may set in. It feels like there is no escape. Almost everyone experiences one or more bouts of panic about the magnitude of the commitment.

Under the pressure of the final days, some people head for the exit sign. In fact, over a fifty-year period in New York City, a steady 5 percent of those who take out marriage licenses do not get married within the required sixty-day period.[2]

For the large majority who go ahead with marriage, there is an obstacle course of worries during the final days of being single. Although premarital anxieties are common and in most cases a healthy sign of adjustment, there is a persistent tendency to deny them.

One of the most prevalent feelings that couples try to avoid is doubt. Most of us hate to admit that we're worried about doing the right thing. After all, aren't we supposed to be totally certain when we take that marriage vow to commit ourselves for life? It's hard to admit that we're feeling ambivalent, especially in the last few weeks when plans are set and invitations have already gone out. Yet, is it really abnormal to worry when the divorce rate is over 50 percent? Is it pathological to be concerned about whether your spouse will be a loving parent to your children? Is it strange to be apprehensive about repeating your parents' pattern of endless bickering and emotional alienation?

Many couples focus their energies and anxieties on the external demands of organizing the wedding and neglect the profound inner transformation that is taking place. They're so busy planning the huge expenses and ritualistic events that they may not look deeply at their feelings. Besides that, they may have two families breathing down their necks with endless expectations and advice.

Before the wedding, our dreams act like an inner radar, exaggerating the very feelings that are most difficult to admit or accept. When we allow our dream radar to alert us to hidden fears and deeper dimensions of our feelings, we may harvest subtle yet important insights. We may even be inspired to make changes in marriage plans and preparations that express our true needs and feelings. Occasionally, a dream or series of dreams will even stimulate a person to delay or cancel an engagement or wedding.

In this chapter, we'll explore the most common prewedding dreams and learn how they can help you to cope with the inner experience of marriage. We will see how sharing and exploring dreams can offer an antidote to your anxieties by helping you to:

* recognize and communicate your feelings and needs to your fiancé over issues such as conflicts related to the wedding's details, performance anxieties about the wedding day, and tension with family and in-laws

* deal with fears of intimacy and commitment, such as a sense of panic about whether you are choosing the right person (is there someone more suited to you, or will your prince turn out to be a frog in disguise?); the grief of losing the personal and sexual freedom of being single; and fears of repeating unhealthy patterns from your parents' or your own past relationships

* resolve anxieties about changes in identity and roles, including changes in name, relationships, religious orientation, and status in the community

* savor the joy and the spiritual dimension of the marriage preparation and ritual

Ceremonial Disaster Dreams

Dreams about mishaps and misfortunes at the ceremony and reception recur frequently during the period just before the marriage. These Ceremonial Disaster dreams are a direct reflection of the most common conscious anxieties about planning a wedding. They portray every imaginable calamity that could spoil our enjoyment of the event.

For example, Robin, age twenty-five, had been working with her mother to plan an elegantly catered affair. They'd been having many stormy arguments because Robin didn't want the wedding to be as formal as her mother did. She was resentful, moreover, of her mother's attempts to control every detail of the wedding but at the same time secretly worried about pleasing her.

tacky food at my wedding

We're sitting at the head table at the reception, and I notice that the waiters are serving canned spaghetti directly from the cans. I'm horrified, and I don't know what to do.

Robin woke with a feeling of humiliation and panic. After all the planning and verbal battles, would they really end up with canned spaghetti? Would she be mortified in front of her family and friends and disappoint her mother?

Robin's panicky feeling began to subside when she told her dream to her fiancé, who laughed out loud when he heard it. Life would be easier, he said, if they *could* just serve canned spaghetti at the reception. He also reminded her that when they went on their first camping trip the summer they met, she had brought along canned spaghetti, and they had enjoyed it. In discussing the dream further with her fiancé, she realized that she wanted her wedding to be more down-to-earth with an emphasis on sharing the emotional experience rather than on obsessing over expensive and showy material details.

The absurdity of the spaghetti banquet made Robin aware of how much tension had built up between her and her mother. As long as she could remember, her mother had been nervous about how the food would turn out at any party she was throwing. Robin realized that she too had succumbed to her mother's emphasis on how things look and what other people think.

Robin's dream also stimulated her to think about the deeper changes that were occurring beneath the conscious conflicts in her relationship with her mother. Robin had desperately wanted her mother's approval of her marriage plans, but her mother had initially been critical, saying Robin was too young. Robin realized now that her mother was having a difficult time accepting the marriage because it represented a separation. Financing and planning the wedding was a way for her mother to reassert the control over Robin she feared she was losing.

In any case, Robin began to insist on toning down some of the expenses and formalities of her wedding reception. This initially led to further arguments, but Robin was gradually feeling more sure of what she wanted. Ultimately her mother acceded to Robin's demands, and they were able to work collaboratively, with Robin taking more of the lead.

Understanding her dream helped Robin become assertive in a new way, a way that changed her relationship with her mother. She felt that she was no longer just her mother's daughter but would be on more equal footing with a husband and eventually with a family of her own.

Ceremonial Disaster dreams take many forms. Forgetting one's lines during the ceremony is another common theme. Prior to my own wedding, I had a series of dreams that depicted variations on this theme.

forgetting my Lines

The wedding is beginning, and everyone is watching us. I begin to panic because I realize that we have never rehearsed, and we forgot to even write our vows. I don't know what to do or say next.

At that point in our wedding planning, we had in fact neither rehearsed nor written our vows. Soon afterward, we spent a weekend in Yosemite, writing our vows and planning the final details of the ceremony. Even this didn't cure me of my wedding anxiety dreams. I continued to have dreams about forgetting to rehearse and forgetting my lines. I was becoming increasingly nervous and impatient.

A final Ceremonial Disaster variation occurred twice within two weeks of the wedding. In these dreams, the ceremony seemed to be flowing well and I knew my lines, but something was missing. I felt that I should be having stronger feelings. I didn't feel ready. At this point my optimism was shaky. Was I doing the right thing? Finally, during the last week before the wedding, a resolution of these fears appeared.

fINDING my LINES

The wedding ceremony is beginning. It isn't at the hotel. It is outside, near the ocean. Everyone is surrounding us in a circular formation. I'm worried because I forgot to bring our vows and the *Ketubbah* (the Jewish wedding contract). As I speak, I am ad-libbing, making up new lines and new vows to Tracy that seem more meaningful and more emotional than what we had written. I feel incredibly excited, and everything is working out perfectly.

This dream begins with the fears that had been plaguing my dreams for weeks—forgetting my lines and performing poorly in front of family and friends. But then at the crucial moment, I find my inner voice and declare my love for my wife in a more heartfelt and highly original way. This dream was consistent with a lifting of anxiety in the days preceding our wedding. Our material and emotional preparations had helped me to feel ready for the marriage ritual.

Finding my voice in this dream left a glow of confidence that carried me to the joyful day itself. The dream represented an emotional breakthrough for me. It was parallel to my Sacred Totem Poles dream (see introduction), through which I discovered a reservoir of confidence and creativity at a moment of self-doubt.

If you have a Ceremonial Disaster dream, it may appear at first glance to be nothing more than an inner reminder to memorize your lines, pick up the wedding rings, make sure you are on time, and so on. Closer examination, however, often reveals that these dreams are only the tip of the iceberg. Lurking just below the surface is an underworld of upsetting feelings. These include anxieties about how you will "perform" in the new role of husband or wife, fears of being judged by family and friends, grief about your loss of independence, and for some, a paralyzing sense of not being ready for the finality and commitment of marriage.

Anxiety is a universal feature of turning points. It may be a sign of an emotional impasse, but in most cases it's a normal feature of confronting profound change. When the performance anxieties of Ceremonial Disaster dreams are denied or downplayed, the anxiety may increase and dampen the joy of the marriage ceremony and the honeymoon. When the source of your performance anxieties can be consciously identified by remembering and exploring dreams, you have a much greater chance of getting at the root of the problem before the wedding.

Resolving your anxiety may require actual changes in the wedding plans, like those Robin made when she realized that she was more anxious about living up to her mother's expectations than her own. In other cases, our dreams are reminding us that we need to do our emotional homework, such as in my own prewedding dreams about forgetting (and ultimately finding) my lines. These dreams were reminding me that I needed not only to rehearse my lines, but also to deal with my fears of commitment and my unfamiliar new identity as a married man. When I began to talk about these fears with my fiancée and close friends, I began "finding my lines" in my dreams.

Sexual Adventure Dreams

Many infidelities and erotic adventures occur in the dreams that precede marriage. Sexual Adventure dreams feature sensual or directly sexual liaisons, often with partners other than your intended spouse. These may involve old flames, unknown or anonymous partners, friends, relatives, or even colleagues.

Julia was only eight days away from her marriage to Bruce when she had the following dream.

THE KISS

There is a muscular-looking man who is with me in my office at work. He looks sort of like Tony, an associate at my company, but he seems much more attractive. We are kissing, and at first it seems strange because we work together. But somehow that doesn't matter. He is kissing me with his tongue, and it seems like we are in a bedroom. His kiss is incredibly pleasurable and seems to go on for a long time. Right in the middle of this sexy interlude, the scene changes and I hear the phone ringing, and I think it is Bruce on the line, but it's all static and I can't hear his voice well. I wake up saying out loud, "Is that you, Bruce?" (and coincidentally the phone is ringing when I wake up, and it really is Bruce on the line).

Julia experienced the first part of the dream as surprisingly pleasurable, though Tony was a man she had rejected in the past. In fact, Tony had tried to take advantage of their professional relationship by making sexual advances. Although Tony's macho tendencies were repugnant to her in waking life, she found herself consenting to his advances in her dream.

Julia wondered why she was making love in this dream with her work associate and not with her fiancé. She felt no conscious desire to be sexually intimate with Tony or any other man except Bruce. In fact, she remembered that she had recently told Bruce that her working relationship with Tony had improved considerably since she had announced their engagement.

At times, overtly sexual dreams may symbolize nonerotic themes. This dream mirrors the rapprochement that Julia had achieved with Tony in their working relationship, but there was something more in the dream that had to do with her sexual relationship with Bruce. In the past, Julia had become sexually involved with men who were brusque and not very open emotionally, like Tony. Bruce was dramatically different, more emotionally expressive and caring. Julia felt that the dream was telling her that she had begun to escape her old pattern of picking macho men. The sexual pleasure in the dream was more like the new kind of erotic warmth she was feeling with Bruce, a feeling she never had in any previous sexual relationships. After exploring her Sexual Adventure dream, Julia concluded that it was not so much about Tony, as about breakthroughs in her ability to be intimate with Bruce.

Fear and anxieties about the meaning of loyalty are common stumbling blocks on the road to marital commitment. As the wedding date approaches, themes of sexual fidelity and infidelity abound in both men's and women's dreams. A frequent theme is of a spontaneous erotic encounter interrupted by an awareness that you are now engaged or married, making such behavior taboo.

Dennis's premarital Sexual Adventure dream featured an anonymous younger woman. Dennis awoke with feelings of guilt and anxiety three weeks before his wedding.

I CAN'T; I'M AN ENGAGED MAN

A young attractive woman comes up to me and makes seductive overtures, and we engage in some making out and light petting. I feel anxious because I know it isn't right for an engaged man to be making out with someone else. I am suspicious of the young woman's motives; I call it off, and she leaves.[3]

Dennis worried that he would still be attracted to old lovers and wouldn't be able to maintain his loyalty after so many years of being single. Would he be tempted in real life to taste forbidden fruit and engage in sexual infidelity?

One way to understand this type of dream is as a form of unconscious rehearsal for maintaining self-control in an exclusive sexual relationship. As we enter into a marriage, our dreams frequently remind us of our newly formed commitment by contrasting our impending vows of fidelity with images of infidelity.

If you have a blissful or warm Sexual Adventure dream with your fiancé or during any important new relationship, it may reflect a period of sexual passion that you are enjoying. But even during a passionate period in your sexual relationship, you may have dreams of other sexual partners. This nocturnal wanderlust is not necessarily a sign that your partner can't satisfy you. It may be a way of representing the depth, variety, and newness of your current sexual relationship.

There are other issues to keep in mind as you explore your own Sexual Adventure dreams. Just as symbols in nonerotic dreams may have camouflaged sexual meaning, overtly sexual dreams may have hidden meanings that relate to issues other than sex. For Julia, her dream affair with her colleague reflected changes in her waking relationship with Tony, but more profoundly it was evidence of a new emotional openness with a man. The wonderful sensuality of her dream kiss gave Julia confidence that she had chosen a man who would treat her well.

Sexual Rejection Dreams

Six weeks prior to his wedding, thirty-four-year-old Brian began to have a series of vivid dreams about sexual encounters with old girlfriends. When I met with him to discuss his dream series, he was ashamed about his persistent dream infidelities. He was not only feeling guilty, he also had been experiencing signs of depression such as disturbed sleep, loss of appetite, irritability, and persistent sadness. He was beginning to feel that his dreams and his depression were telling him that the marriage was not right.

As he shared his dream series with me, I noticed that his initial dreams involved liaisons with women with whom he had been involved just prior to his engagement. Subsequent dreams portrayed earlier girlfriends from his twenties, high school, and even junior high.

BACK WITH MY HIGH SCHOOL GIRLFRIEND

I'm back in my hometown visiting Andrea, my high school girlfriend. She wants to make love and tells me she has loved me all these years. "Aren't you still married?" I ask her. She doesn't answer, but I have a feeling that she has left her husband.

Brian was especially troubled by these dreams and wondered whether they were telling him that he still had wild oats to sow or that he wasn't ready for the commitment of marriage.

A series of repetitive dreams usually reveals unresolved emotional issues. As Brian reread more than a dozen of these dreams in his journal, he began to see a pattern. In over half of the related dreams, his sexual partner would reject him toward the end, becoming cold or appearing with another man. In one dream, Brian was seduced and then scorned by Arlene, a woman he had lived with in college. Their relationship had ended when she left him for another man.

JILTED AGAIN

I am back living with Arlene in our old apartment in New York. I can see her naked body. She still looks young, as if she hasn't aged at all. I feel very sexual. Maybe we have just made love or are about to. She suddenly says that she has to leave and starts to get dressed. I ask her if there is another man. She is reluctant but finally says yes as she is about to leave. I feel incredibly sad.

In waking life, Brian's sexual relationship with his fiancée was still passionate. He wondered what could be causing his mind to focus on old lovers and especially on being rejected. Brian had always feared rejection. In two previous serious relationships, he had experienced rejection when the woman decided to end the relationship. As the middle child in his family, in fact, he had always secretly felt that his older sister and younger brother had gotten more of his parents' love. Consequently he had always felt insecure in close relationships.

As he explored this series of dreams, Brian realized that they weren't really expressing desires for sexual infidelity, nor were they literal predictions that he would face rejection if he went through with the marriage. Rather, his guided tour of being teased and rejected by old flames was a persistent message about his fear of rejection. On the threshold of making a lifelong commitment, deep fears of abandonment were surfacing.

Sharing and exploring his Sexual Rejection dreams helped Brian understand how his deeply rooted fears of abandonment were blocking him from being able to accept the emotional commitment of marriage. By acknowledging his fears and seeking emotional support, Brian was able to restore his optimism about the wedding and alleviate his depression.

As you explore your own Sexual Rejection dreams, you may discover that you are still vulnerable to old wounds of being rejected or abandoned. These emotional wounds may come from adult experiences of being rejected in love, or they may date back to childhood traumas, such as the birth of a younger sibling or separation from a parent or other significant relative due to divorce or death. They may also relate to lingering Oedipal conflicts. According to Freud, such conflicts occur when a child's normal feelings of attraction toward the opposite-sex parent and rivalry with the same-sex parent are not adequately resolved.

Dreams of Losing Valuables

Sarah had been looking forward to her marriage with David and to the long-cherished hope of having a child. They had been getting along well, and both families approved of the match. They decided to move in together after getting engaged three months earlier. As her wedding date approached, however, Sarah became preoccupied with an uneasiness that she couldn't explain. Her dreams, which had initially been joyful, gave way to a series of troubling nightmares. Two of Sarah's Ceremonial Disaster dreams are described at the beginning of this chapter.

Sarah tried to suppress her anxieties. She felt ashamed of getting cold feet at this late date. But as much as she tried to deny her doubts about the marriage, the nightmares kept increasing. She began to have a recurrent dream, which was always followed by feelings of helplessness and depression.

Losing my purse

I want to go out by myself. I realize that I can't find my purse anywhere. I look frantically for it but can't find it. Suddenly, I remember that I left it in the trunk of David's car. I won't be able to go anywhere until he gets home. I feel trapped.

Sarah discussed her dreams with her fiancé. He became quite worried that she had changed her mind about the wedding. After confiding in her friends, she decided to seek guidance from a psychotherapist and came to see me.

The meaning of her repetitive nightmares did not seem obvious at first. I encouraged Sarah to brainstorm about what the dream was telling her. Her first thought was that David was very possessive about his car and didn't like her to drive it. Then she said she couldn't remember losing a purse or leaving anything in his trunk. She decided to focus in a general way on what else she might be losing. Before the word "losing" had rolled off her tongue, her mind began to click on a number of possibilities.

Sarah had been secretly upset about giving up her apartment of seven years and moving in with David. Her old apartment had been decorated with souvenirs from trips she had taken to Europe and Asia. David said he would allow her to redecorate parts of his house with her artifacts, but so far they had never had the time to do so. In fact, she had even been reluctant to unpack her belongings. She felt as if she was losing the strong identity of her old home and with it a hard-earned sense of independence and separateness.

Discussing her Losing Valuables dream also allowed Sarah to become aware of mixed feelings about the religious aspects of the wedding. She had agreed to be married in the Catholic church where all of David's family were members. Sarah realized that David and his family were overwhelming her. She felt as if she was losing her connection to her own familiar religious and cultural traditions.

"Talking about these dreams made me realize that I was afraid of losing my independence and being dominated by David and his family. When I finally put my finger on what was bothering me, I knew I could at least try to do something about it," she said.

The dream of losing a purse or wallet is one of the most common themes worldwide. A purse or wallet is something that you keep with you and protect. It contains identification, valuables, and photos of important people in your life. Dreaming that you lose your wallet or purse often symbolizes fears about changes in your identity or losing a connection to religious, moral, or cultural values that may be important to you.

Sarah did not call off the wedding. She did, however, take a more assertive stance with David and his family. She insisted that David help her begin redecorating the house with some of her belongings and that they spend less time visiting his family on weekends. She also took a stronger stance with David's mother on planning the wedding reception. These actions did not completely resolve Sarah's fears of being dominated by David and his family, but they did make her feel hopeful that she could maintain her sense of independence and work out issues in the future. Sarah's depression improved substantially, and her nightmares subsided as the result of confronting these issues.

If you have dreams of losing valuables such as wallets, purses, money, jewels, or other precious possessions, you may want to consider what emotional losses you are experiencing. The types of losses may vary at different turning points, but fears about losing one's identity and independence are especially common prior to marriage.

Bride of Frankenstein Dreams

Dreams exaggerate our fears and doubts about our marriage partner. A common expression of these fears is dreams that portray our partner with some previously unknown, unacceptable—even grotesque—quality. These dreams often have more to do with the dreamer than with the marriage partner. For example, a woman named Diane had the following dream.

BLUe sueDe suit

My fiancé shows up dressed in a horrible blue suede patchwork jacket and announces that he is feeling trapped. He feels that if he married me, he couldn't be wild. I think this is odd, since before he arrived, I'd been flying through the air in a convertible.[4]

As she awoke from this dream, Diane found herself upset about her fiancé's bizarre outfit and his expressed desire for more freedom. She also worried that after they were married he would suddenly show an unknown side of his personality that might embarrass or betray her. Because her fiancé was five years younger than her and had less experience in relationships, she also began to worry that he might be jealous of her past adventures and feel tied down by the marriage.

As Diane wrote down and reread her dream, her attention was drawn to the last part where she had been flying through the air in a convertible. At age thirty-five, in contrast to her fiancé, Diane had dated extensively before deciding that she wanted to settle down. She realized that the dream was emphasizing her own doubts about losing her wild side rather than fears of her fiancé finding his. Despite her conscious desire to settle down, Diane had begun to have mixed feelings about the commitment of marriage.

This dream represents what Freud called reversal. When reversal is at work, the emotional message of a dream takes on an opposite form. In this case it's not her fiancé but Diane herself who wants to fly through the air in convertibles and wear wild and crazy clothes. Reflecting on this dream helped Diane to better understand her own ambivalence about losing her independence as a single person.

In her study of women's dreams, Patricia Garfield describes an attractive woman who dreamed that her fiancé announced that he wasn't going to marry her because she was ugly. He then turned into a terrifying monster. In the dream the woman thought she'd have to cancel the wedding but was horrified at the prospect.[5]

In some instances, this kind of dream could be considered as a warning that some unknown attribute of the marriage partner may prove disastrous for the marriage's success. In this case, however, the dream was not a premonition of her fiancé becoming a verbally abusive or rejecting husband; Garfield reported that the couple was happy three years after the wedding.

Knowing the happy outcome, we can speculate that this dream was rather a reflection of wounds the woman had suffered earlier in her life. On the threshold of commitment, fears of reliving harsh parental criticism, abandonment, or even physical abuse may surface and limit the bride or groom's ability to be intimate. This bride was able to identify and overcome her fears. Until they are acknowledged, however, such fears can exert a hidden influence that may limit our emotional readiness for marriage.

In a related dream analysis, Carl Jung writes of a university student who developed a severe difficulty in swallowing after becoming engaged to a girl from a good family. He was also unable to study for his final exams. Jung requested that the man remember and report his dreams in an effort to discover the source of the physical symptoms. When the man related his dreams to Jung, he was stunned to observe that his fiancée frequently appeared as a prostitute or in other unflattering circumstances.

In this case, Jung had an intuition that the dreams contained a kernel of truth. Although the patient strenuously objected to the suggestion that his dreams were based on fact, an investigation of the woman by a private detective revealed that the dreams were accurate. According to Jung, the "shock of the unpleasant discovery did not kill the patient. On the contrary, it cured him of his neurosis and also of his bride."[6]

Even a dream that has an objective basis should be considered on a more subjective level. In the book *Dreams: A Portal to the Source,* Jungian analysts Edward Whitmont and Sylvia Brinton Perera discuss this same patient further. In their view, his dream may have revealed what his heart had known but was unable to admit. They speculate that the dreamer may have unconsciously chosen a partner lacking in integrity or commitment because he was unable to face those very attributes in himself. Or perhaps he had been prostituting himself by engaging in marriage plans for some expected financial or social gain.[7]

Bride of Frankenstein dreams present grotesque and even humorous caricatures of the prospective partner. When you have a dream of this nature, consider whether it is about some upsetting feature of your partner or whether it may be a parody of some unexplored aspect of your own character.

Clothing and Nudity Dreams

Clothing and Nudity dreams are common throughout the life cycle. At turning points that require us to take on new roles, such as marriage, Clothing dreams often represent explorations of new appearances. Nudity dreams in general suggest a feeling of being exposed or psychologically vulnerable. They also correlate with a sense of openness and sincerity. Clothing or the lack of it is a frequent theme in prenuptial dreams. A woman may have fantasized for many years about how she will look in her wedding gown.

Consequently, anxiety about being improperly dressed or in some state of nakedness is common. One woman dreamed that she looked down during the ceremony and noticed that she was wearing one blue shoe and one white shoe. Another woman dreamed that she had completely forgotten to hem her dress, which had ragged edges. Another one dreamed that while putting on her wedding dress, she noticed that it looked like a huge, very unflattering padded bra.

Dreams such as these are a variation on the Ceremonial Disaster dream. A focus on clothing, new hairstyles, or improper attire appears frequently in dreams of people who are going through transformations in their identity. Changing clothing often symbolizes an inner rehearsal of new roles. These dream rehearsals don't usually proceed smoothly. As in the dreams above, there is often an anxious moment of awareness. An appearance or a role that we thought we could fit into suddenly seems impossible.

Appearing naked in public is another theme common to many cultures. Although the meaning may differ for each dreamer, this type of imaginary embarrassment often occurs when the dreamer is afraid of exposing some emotional vulnerability in waking life. Frequently associated with a feeling of being unprepared, it is another variant of the performance anxiety theme of Ceremonial Disaster dreams. A common premarital variation is dreams that feature the bride or groom in underwear, being exposed or partly naked at the wedding ceremony, or in other compromising circumstances.

Dream researcher Dale Westbrook examined the issue of Clothing dreams in her study of the premarital dreams of men and women over the age of thirty-five who were marrying for the first time. The grooms-to-be had clothing references in 28 percent of their dreams, as compared to only 2 percent for a matched control group. Phrases such as "feeling well-suited" and trying to "fit in" to new clothes were typical.[8]

Andrew, a thirty-nine-year-old man in Westbrook's study, had two dreams in the same week that related to changing roles and identities. Andrew had been rebellious in his twenties and thirties, refusing to conform to the social norms that he perceived to be a part of mainstream society. He had refused to work in a traditional career or to dress in a conventional manner.

In Andrew's first dream, he found himself with his fiancée, Nancy, in a neighborhood of older homes.

naked in a world of traditional values

I'm naked. At first this is OK. Then I realize how easily I could be spotted on the street. I ask Nancy to go to the enemy's headquarters and sneak out clothes for me. She could try this because they wouldn't suspect that she was helping me.[9]

In this dream, Andrew has no secure role within the world of mainstream commitments. He is oblivious at first, but suddenly experiences fear at his nakedness. To resolve his sense of vulnerability, he uses his fiancée as an infiltrator in the world of his former enemy: traditional values.

Later that week, Andrew had the second dream in this series.

DESIGNING my NEW UNIFORM

I have been given a promotion at my job. I'm designing a new uniform for the position. It will consist of yellow tennis shoes with black soles and laces, yellow pants, yellow shirt, a pleated coat/shirt that is black on the outside and yellow on the inside. I don't know whether the tie is to be yellow or black.[10]

Andrew felt "excitement and preoccupation" as he described his new uniform. He had not actually received a new job or promotion, but he felt that this dream symbolized his efforts to fit into social norms. Andrew's yellow uniform is a far cry from a pinstripe suit, and he is clearly not ready to adopt a totally traditional lifestyle. But his dream does suggest that he is engaged in an inner struggle to develop a new look, a new way of appearing to others and of experiencing himself in the world.

The necktie is another recurrent symbol of "tying the knot" for men who are entering into marital commitments. One groom dreamed that he was struggling to tie a yellow tie. Another dreamed his tie was too tight. In reality, he ultimately broke off the engagement. Neckties, inappropriate wedding attire, and appearing nude or partially disrobed are all wedding-related variations of two universal dream themes, clothing and nudity.

Dreams of Mortal Threat

A common focus of anxiety in prewedding dreams is fear of physical danger or even a mortal threat to oneself or one's fiancé. Such dreams may relate to actual fears for the partner's safety. A spouse who works in a dangerous occupation—a police officer, for example—may inspire this kind of dream. More often, dreams of danger have a symbolic meaning that has to do with perceived emotional threats to oneself or to the relationship.

In the following example cited by Westbrook, Allison, a thirty-five-year-old woman, was coordinating the arrangements for her $10,000 wedding and was feeling happy about her upcoming marriage. Consequently, her dream about needing heart surgery came as a shock.

I was scheduled for heart surgery. The nurse had a piece of paper that she asked me to sign saying, "Do you want the doctors to do everything they can regardless of cost?" The paper stated that they would spend up to $10,000 to prolong my life, but no more than that (in case something went wrong). If they did use all means to prolong life, I would be billed. I really struggled with what to do, even whether or not to have the surgery. I had already been anesthetized and was getting very sleepy, yet I was struggling to stay awake to tell them that I wasn't sure whether I wanted the surgery.[11]

Allison was upset after this dream and at first wondered whether she might be facing a serious illness or perhaps surgery. As she was writing in her journal, she stared at the words "heart surgery." Suddenly it occurred to her: "Of course, my wedding is an operation of the heart, and it's going to cost $10,000."

This flash of insight revealed the key metaphor of her dream. As she discussed its possible meanings, she was struck by her ambivalence to this heart surgery. Could she afford it emotionally? Would the surgeons damage her heart?

Then Allison remembered her father's bypass surgery two years earlier. She had been terrified about the outcome. Getting married, however, didn't seem like a life-or-death situation. The dream was exaggerating a physical danger to make her aware of the emotional risks. Worrying about planning the details had been like the anesthesia, keeping her from awareness of fears related to the wedding.

Allison's anxiety dreams did not cause her to question her marriage. They did motivate her to take time out from the planning to focus on her feelings and share them with her fiancé.

Getting married represents an emotional transformation, a permanent change in loyalties of the heart. Even in well-matched couples who enjoy a happy marital adjustment, dreams often show fears about the emotional commitment and a sense of loss of identity as a single person.

Dreams of Mortal Threat or physical danger offer an opportunity to examine whether there are physical dangers to you or your loved ones. When realistic physical danger or illness are not present concerns, your dreams are probably indicating a perception of danger to your emotional well-being.

Culture Clash Dreams

Mixed marriages have become increasingly commonplace. Many couples of different ethnic or religious backgrounds establish a family life that integrates important rituals and wisdom from both cultures. In order to forge a blend of cultures, couples must take time to communicate their expectations and be willing to compromise.

Many couples underestimate the conflicts they may encounter. They hope that if they behave in a low-key manner or try to avoid religious or ethnic confrontations, everything will work out. But cultural differences do not evaporate easily. Strong preferences often assert themselves at turning points. These issues cannot necessarily be solved before marriage. They tend to simmer underneath the surface as the wedding approaches. Dreams can reveal these issues and point out emotional sore spots that require discussion and resolution.

Roger, a Presbyterian, was about to marry Sandy, a Jew. Roger played down their cultural and religious differences. He had agreed to be married by a rabbi because "neither of us is very religious." He didn't expect any problems to arise. But one month before the wedding, he had an unsettling dream.

MIDDLE EASTERN INVADERS MOVE INTO OUR HOUSE

A group of dark-looking people from a country in the Middle East come to stay at my house. They say they are moving in and are going to take over my house and live there. I try to talk to my fiancée, but she doesn't seem to be able to help me get them out. They may have even captured her in some way, so she is loyal to them.

When Roger was asked to free-associate about the image of the Middle Eastern invaders, his first thoughts were of his fiancée's parents, whom they had recently visited. His future in-laws had shown him a treasured photo album of their numerous trips to Israel, including visits to relatives who were Holocaust survivors. Although Sandy's family was not dark-skinned, many of the photographs were of deeply suntanned Israelis.

The invading Middle Eastern family was an exaggeration of Roger's unconscious concerns. Would Sandy's family's cultural traditions dominate their family life? Would she be loyal to him on crucial issues or would she side with her family? Discussing this dream helped Roger to see that his differences with Sandy were not trivial. He did feel a little unsettled about being married by a rabbi, and he had been touchy about some of the wedding plans. As a result of examining this dream, Roger became more open about his concerns. Subsequently, Sandy agreed to have further discussions about the wedding ceremony and about Roger's general feelings on religion and child rearing.

Not all cultural differences are a source of anxiety or alienation. In some instances the cultural differences may be part of the attraction. A cross-cultural marriage may bring a sense of warmth and acceptance that a person may not have in his or her own family of origin.

For example, Bob, an Anglo man, was about to be married to Yolanda, whose family was from Nicaragua. Bob's dream helped to confirm the feelings of warmth that he had experienced with Yolanda's family.

the hopi indians welcome us

Yolanda and I are on the Hopi Indian reservation. The Indians we meet are helpful and warm. I think to myself that they have accepted us. Yolanda and I discuss this with excitement. Several men and women help us. They treat us as if we are part of their tribe.[12]

Both of Bob's parents had been alcoholics. His father had been physically abusive, and his mother was often depressed. Bob had participated in groups for Adult Children of Alcoholics and realized that his previous reluctance to make a commitment had been related to fears about aggravating the wounds that he suffered in childhood. He also worried about the possibility of inflicting similar damage on his children.

For Bob, the Hopis symbolized the warmth and acceptance of his new in-laws. The dream bolstered his confidence in his decision to marry Yolanda and left him feeling excited and positive about the wedding.

Culture Clash dreams are common in people who are about to marry someone from an ethnic, religious, or economic strata different from their own family's. They may occur even in marriages that are not mixed, symbolizing the emotional or physical difference between the two families.

Couples who spend time openly discussing and learning about the differences in their backgrounds will be better prepared to resolve the inevitable conflicts. Culture Clash dreams provide us with an opportunity to appreciate the richness of our own and our spouse's cultural identity. In so doing we can forge a healthier identity for our marriage and our children.

How to Use Wedding and Relationship Dreams

We tend to put on a happy face when we make the commitment to marry, throughout the wedding preparations, honeymoon, and aftermath. It's hard, therefore, to admit the normal and expectable anxieties that we inevitably experience. It's important to keep in mind that upsetting dreams and even occasional nightmares are normal. They may even be a positive sign that we're actively wrestling with important feelings that need to be worked out.

Examining patterns in wedding and relationship dreams reminds us that making a commitment is not an easy task. We often feel passion, intense joy, and fulfillment. But we may also experience ambivalence, fears about intimacy, struggles for power and control, stress over assuming new roles with family and friends, and grief over the loss of the single life.

Nightmares and recurring anxiety dreams are an SOS from the unconscious. They emphasize feelings that we have been unaware of or are denying. In most cases, the feelings are appropriate and normal and can be worked through as part of the preparation for commitment. Occasionally, a series of dreams or nightmares will help us discover unrecognized feelings that suggest that delaying or canceling marriage plans may be prudent.

Because of the predominance of anxiety dreams prior to and during a turning point and because of the tendency for dreams to be exaggerated and distorted, it would be unwise to base any rash decisions about your commitment to marriage or a relationship on a single dream. A Ceremonial Disaster dream should not be taken as an accurate psychic prediction that your wedding ceremony will turn into a fiasco. Nor does a Bride of Frankenstein dream mean that you will awaken one night to find your groom transformed into a monster.

To appreciate the hidden meaning of relationship and prewedding dreams, you need to look behind the obvious and conscious anxieties and see whether your dreams reveal symbols, distortions, reversals, or disguises for your deeper feelings and needs. A Sexual Adventure dream may reveal ambivalence about sexual fidelity or a fear of abandonment; the shock of dreaming about being naked at your wedding may expose a performance anxiety or other vulnerability; when your fiancé turns from Dr. Jekyll to Mr. Hyde in a dream, it may illuminate your own fears of commitment and not his.

To reveal the deeper meaning of your prewedding dreams, try to devote some time to remembering, communicating, and exploring them. For couples preparing for marriage, remembering and sharing dreams provides a special forum for expressing feelings.

Positive dreams remind both partners about the emotional and spiritual depth of the marriage commitment. Anxious dreams and nightmares are also a vital source of information. Sharing anxious dreams and other upsetting feelings can bring about a sense of empathy and collaboration that will form the basis for successful problem solving and a resilient marriage in future years together. Helping each other to understand your dreams may even guide you to take new approaches to planning your wedding and honeymoon, dealing with your families, or planning when to have your own family.

A vast amount of time, energy, and financial resources is devoted to preparing for a set of marriage rituals that last for a few hours. Much less time is set aside for emotional preparation for a marriage commitment that is meant to last a lifetime. Exploring dreams with your partner can help both of you to work through the profound changes that you are experiencing and to establish a solid foundation for your marriage.

4. from conception to birth
dreams of expectant mothers and fathers

With joy and trepidation we dream our children into existence. From the moment of conception, expectant parents dream about many aspects of their unborn child. In our pregnant dreams, we envision our child's face, their name, the feeling of their skin. We burst with pride when our dream child talks precociously. As expectant parents, we dream that we risk life and limb to protect our children from danger. Anxious about whether we will become good parents, we dream we blow it, neglecting or losing our dream children, forgetting to feed them, and causing them injury.

Many pregnancy dreams are filled with anxieties about our child's well-being and with doubts about our competency as parents. It is very distressing to see every fear and worst-case scenario played out in our pregnancy dreams. However, there is an amazing paradox in these vivid worrisome pregnancy dreams. Despite how distressing these nightmares are, they are actually helping us to prepare for the indispensable role we must play as parent to our helpless newborn child. A crucial function of pregnancy dreams is to rehearse and develop our parenting skills and form an inner relationship with our unborn child.

Pregnancy is a turning point in life that's likely to be filled with compelling dreams. The vivid themes of pregnancy dreams have been studied in more depth than those of any other turning point. In this chapter we'll examine the remarkable patterns in the dreams of expectant mothers and fathers and demonstrate how awareness and exploration of these dreams can enhance our emotional preparation for parenting.

The first two dreams we will look at are Animal Birth dreams which were collected from women in the final stage of their first pregnancies. Although a century apart, both have elements that are common to the dreams of late pregnancy: the presence of water and the arrival of furry mammals. The first dream is taken from Sigmund Freud's *The Interpretation of Dreams* and was probably the dream of a Viennese woman near the end of the nineteenth century.

the trapdoor seal

A subterranean channel led directly into the water from a place in the floor of her room. She raised a trapdoor in the floor, and a creature dressed in brown fur, very much resembling a seal, presently appeared.[1]

In the briefly reported associations to this dream, Freud noted that the "creature turned out to be her younger brother to whom she had always been like a mother."[2] Freud did not elaborate at length on this dream, except to note that the subterranean channel and the water represented the birth canal and the amniotic fluid.

The second Animal Birth dream, from the end of the twentieth century, is Jennifer's, a San Francisco nurse in her eighth month of pregnancy.

the otter's smooth skin

I'm in labor and I am lying on a beach. The tide is coming in, and big waves are washing up onto shore. I keep calling for my husband. I know he's there, but I can't see him. The waves are getting bigger and more dangerous. Just when the waves seem like they are going to drown me, I see a little sea otter next to me. I know it was supposed to be my baby, but I am confused that it looks like an otter. I touch its skin, and it is incredibly smooth.

Jennifer worried that her Animal Birth dream might signify something abnormal about her baby, perhaps a premonition of some malformation. But as she told her dream at one of my workshops for nurses and childbirth educators on the psychology of pregnancy, there were many looks of recognition on the faces of the other women in the class. They quickly volunteered that they, too, had had frightening dreams during their pregnancies.

As Jennifer listened to the other women discuss the details of their worrisome dreams, she was reassured. She saw the dream as representing not danger, but joyful expectation of holding her baby and touching its wonderful soft skin.

Jennifer's dream also contains a number of other themes common to women in their last trimester of pregnancy. The imminence of labor is often represented by waves, earth tremors, other powerful movements, and a feeling of losing control.

During the second and third trimester of pregnancy, many women also have heightened fears about their spouse's well-being. In Jennifer's dream, her husband's presence is sensed, but he is unable to arrive soon enough to protect her from the dangerous waves of labor.

Dreams also focus on anxieties that haunt both men and women even during a healthy pregnancy. These include themes that exaggerate the dangers of labor and delivery and fears about birth defects. Dreams also express marital tensions, feelings of rejection, and fears about being an incompetent parent.

For example, early in his wife's pregnancy, one man who was in the process of wallpapering a room for his child-to-be had a nightmare that he entered the room and saw his baby stuck to the wall with glue.[3] Another woman nearing her delivery date was horrified by a dream that a little boy ran away from his mother and fell off a cliff into a turbulent ocean.

These and other pregnancy nightmares do not necessarily predict disaster. In fact, remembering a disturbing dream may be a positive sign that the dreamer is actively coping with the emotional challenges of becoming a parent. As horrifying as they may feel, troublesome dreams and nightmares during pregnancy provide us with an early warning system that alerts us to the fears and concerns that we need to work out.

You may feel reassured to know that women who have more frequent dreams involving anxiety or threat had shorter labors and healthier deliveries with fewer complications than women who did not report such dreams. A study of seventy women, by researchers Carolyn Winget and Frederic Kapp, concluded that troubling dreams may be evidence of important conflicts that were being resolved. When fewer distressing dreams were remembered, women tended to have longer labors and more complications. Those women who recalled more troubling dreams appeared to have worked out the normal anxieties that accompany the final stage of pregnancy.[4]

Medical breakthroughs have given us the technology to diagnose and treat risk factors during pregnancy and delivery. With electronic sensing and imaging, we can listen to our baby's heartbeat and actually look into the womb to see our baby very early in the pregnancy.

Technological advances, however, are not the only resources we have for understanding what's going on with us during pregnancy. We can also use our dreams as an emotional ultrasound. They provide a way to look into our unconscious and see how we're responding to the changes in our identity, our marriage, our relationships with family and friends, and our newly forming attachment to our unborn child.

In the sections that follow, we'll explore how remembering, sharing, and exploring dreams can help expectant parents to:

* understand and enhance the powerful prenatal emotional attachment to the unborn child

* recognize unique patterns in dreams during the three trimesters of pregnancy and become aware of how they relate to the emotional stages of becoming a parent

* understand the similarities and differences between men's and women's psychological conflicts and fulfillments

* generate mutual understanding and empathy for emotional reactions to pregnancy and rekindle communication on issues that often create tension and confusion

* explore patterns in their erotic dream adventures and misadventures, and to use these dreams to help resolve confusion and misunderstandings that may arise in the couple's sexual relationship

* recognize how identity changes and new roles linked to parenthood will cause them to experience themselves in new and unaccustomed ways with family and friends

Dreams of Conception, Pregnancy, and Birth

Pregnancy is a major turning point in the lives of both the expectant mother and the father-to-be. Consequently, each night during pregnancy, a kaleidoscope of images dance in front of the sleeping eyes of expectant parents. As the fetus grows, a new psychological relationship is growing, a powerful attachment that is vividly pictured in turning-point dreams.

Many dreams make direct references to pregnancy, childbirth, the baby's appearance, and the parents' roles. Other dreams are symbolic of the fetus, its experience in the womb and the birth canal. Themes of fertility, virility, dances, and other celebrations express the joy and pride that accompany parenthood.

There are distinct differences between the dreams of early pregnancy and those closer to delivery. Dream images closely parallel the biological milestones of pregnancy. When a woman misses her period or feels the first signs of pregnancy, when she senses the first movements of the baby in the womb, when her body grows progressively larger, or when labor contractions are felt, the unconscious minds of the expectant mother and father generate dreams that tell the story of their varied responses.

Fetal Identification Dreams

Some dreams tend to occur more frequently at certain stages of pregnancy. Others happen throughout pregnancy, but their form changes as the pregnancy progresses. An example of the latter is what I call Fetal Identification dreams, which are common for both men and women throughout pregnancy. In these dreams, the dreamer experiences a fantasy version of what the fetus might be undergoing.

Early-pregnancy Fetal Identification dreams may focus on a quiescent fetus lolling about in a fertile womb. For example, one father-to-be during the first trimester of pregnancy described a dream in which he was floating in an enclosed body of water with fertile vegetation and rose colors at the horizon. In contrast, late-pregnancy Fetal Identification dreams focus on the dangers of the journey down and out of the birth canal. Third-trimester examples include dreams of being trapped or suffocated in small spaces, perilous escapes from caves, and swimming downhill.[5]

Pregnancy Identification Dreams

In addition to Fetal Identification dreams, both men and women have Pregnancy Identification dreams, which begin around the time of conception and continue unabated until birth. These dreams feature references to every aspect of the biology of pregnancy and birth. Some of these dreams are realistic depictions; others are cloaked in exotic or even humorous symbolism.

Conception Dreams

For most people, the beginning of pregnancy unleashes a wave of fantasies and dreams after the confirming test. It can be fascinating to reread your dream journal from around the time of conception. Many women have noted themes related to impregnation at this time. Fish or amphibious animals swimming up narrow channels and objects or people merging together are common themes at the time of conception.

Around the time of conceiving our daughter Zoe, my wife, Tracy, had a dream that evoked a powerful feeling that she had indeed conceived a child.

embryonic journey

I am in the ocean and have to swim down this channel to get to the shore. As I swim down the channel, whales and big boats pass me. I am bodysurfing on three-foot waves that are very scary. When I get tired of bodysurfing and want to get out of the water, I get really scared because the waves are very high and are crashing up against the shore.

When Tracy awoke, she was anxious but quite exhilarated to have escaped the water. This feeling was similar to how she felt after getting off a roller coaster. Two weeks later, after confirming that she was pregnant, Tracy reviewed her dream journal. Her Embryonic Journey dream had occurred the day after she thought she had ovulated. She felt that the imagery of that dream symbolized the perilous journey of the egg down the fallopian tube. As in the Fetal Identification dreams discussed above, she experienced the uterine environment in a personal way.

Fertility Dreams

In the first trimester of pregnancy, the excitement and sense of creativity are often evident in dreams. For women and sometimes for men, dreams of incredible fertility appear without direct reference to the fetus. One woman whom I interviewed dreamed that while swimming she saw a beautifully pruned pear tree with gorgeous fruit that appeared to be shaped like a uterus.

In Dr. Myra Leifer's excellent book on first pregnancy, *The Psychological Effects of Motherhood,* she describes the following Fertility dream.

my breasts are blossoming

I dreamed about my breasts having all these big, bright flowers flowing out of them. It was just beautiful. I was in a swimming pool, and I must have taken myself for a water lily, and these flowers were blooming from my breast. Then I came out, and everyone—men, women, and children— was looking with great admiration at my flowers.[6]

Fertility dreams symbolize the body's creative powers during a period of rapid growth of the fetus. In Arthur and Libby Colman's groundbreaking book, *Pregnancy: The Psychological Experience,* they assert that acceptance of the reality of the pregnancy is the most important psychological task of the first trimester.[7] Remembering and sharing Fertility dreams with your loved one can enhance your mutual positive feelings about the pregnancy and hasten the process of accepting its reality.

Aquatic Dreams

There are no droughts in pregnancy dreams. Water is everywhere: tidal waves, coursing streams, warm amniotic fluids, swimming pools, and one of the most common water dreams—the washing machine dream.

The washing machine is, of course, useful to have for the diapers and extra laundry of infancy. But why would the unconscious mind of so many expectant parents focus on an appliance? Because the watery inner space of a washing machine is a symbol of the pregnant womb.

With the advent of high-tech methods for observing a fetus, washing machine dreams may coincide with ultrasound diagnosis. For example, prior to an appointment for an ultrasound exam, Kathy, a thirty-year-old teacher, dreamed that she was looking inside an old-fashioned glass washing machine and saw a boy waving at her.

Joel, a computer programmer in a large urban hospital, had a humorous version of a washing machine dream.

A WILD RIDE ON OUR WASHING MACHINE

My wife and I are at an amusement park full of household items that are giant-sized. We are riding a giant washing machine agitator. My wife is trying to hang on. She laughs and says that she used to do this as a child.

Joel was amused by the dream. His first association was how both he and his wife enjoy the rides at Disneyland and go there every year. The dream brought back positive memories of visits there with his parents and stimulated fantasies about how wonderful it would be to share the fun with his own child.

As he continued to explore this dream, Joel remarked that he and his wife were experiencing what it must be like for their child in the womb— floating around and being shaken by the mother's daily activities. The agitator arm made him aware that the pregnancy was bringing some agitation. At times, as in the dream, it felt hard to hold on and stay above water emotionally.

Body Image Dreams

While some dreams are filled with disguised symbolism of pregnancy and birth, other dreams make direct reference to pregnancy. Despite reassurances from others, many women feel that their changing bodies are unattractive.

One woman dreamed that her mother accused her of gaining too much weight during pregnancy. Another woman dreamed that she looked in the mirror and saw herself as incredibly bloated, like the fat woman she had seen in a circus.

Toby, an attorney, had not yet announced her pregnancy to her coworkers because she wanted to wait until all dangers of miscarriage were past. At twelve weeks, many of her clothes were already too tight, and she was beginning to feel dowdy, dressing in more loosely fitting clothes. She had two upsetting Body Image dreams about her mother criticizing her for being too fat. She woke up from the following dream in tears.

NOTHING TO WEAR

My husband, Andrew, is telling me that we are invited to a dinner party at an elegant restaurant with his business associates. I see him changing into a tuxedo, and I suddenly see the other women as we are arriving at the restaurant. They are all wearing very fancy dresses with velvet and sequins. My outfit feels old and frumpy in comparison, and my stomach is sticking out even though I know I am only a few weeks pregnant. I burst out crying and run sobbing to the bathroom.

Toby was agitated and tearful as she told this dream to Andrew. She could not stop thinking about feeling physically unattractive. Andrew tried to reassure her about her attractiveness and pointed out how exaggerated the contrast was between her frumpy old clothes and the elegant gowns of the other women.

As Toby calmed down, she began to realize how hard it was to accept the physical changes that accompanied being pregnant. As we observed in prewedding dreams, changes in clothing may represent changes in identity.

The lack of social acknowledgment may have hampered Toby's ability to accept the changes in her pregnant body. After discussing this dream, Toby and Andrew decided it was time to inform her coworkers about her pregnancy and to buy or borrow some attractive maternity clothes.

Because of our nearly universal standard of being slim and fit, many women are ashamed to gain weight, even during pregnancy when it is essential for the child's health. Exploring Body Image dreams that exaggerate the physical changes of pregnancy can help a woman accept not only her own altered body image but the psychological reality of the pregnancy. By sharing dreams related to weight gain, a woman can receive reassurance that these worries are a normal part of adjusting to the physical changes that occur during pregnancy.

For women who have had mild or serious problems with anorexia or bulimia, dreams that emphasize the issues of weight and body image are especially important. Eating disorders may get stirred up during pregnancy, and these dreams emphasize the need to work out responses to pregnancy's inherent physical changes. If dreams and anxieties about eating or body changes persist, it may be important to seek professional support.

Labor and Delivery Dreams

As the due date approaches, women's and men's dreams begin to focus on the symbolism of labor, traveling through the birth canal and giving birth. Whereas early-pregnancy dreams of floating and swimming are more tranquil, late-pregnancy dreams portray labor's powerful contractions, including themes of earthquakes, powerful tides, and overwhelming waves. Experiences of loss of control may be seen in dreams of falling, cars going out of control, or drowning. These labor and delivery dreams may be a direct anticipation of labor but may also warn us that we are feeling emotionally overwhelmed.

Dreams depicting physical danger or actual pain or injury to the mother or child increase in late pregnancy. Dreams of damaged buildings and other architectural features symbolize the structural damage that is feared in the birth process.

Traveling in and emerging from narrow passageways is the late-pregnancy version of the Fetal Identification dream. Caves, tunnels, and interior hallways represent the birth canal. Many swimming dreams and narrow-passage dreams feature downhill motions that parallel the downward journey of the fetus through the birth canal.

Two weeks before her due date, Maureen had a frightening dream that she did not immediately associate with her pregnancy.

escape from the jungle gym

I am playing on top of a jungle gym with a friend from elementary school whom I haven't seen for years. Even though I am very pregnant, I'm still able to climb up and around. Suddenly I start to lose my grip and fall through the bars. I am all tangled in the bars and can't seem to get out. I slowly work my way downward on the bars till I come out of a larger hole near the bottom that someone had pulled apart. I am incredibly tired from the exercise and from how scared I was about falling.

Maureen associated the anxiety in the dream to her fears about something going wrong at the birth, such as needing a cesarean section or having a prolonged labor. As she told her dream a second time, however, she began to see the emergence from the jungle gym as an image of what it must be like for her baby to make its way out of the labyrinth of the womb.

Maureen was puzzled about why she dreamed about a jungle gym and a friend she hadn't seen for so long. As she allowed her mind to associate, she remembered that she had fallen off of a jungle gym in elementary school, chipping a tooth and suffering a mild concussion. After that she had developed a phobia about jungle gyms and other similar playground equipment.

Maureen's dream had drawn an image of danger from her long-term memory banks and associated it with birthing. Acknowledging the nature of her fears did not make them evaporate because she knew there is real danger at the time of birth. A certain level of fear is normal and helps to mobilize us to action when we are facing a difficult situation. Maureen felt that exploring her Labor and Delivery dream helped her to ventilate her feelings, reduce her level of fear, and become more prepared for the birth.

Dreams about Babies and Children

A vital part of the process of forming an emotional bond with our child occurs during pregnancy. In dreams and in waking fantasy, we are preoccupied with images of how our baby will look and what our relationship with our child will be. In daydreams we may dwell upon feeding or brushing hair or playing ball in the park. At night, our dreams continue where our conscious fantasies leave off.

In fact, babies are featured in up to 40 percent of pregnant women's dreams, versus only 1 percent in a comparative study of other young women.[8] My own research revealed that 21 percent of expectant fathers had dreams about babies during a two-week journal-keeping period.[9]

Animal Birth Dreams

Studies of pregnant women's dreams have shown that 17 percent contain animals, more than twice as many as in a nonpregnant group.[10] Dreams of giving birth to furry mammals such as puppies, kittens, and seals are common during pregnancy. The endearing creatures symbolize the vulnerable newborn who will soon need the parents' tender care. These Animal Birth dreams reveal an inner rehearsal that prepares the dreamer for a new or renewed role as a parent.

In addition to cute furry mammals, a wide variety of other dream creatures may appear. Fish and amphibious creatures tend to represent the water-dwelling fetus that eventually makes its way to land. Common farm animals such as chickens and pigs may represent an exaggerated image of fertility, as we often picture them teeming with offspring. Injured or defective animals represent fears about birth defects.

Animal Birth dreams, like most common pregnancy dreams, change over the course of the pregnancy. For some women they may even follow a course similar to the evolution of the species, which began in water and gradually moved onto land. Early in pregnancy, dream animals tend to be smaller.[11] Aquatic animals such as fish and tadpoles are common. Insects such as spiders, which are known to have multiple births, also appear. As the fetus grows and begins to move around during the middle of pregnancy, dream animals grow larger too. As the due date approaches, larger species such as seals and monkeys and other large mammals are more common.

In my research, I found that men do not have more frequent Animal Birth dreams during their wives' pregnancies. The animal dreams they do have, however, relate directly to fantasies about the child and the birth process. Neal, an architect and oldest of four children, had the following dream late in his wife's pregnancy.

the old dog under the sea

I am fishing at the beach with Will, my younger brother. Out of a bubble comes a "boo" sound, which startles me. As I pull in my line, I feel no resistance. There is a white, fluffy, ripply thing attached to the end. Then I get it up on the beach, and I see it's a very old dog. It is alive. I have a feeling that it lived in the ocean to be protected so no one knew that it was alive.

Although there is no specific mention of children or birth, Neal's dream is filled with images of pregnancy and birthing. It portrays the mysterious arrival of an animal, barely alive, that was hidden under water for protection. Emerging from a placenta-like bubble with a shout, Neal's dream dog is clearly a symbolic vision of his child's coming arrival.

Like many expectant fathers, Neal was puzzled by what his dream might be telling him. He did not immediately connect the dream to his feelings about the pregnancy. When I explained that animals often serve as symbols of the baby during pregnancy, Neal became quite animated. The whole dream seemed to make sense to him, and he was pleased that he had had a dream related to the birth of his child.

The presence in the dream of his younger brother reminded Neal of his brother's actual birth when he was four. His mother's return from the hospital with Will was one of Neal's first memories. According to his parents, Neal did not adjust easily to his brother; he was frequently angry and threw tantrums.

Discussing this Animal Birth dream helped Neal realize that he was harboring hidden fears about his child's impending arrival. Although he very much wanted to be a father, he discovered that he was also afraid of being emotionally displaced by a baby, which is what he experienced after the birth of his brothers.

Neal talked to his wife about his fears and his positive sense of being touched by the pregnancy. She was sympathetic and in fact admitted to him that she had been so busy dealing with her own reactions that she hadn't stopped to think about his. Finally, in an attempt to follow through on the dream's message, he enlisted his mother's help to review how he had reacted when his brother was born.

Some animal dreams are unpleasant or nightmarish. In *Pregnancy: The Psychological Experience,* the Colmans reported a pregnant woman's dream that depicted a cat leaping up to claw the dreamer. In retaliation, the dreamer flung the vicious cat against the wall.[12]

Dreams of violence or injury toward an animal may represent fears of injury to the baby. They also may represent feelings of aggression toward the child. Despite our positive feelings about pregnancy, we have mixed feelings about the upsetting physical and emotional changes that the pregnancy is causing and about how the baby may intrude upon the stability of our relationships and career, not to mention our sleep.

Animal Birth dreams during pregnancy are closely related to feelings about the fetus and the pregnancy. Even when such dreams are troubling, they are directing the expectant parent to focus on preparing for the new relationship.

Dreams of Forgetting the Baby

One of the most troubling types of pregnancy dreams typically culminates with the shocking realization that you've left your baby somewhere, unattended or in dangerous circumstances. Frequently the dreamer has gone on to some other activity, oblivious of the fact that he or she is now a parent.

Anna, age thirty-six, a junior high school principal, had been married for less than a year when she became pregnant. Although her pregnancy was planned and both she and her husband were looking forward to their daughter's arrival (the gender confirmed by amniocentesis), Anna had been troubled by fears about how she was going to balance her successful career with the demands of parenthood. She had been granted a six-month maternity leave but wasn't sure that it would be enough time to establish a relationship with her daughter. She didn't see how she could handle a demanding job, which often required overtime, and care for her child as well.

In her ninth month of pregnancy, she had a nightmare that left her anxious and shaken for days. It occurred three weeks before her due date, on her last day at work before her maternity leave.

the abandoned baby

I am walking along the waterfront, pushing a stroller with my baby in it.
I think it is a girl. A brightly lit yacht pulls up nearby, and a woman in a
professional suit offers me a ride on the boat and a luxury trip to Hawaii.
I accept and am suddenly on board, sailing in the open sea. All of a sudden,
I realize that I left my baby alone on the dock. I panic and start shouting,
trying desperately to get the boat to turn around, but no one will listen. I
wake up crying and feeling incredibly guilty.

Anna was worried and occasionally tearful for days after she had this
Forgetting the Baby dream. Although she saw herself as a responsible person,
something about the dream touched off irrational fears that were haunting
her. She was desperately afraid that she would act in life the way she did
in the dream: like a hedonistic woman who would recklessly abandon her
baby. She was afraid to share her fears with anyone, including her husband,
and was beginning to wonder whether she had made a mistake by getting
pregnant.

In a dream workshop, as Anna visualized the first part of her dream,
where she was tempted onto the Hawaiian cruise boat, she was reminded of
a number of trips she had taken during school vacations. On a couple of
occasions she had spontaneously embarked on a trip to Hawaii at the last
minute with a group of friends. As she continued to recount some of the
travel adventures of her younger days, Anna realized that this part of the
dream was reminding her that she would no longer have the freedom to
travel spontaneously.

The most compelling moment in the Forgetting the Baby dream, however, was her sense of panic when she realized that she had left her baby on
the dock and was screaming, trying to get back. As she explored the image
of forgetting her baby, Anna began to see the dream as an exaggeration of
her fears about being a responsible parent and not a prediction that she
would be a negligent mother.

Starting with her role as the oldest of four children, Anna had always
been efficient at caring for others' needs. On the other hand, she found it
hard to ask for help for herself at work or with friends. Discussing this dream
and her fears about being an inadequate parent and about balancing work
and mothering helped Anna realize that she needed emotional support.

Because Anna had been busy at work prior to her leave, she had not had
time to read books on parenting or to talk at length with friends who were
parents of young children. She understood now that she needed to spend

much more time talking with her husband and with other parents. Although she was on the phone with her mother more frequently, her family lived two thousand miles away. Because she lacked good contacts with friends or relatives with small children, I encouraged Anna to seek out a support group for new parents. As a result of discussing this dream, Anna also resolved to extend her maternity leave, then work part-time in her present job and seek other related work that did not require a lot of overtime.

Forgetting the Baby dreams exaggerate our worst fears about being inadequate parents. At the same time, they can provide us with a stimulus to become more prepared by seeking emotional support and guidance from others.

Dreams of Losing Valuables

Dreams of finding, carrying, and losing valuables are a universal dream theme that is especially common among pregnant women. In most pregnancy dreams with this theme the valuable item has womblike attributes—purses, pouches, and suitcases, for example.

During pregnancy, dreaming of losing or sustaining damage to a precious item is thematically similar to Forgetting the Baby dreams and Endangered Baby dreams (see below). Generally this kind of dream can be linked to anxieties about the responsibilities of carrying such a precious inner cargo. Many pregnancy dreams of this type feature the loss of precious items, and some depict dangerous quests to retrieve them. For some expectant parents, repetitive dreams of losing or missing valuables can be a sign that grief about past losses is bottled up, jeopardizing the psychological well-being of the mother and the physical well-being of mother and child.

While working as a psychological consultant to a high-risk maternity clinic, I was asked to consult with Denise, who was seven months pregnant and suffering extreme anxiety and depression. In talking to her obstetrician, I learned that her first child had been born without kidneys and had only lived for ten days. In a stroke of cruel irony, Denise's second child was scheduled to be delivered by cesarean section on the first anniversary of her first baby's death.

Denise refused to talk about her first child but was frequently tearful. According to her family, she had made no preparations for her baby's arrival, was eating poorly, and had been forced to quit her part-time secretarial job because she was so preoccupied. Her doctor was concerned about her health and her baby's well-being. She repeatedly refused to speak with a psychologist or social worker, insisting that she wasn't crazy and didn't need to talk to a "shrink." As her condition worsened, she began to have repetitive nightmares. When she learned that I was a "dream expert," she requested a meeting with me.

With little introduction, she tearfully told me her nightmare. Almost every night she would wake up sweating and crying, unable to sleep after her dream.

my suitcase is missing something

It is almost time to go to the hospital, and I search for my suitcase to prepare to leave. As I desperately throw things into the suitcase and try to push it shut, I panic because it is time to leave and there is something missing.

Through her tears, Denise pleaded with me to help her with her terrible nightmare. I suggested to her that if it were my dream, I would feel that there was something I wasn't ready for. Upon hearing my words, Denise launched into an emotional description of her fears about the upcoming birth of her child. She tearfully confessed that she didn't feel ready. She knew that her family and her husband were worried, but she didn't know what to do to prepare.

Talking about her Losing Valuables dream allowed Denise to access her grief and guilt. I asked her how she would feel if something was missing from her suitcase. She spontaneously realized that the suitcase with the missing item represented the baby who had died. She was finally able to talk about her guilt. For months she had blamed herself for her baby's death even though the doctors had assured her it was not her fault. She was terrified that her second child would also die and that it would again be her fault. Over the next hour, as Denise poured out her feelings, her mood and demeanor visibly lifted.

Exploring the elements of her Losing Valuables dream allowed Denise to feel more secure about discussing vital feelings that had terrified her. She was increasingly receptive to talking with the nurses in the clinic and with her family about her guilt and grief. The date of her cesarean delivery was changed, and she gave birth to a healthy child. Although Denise was resistant to ongoing counseling, sharing and working on her dream allowed her to break out of the mire of a turning-point impasse and move toward forming a healthy connection with her new baby.

Deformed and Endangered Baby Dreams

Even to those people who don't consider themselves superstitious, having a dream about a deformed or injured baby is likely to induce a feeling of worry or panic. Although these dreams are quite common and usually not a danger sign, nightmares about endangered babies can leave an emotional residue of anxiety and depression.

Joel, whose washing machine dream we discussed above, had listened to his wife talk about her fears of giving birth to a Down's syndrome child. Joel was sympathetic but didn't pay much attention. He figured that at thirty-one, she wasn't at risk according to the statistics he had read. Joel was finding it difficult, however, to watch the eleven o'clock news, especially stories of children injured in auto accidents. When a special documentary came on TV about premature babies, he was surprised at how quickly he wanted to change the channel.

Early in the second trimester of his wife's pregnancy, Joel had the following dream.

the clinic for retarded children

I am in a medical clinic where everyone speaks Spanish. I am on a lengthy tour of the place and am being shown new techniques to deal with mentally retarded children. I am saddened but very relieved that our own baby, who is now a year old, was born normal. I want to get out of the place, but the director drones on and on and I don't want to offend him.

Joel's dream helped him to accept the fact that he, too, was fearful about something being wrong with the baby. Although Joel's Deformed Baby dream appears to be reassuring him that his baby will be normal, it also clearly shows his anxiety.

As in many pregnancy dreams, Joel's baby is not depicted as a newborn. Seeing your child as a few months or even a few years old in pregnancy dreams is usually associated with an attempt to skip the anxiety over the dangers of labor, as well as the fears about adjusting to the early weeks of parenting a newborn.

Joel was perplexed about why everyone was speaking Spanish in his dream. He realized it had something to do with the way he felt about pregnancy. He felt out of place when he and his wife took a tour of the maternity ward and when they went to the obstetrician's office. He felt like an outsider in a foreign country.

This dream helped Joel acknowledge his fears and his feeling of being an outsider. By being consciously aware of these issues, Joel became more assertive about being involved as the pregnancy progressed. He insisted on going to all of the doctor visits. He went to the classes at the hospital, and he talked more to friends who were fathers.

Paying careful attention to dreams about deformed or endangered babies can help us identify fears we find difficult to admit consciously. It can be deeply reassuring to know that the fears and nightmares that afflict us are part of the normal process of psychologically preparing for parenthood. When we stop denying the stresses of having a baby, we can turn our attention to seeking the extra support that is essential during pregnancy.

Psychoanalyst Robert Gillman's 1968 study of pregnant women's dreams found that one in eight women dreamed of deformed babies.[13] Dreams of endangered babies appear to be even more common.[14] These dreams are profoundly disturbing to expectant parents. No matter how much we try to tell ourselves that "it's only a dream," we have a powerful tendency to believe that our nighttime visions are predictive of real disaster.

Breaking the spell of these nightmares can help us understand our fears and motivate us to prepare more thoroughly by monitoring our nutrition and seeking medical, educational, and psychological support to reduce the chances of endangering our baby's health.

Dreams about the Baby's Name and Gender

Many baby dreams focus on the baby's identity. This includes dreams about naming the baby or about the baby's physical or emotional characteristics. Whenever I speak to groups about dreams and the psychology of pregnancy, one of the most frequent topics raised is whether dreams can predict gender. Every culture and every family seems to have its own criteria for determining the baby's gender, and dreams are often part of the formula.

Dreams that identify the baby's gender are very common.[15] A 1986 study found a 50 percent accuracy rate for pregnant women who dreamed about the gender of their unborn. Gillman's study showed a much lower accuracy rate. In that study, women's baby gender dreams disproportionately featured male children by a ratio of two to one.[16]

Of course, those of us whose dreams correctly identify the baby's gender are convinced that the dream was a precise predictor. Those whose dreams turn out wrong aren't so sure. In my experience, the value of these dreams is not their predictive accuracy. The deeper meaning has to do with the process of forming a prenatal bond with the child and the parent's ability to accept and relate to a male or female child.

Despite her desire to have a girl, Linda had repeated anxious dreams of giving birth to a boy who was extremely active and hard to discipline. In one of her upsetting dreams, the rowdy boy had a name that puzzled her.

a brat named island

My baby looks like he is almost two years old. It doesn't seem like I know him very well. My neighbor is there looking very angry. He says that Island broke some things at his house. Then he yells at me for having such a bratty kid and not controlling him. I'm very upset and confused, and I don't know how this happened.

Linda was disturbed by the bratty boy in her dream. Although she didn't believe in precognitive dreams, she had become preoccupied with wondering whether the dream was predicting not only the gender but the temperament of her child. The offbeat name, Island, seemed very odd to Linda; she and her husband had been considering traditional names such as James and Ellen.

As she thought about the name Island, Linda linked it to Ireland, the place of origin of her father's family. This association helped her clarify the nature of the dream's meaning. Linda's father had been abusive to her mother and had gone on occasional drinking and womanizing binges. He left the family when Linda was fourteen and rarely saw them after that. She feared that a male child would somehow be like her father, uncontrollably violent and destructive.

Understanding this Baby Name dream stimulated her to talk more about her relationship with her father and the pain that he'd caused her. She even contacted him after five years of not being in touch. Although he wasn't very warm, he expressed interest in seeing her and her baby. Although her father hadn't changed much, the experience of focusing on her relationship helped Linda resolve some of the grief and anger she had harbored toward him.

Because of the repetitive nature of her dreams, Linda was surprised when she had a girl. Although she was very pleased with her daughter, she felt that focusing on her dreams had helped her work out conflicts related to having a male child. She now felt that she would like her second child to be a boy.

For expectant fathers or mothers who have a strong preference for either a boy or girl, baby name and gender dreams can serve a vital purpose. They call our attention to the unconscious reasons we may prefer one sex over the other. Exploring these dreams often unearths strong feelings about our own identity and how we feel about our parents and siblings; for example, "My father had a violent temper, and he (like other males) can't be trusted," or "My mother (like other females) was domineering and never left me room to breathe or to be myself." Feelings, ideas, and memories like these, along with cultural conditioning, create strong gender preferences in some people.

Whether we admit it or not, we all have distinct feelings about what it would mean to have a male or female child. These feelings are influenced by the nature of our early relationships with our parents and siblings. Our dreams reveal our preferences and can help us prepare to accept and establish a strong relationship with a baby of the less-preferred sex.[17]

Dreams about the baby's name and gender are connected with our growing images of what it will be like to relate to our child. Exploring these dreams can reveal positive aspects of a growing prenatal bond. They can also alert us to potential conflicts in our ability to form a healthy attachment with our child.

Dreams and the Expectant Father's Secret Life

The strength of men's emotional experiences during pregnancy has only recently come to light. Beginning with the confirmation of pregnancy, powerful feelings and dreams emerge. Some of these responses are similar to those of women. Others are unique to men.

Awareness and discussion of these dreams can help transform what frequently is a sense of alienation for expectant fathers. Dreams are a resource for helping men to feel more secure about their role in pregnancy and to forge a closer bond with both wife and child.[18]

In 1981 I began the first systematic study of the patterns in expectant fathers' dreams. Using the two-week dream journal procedure (see chapter 12), I compared expectant fathers' dreams with the dreams of a matched group of married men who were not fathers and were not expecting. Using content analysis to compare the dreams of the two groups, I found striking differences. From the earliest days of the pregnancy, the expectant fathers' dreams were replete with vivid imagery of pregnancy, birth, and babies. Dreams of rejection and exclusion were especially prominent throughout the pregnancy, as well as many dreams of graphic sexual and homosexual adventures and wild celebratory birthday parties.

This finding challenges the notion that the expectant father faces no significant emotional upheaval until later in the pregnancy or after the birth. In reality, throughout the pregnancy a father's dreams are intimately related to his role as a father, his changing relationship with his wife, and his newly forming relationship with his child-to-be.

Left-Out Dreams

One of the most common issues in expectant fathers' dreams is the theme of feeling left out, misunderstood, deprived, or threatened in other ways. These dreams reveal old wounds and sensitivities to rejection that are reopened by fears of being displaced by the baby's arrival.

Joel, whose dreams we discussed earlier, had increased his hours at work to try to make more money to pay for his child's expenses. When Joel's wife was five months pregnant, he had a troubling dream that took place during a baseball game at Candlestick Park in San Francisco.

banished to the back of the stadium

In the middle of the game, I get up to get some beer. When I return, I can't find my seat. I look around for a new one, but many of the women in the stands are pregnant, and they are taking up two seats. I have to go to the back of the stadium and stand. I am very annoyed.

Joel was upset and puzzled by this dream. He wasn't much of a sports fan, and he generally avoided alcohol because his father had a drinking problem. "The feeling I have in this dream is that of being left out. There is no room for me with all these huge pregnant women." Joel was able to laugh at the absurdity of a stadium full of pregnant women crowding him out. Even in the generally male domain of beer and baseball, he felt like an outcast, rejected and forced to the back of the stadium.

Exploring this Left-Out dream helped Joel to understand that he was having a strong emotional reaction to his wife's pregnancy. Despite his positive conscious reaction to becoming a father, he was feeling excluded by his wife, which is a painful phase of pregnancy that many men suffer through. The dream's message was not about baseball; it was about Joel's sense of exclusion and his need to find more ways to be involved in the pregnancy and planning for the baby. After discussing this dream, Joel was able to express his left-out feelings more directly to his wife. They decided that he would cut back on overtime hours at work so he could spend more time with her and be more involved in preparations for the baby's arrival.

Male Pregnancy Dreams

Dreams of actually being pregnant or giving birth are dramatic evidence of men's psychological involvement in pregnancy. Until the 1970s, male symptoms of pregnancy were generally viewed as pathological, as womb-envy as opposed to a wish to share and be involved in the pregnancy. Men were not expected to have any unique or strong feelings, especially early in the pregnancy.[19]

Many men experience what is known as the couvade syndrome, which is a cluster of physical and psychological symptoms mimicking a woman's experience of pregnancy.[20] Studies by Jacqueline Clinton, a professor of nursing at the University of Wisconsin, have shown that over 90 percent of expectant fathers experience one of the signs of couvade, such as weight gain, nausea, stomach bloating, food cravings, fatigue, and irritability.[21] Pronounced cases of couvade syndrome involve multiple symptoms and occur in approximately 10 to 30 percent of expectant fathers. These symptoms are considered to be characteristic of the pregnant female, yet some men have more of them than their wives.[22]

Anthropologists who study primitive cultures have found widespread evidence of couvade rituals, in which expectant fathers engage in elaborate dietary and behavioral practices that mimic aspects of pregnancy. In some cases the men go into huts and simulate the pain of labor. These rituals are thought to be a form of sympathetic magic, a way of distracting and fooling evil spirits and thus protecting the wife. In addition, couvade rituals establish that the man is indeed the father and give him an important role to play in the pregnancy and birth.[23]

In our culture, we have few roles or rites of passage to help men understand and integrate the experience of becoming a father. Without couvade rituals, it appears that men's unfulfilled wishes for involvement are converted into an unconscious male version of pregnancy.

In some men, Couvade dreams take the form of actual pregnancy or of giving birth. Alex, a thirty-three-year-old engineer, felt that he was having difficulty accepting the pregnancy's reality. Even after the baby began to move, he did not feel that the pregnancy had made much of an impact on him. Late in the second trimester, he had the following Couvade dream.

IT'S MY BABY

I am standing on a street corner carrying my baby fetus under my shirt against my chest. I have my hands cupped over the fetus to protect it. It is moving, and people ask what it is. I say, "It's my baby!" Someone tries to smash the fetus by hitting my chest. I become enraged at the person and pick him up and throw him into the street.

The powerful feeling of protectiveness in this dream occurs in many expectant fathers' dreams. Alex not only appears pregnant in public, he is ready to fiercely defend his baby against threats. Alex did not ordinarily remember his dreams. He was surprised by the intensity of his protective feelings and by the fact that he was pregnant in the dream. After exploring his feelings, Alex realized that he might have been denying some of his reactions to the pregnancy because he felt that he should be the strong one to help out his wife while she was nauseous.

I have collected many other dreams with direct pregnancy references in which men show strong feelings of protectiveness toward their wives and unborn children. This form of Couvade dream, which I call a Magical Protection dream, often portrays creative and sometimes amusing solutions to the fears of pregnancy.

In the first trimester, the danger of miscarriage is high. Don, whose wife had experienced a previous miscarriage, had three dreams in a two-week period that suggested magical solutions to his fears about the pregnancy's progress. In one dream a neighbor advised him to find a doctor willing to make home visits in case his wife was too tired to go to the office. In another, he fashioned a bowl that would provide protection for his child inside his wife's growing belly. His final dream is also an early version of an Endangered Baby dream.

miscarriage prevention

My wife is telling me that she has been using a tampon every day. She doesn't explain it, but it makes sense to me that it was a way of making sure that there's not a premature birth.

When Don looked over his dream journal entries, he was shocked at how many different ways he was trying to protect his wife and baby. Seeing the persistent pattern in his dreams was irrefutable evidence that he was involved in the pregnancy. Knowing this helped Don to convert his dream protectiveness into more conscious protection and support for his wife in the early months of the pregnancy.

Many men may be unaware that they are having symptoms directly related to pregnancy. Because their experience is not socially validated by women or by the medical establishment, their fierce feelings of protectiveness and their actual physical symptoms of pregnancy may go unnoticed. On the other hand, when a man's protective fantasies are acknowledged, he is likely to feel gratified by becoming consciously aware of his protective instincts and may be more inclined to express his involvement in waking activities. Discussion of Couvade and Magical Protection dreams can help a man acknowledge his unconscious preoccupation with pregnancy and convert it into more active conscious involvement with his wife and child.

Sexual Adventure Dreams

Sexual experiences appear frequently in the dreams of both men and women during pregnancy. They may experience exquisite sensuality, award-winning orgasms, and animal passions in their dreams—with their spouse, old lovers, colleagues, or friends.

The biological necessity for sexual relations is fulfilled once conception occurs. However, the psychological importance and influence of our sexual feelings does not subside during pregnancy. Judging by the increase in dreams and fantasies with sexual themes, a massive alteration of our sexual identity and appetites occurs as pregnancy progresses.

Many couples have achieved equilibrium in their sexual and emotional intimacy prior to pregnancy if they have been together for a long time. In early pregnancy, the joyful news of conception often fuels the marriage's erotic flames. Experimentation, increased closeness, and enhanced communication may grow out of the excitement of pregnancy.

My study of expectant fathers revealed some exotic Sexual Adventure dreams, including a ménage à trois after hours at Disneyland, necking furiously with a young blonde on a spaceship, and a hooker offering a full range of services.

When your dream amour is not your spouse, pangs of guilt may afflict you when you awake. One expectant father, Frank, who had experienced extended couvade symptoms of nausea, food cravings, and stomach bloating during the first trimester, also was having wild erotic fantasies in daydreams and at night. In one second-trimester dream he was aware within the dream that his desires were adulterous.

tHe aLaRm IN my weDDINǥ RINǥ

I am being approached by a voluptuous woman. I can tell she wants to seduce me, and I am very tempted. All of a sudden, I know I am in trouble. An alarm goes off and I think it's my watch, but when I look I realize the alarm is on my wedding ring and I have to get home to my wife.

When Frank's wedding ring alarm goes off, he is torn between powerful desires and a sense of loyalty to his wife. For weeks he had been preoccupied with his own sexual fantasies and physical symptoms set off by the pregnancy. At the same time, he was anxious about his increased responsibilities as a nurturer and provider for his wife and child.

Frank's Sexual Adventure dreams did not inspire him to pursue extramarital sex. Rather, Frank felt that his sexual dreams were related to a feeling of sexual neediness on his part. He recognized that in the past an increase in sexual fantasies had been related to a need to be taken care of and given attention. He felt that his wife had been preoccupied with other aspects of the pregnancy and had rejected him sexually during the first trimester when they had both been feeling ill.

Frank came to see that the alarm was meant to wake him out of his own neediness, his physical and sexual preoccupations, and to focus on improving his marriage so they could be prepared for the baby's arrival. When he shared his dreams and fantasies with his wife, she was able to understand what he'd been going through and they reestablished a greater feeling of closeness that they had both been missing.

Virility and Impotence Dreams

For many men, the general decrease in sexual relations during pregnancy may result in conflicts that linger on, dampening the marriage's intimacy. The balance of intimacy shifts when nausea and other physical changes affect the woman (or the man, if he suffers from couvade syndrome). Confusion and feelings of rejection may surface. Sometimes sexual inhibitions and hang-ups that the man thought had been set aside years earlier reappear.

Expectant fathers' dreams and fantasies reveal sexual preoccupations that often focus on pride or doubts about their sexual powers. Especially in early pregnancy, men have dreams that express their concerns about their changing masculinity.[24] Over 40 percent of the expectant fathers who participated in my study during early pregnancy had what I call Macho dreams. These dreams feature heroic acts by famous football coaches such as Bill Walsh and actors such as John Wayne. In a typical Macho dream sequence, Burt Reynolds crashes a hang glider but emerges unscathed and chipper.

During pregnancy, a man's masculine identity goes through reorganization as he struggles to integrate more nurturing, feminine feelings into his sense of self and to create a new identity as a father. Many men are unaware of the emotional crisis taking place inside them. In behavior as in dreams, they attempt to seek refuge in being macho to compensate for fears of being unmanly, impotent, or homosexual.

Mixed in with dreams of virility, sexual prowess, and macho heroics are dreams that feature sexual inferiority, impotence, and homosexuality. A sampling of homosexual dream themes in the expectant heterosexual fathers I studied included the following: soliciting a man for oral sex; being accused of being gay and being attacked for it; watching a gay doctor dancing in a tutu; and being accused of perverting a group of children.

One man dreamed that his penis was shorter and less experienced than another man's.

I am lying down and looking down at my naked body. I can see another naked man whose penis is larger than mine in spite of perspective. He is taking some course on human sexuality, and as a result his penis is longer than mine.

At a concrete level, these Virility and Impotence dreams are linked to the changing nature of marital sex during pregnancy. The predominance of dreams of virility and impotence suggests a deeper change, confusion about sexual and masculine identity, and a struggle to create a new identity as a man who is less stereotypically macho and more able to nurture connections with his child and his wife.

Despite the so-called sexual revolution, the women's movement, and other forms of consciousness-raising, many of us still find it difficult to talk about our sexual feelings. Even though we understand intellectually that pregnancy and parenting call for sacrifices, we may still feel hurt if our partner is less sexual or can't be aroused in the same old ways.

Tracking your sexual dreams, exploring them in a dream journal, and sharing them with your partner can help you to express your confused and hurt feelings before they turn into bitterness and alienation. If you have ever had tendencies to feel rejected or jealous, these tendencies may surface during pregnancy. It's vital to set aside extra time to communicate, work out hurt feelings, and discover new ways to be intimate at this crucial turning point in your marriage.[25]

Celebration Dreams

A dramatic feature of expectant fathers' dreams throughout pregnancy is the appearance of parties, celebrations, and what appear to be initiation ceremonies related to pregnancy and childbirth. Over half of the expectant fathers in my study had a Celebration dream, contrasted with only one incidence of this kind of dream in my comparison group. These were slightly more common earlier in the pregnancy.

An especially notable aspect of Celebration dreams is that many featured *birth*day parties. These dreams also depicted elaborate food preparation, eating and drinking, water imagery, and relationships with masculine or macho figures. Some of these dreams were associated with completing a creative project, such as a man who dreamed about a big party to celebrate a writing project he had just completed.

One man dreamed about a big circle dance in a Chinese restaurant, which suddenly switched to a hospital labor room. Another man, Gavin, had a dream with a ritual quality designed to initiate him into the role of fatherhood.

BIRtH DAnce

I am watching people all around me dance and play. I am not seen or heard. A group comes near me and all play ceases. This group seems to have control over all. I like them. Their energy is high and has a calming effect on me. They come to me, surround me. One of them comes over to me and gives me a bundle. It is a baby.

At first Gavin felt left out. The part of the dream when he was not seen or heard made him remember painful feelings of exclusion earlier in the pregnancy, as well as other times in his life when he had felt excluded from groups or other relationships.

Gavin was a middle child in a family of ten. As he explored the dream, he wondered whether it related in some way to memories of the birth of his four younger siblings. For Gavin, this dream may be an example of an early-childhood birth fantasy. If this were true, the dream would represent an attempt to understand and identify with the experience of childbirth, while working out early memories of being confused and displaced by the arrival of new siblings.

At the end of the dream, Gavin is surrounded in womblike fashion and is given a baby. He felt that this part of the dream was telling him that he had worked out earlier feelings of alienation from his wife and the pregnancy. At this point, he was feeling extremely excited and ready to take on the role of father.

The lack of adequate roles and rituals to confirm their inclusion and importance causes expectant fathers to feel anxious about where they fit in. Parties are associated with important turning points such as birthdays, graduations, weddings, and accomplishments. They usually involve a sense of specialness or sacredness apart from mundane routines. The preponderance of men's Celebration dreams reflects an unconscious awareness of the specialness and importance of becoming a father. In their Celebration dreams, most men create unconscious rites of passage to express the excitement of becoming a father.

How to Use Pregnancy Dreams

Dreams exaggerate our anxieties about harm coming to our spouse, our child, and ourselves during pregnancy. Sharing and exploring anxiety-provoking dreams (such as Deformed and Endangered Baby dreams, Forgetting the Baby dreams, and Losing Valuables dreams) helps to make us more aware of our fears. When we can articulate what we fear, we have a chance to understand how appropriate and necessary our fears are. When we can share what troubles us with our spouse, family, and friends, we have the chance to feel reassured, to understand and resolve our changing emotional needs.

Awareness of dreams also can help men to convert their unconscious emotional reactions and fears of being excluded into an energetic involvement with the events of the pregnancy and the preparations for nurturing the baby. It is especially important that men be encouraged to participate in prenatal classes, obstetric visits, genetic counseling and amniocentesis, shopping for the baby's needs, and baby showers and other celebratory events.

An invisible drama unfolds in the dreams of expectant parents. When we make this drama visible by remembering and sharing dreams together, we can nurture the marital relationship and prepare for our new role as parents.

Just as proper nutrition and medical care will enhance the fetus' physical growth, extra communication and emotional support will enhance the parents' psychological readiness. Using our dreams to explore hidden conflicts, feelings, anxieties, and joys can be of tremendous value to couples as they prepare to make the crucial adjustment to parenthood.

5. separation and divorce dreams breaking up, recovering, and moving on

For months after her husband walked out on her, Nora was emotionally paralyzed, afraid to let go of the marriage yet unable to find a new identity. After ten years of being married, she was faced with the need to support her two daughters and start a new life. Her shame about the divorce caused her to withdraw from many of her friends, especially her married friends whom she thought were unsympathetic.

Ten months after her separation, she began to have a series of vivid dreams that helped her to break free from the depths of her depression. Initially, all of the dreams were terrifying and unresolved: nightmares of thieves robbing her and threatening her with knives, of being paralyzed and unable to scream for help. On three occasions she had terrifying car crash dreams about the brakes locking on her car. In the first two dreams, nothing would stop the car, not the hand brake, not downshifting, not steering. During the third dream, she grasped the hand brake and it finally worked.

As Nora made notes in her dream journal, she realized that this was the first dream since her separation that had a resolution. Maybe something was beginning to change, she thought. Soon after, Nora had another series of dreams that felt very important to her. They took place at the museum where she had been a docent.

the art heist, i

I am outside the art museum dressed completely in black. Even my face
is blackened. I have a bag of equipment for the job. My challenge is to
scale the wall, cut through the skylight, drop down, avoid the sensor, pick
up a Pieter Bruegel painting called *Peasant Wedding,* and then escape. The
alarms will bring the police within fifteen to twenty minutes. My goal is
just to see whether it can be done, not to steal the art. The dream ends as
I successfully get into the museum.

Nora was puzzled by this dream. She felt a strange sense of physical exhila-
ration when she awoke, a feeling of having accomplished something important. In her journal she wrote: "I had to depend entirely on myself; I know
my limitations and succeed." The dream's physical challenge was related to
facing the emotional task of overcoming her depression.

Nora was surprised when two nights later she had a similar dream.

the art heist, ii

Breaking into the museum again. The same as before, although this time
my face isn't blackened. I secretly know, with one other friend who volunteers at the museum, that this is a test of the security system. The museum
director and security chief don't know it is a test. This time, I not only go
in and get the Bruegel, but I also descend on the museum and crack the
safe for the master drawings and get the most valuable of the collection.
The director and security chief are furious when they find out.

The following night, Nora had a third and final version of this dream. This
time she is even bolder in her efforts to steal the paintings despite the fact
that some people see her. She scales the wall and gets away in the nick
of time.

By this time, Nora was beginning to see that these dreams were telling
her something about how she was finally making a breakthrough in her
recovery from divorce. As we talked about the elements of her first dream,
Nora commented on how striking the image of her blackened face was. It
reminded her at first of pictures of coal miners in Appalachia. She also
thought that wearing black had to do with mourning the loss of her
marriage as she succumbed to the bleakness of depression. Nora felt that her
blackness represented the state of prolonged grief she had endured, a period
in which she had been hiding from her friends and the world. From that
darkness, she found that she had a bag of tools, resources that were now

becoming accessible to her. She also had a challenging job to do—recovering and building a new life.

But why was she trying to steal a sixteenth-century Flemish painting of a wedding scene? She recalled that in her undergraduate studies she had written a term paper on Pieter Bruegel and had discussed that very painting, *Peasant Wedding*. When she traveled in Europe after college, she made a special point of visiting the museum in Vienna where it was displayed. She recalled from her college research paper that *Peasant Wedding* portrayed a superficial appearance of joyful and prosperous village life. A closer examination of the painting, however, reveals an emphasis on guzzling alcohol and overeating. Critics considered the painting to be a social commentary on the vices of drunkenness and gluttony.

Remembering her interest in that painting set off a chain of associations related to her father's and her husband's alcoholism. To the outside world her family had appeared to be a perfect 1950s family. In reality, the illusion was shattered by her mother's depression and passive acceptance of her father's verbal abuse, late nights out at bars, and occasional gambling binges.

Nora's marriage was also considered ideal. Unknown to their friends, however, Nora's ex-husband, Jack, was a heavy drinker, even on the job. A workaholic building contractor, he had become more successful but progressively more distant from Nora and their children. Although she was devastated when he ran off with his secretary, she was now seeing how empty their marriage had become.

Brazenly stealing the Bruegel painting had a number of important meanings for Nora. The fact that the painting portrayed a wedding scene was especially significant. Capturing the painting related to exposing the hypocrisy and alcoholism of her own marriage and that of her parents. She was the child and ex-wife of an alcoholic. She could no longer mask the emotional damage that had occurred. She had to face the role she had played in colluding with her husband's alcoholism and be careful not to choose another partner who would be as emotionally cold.

Nora saw her art heist dreams as a turning point in her recovery, related to recapturing the inner creativity that had been dormant in her marriage. Exploring the dreams gave her hope that she had reached a new stage in recovering from her divorce. She was beginning to move out of the blackness of her months of depression. She could risk breaking out of the security system of her old fears and recapture the precious resources of her strength and creativity.

Separation and Divorce As Turning Points

The way in which we cope with the end of a marriage or an important love relationship can alter the course of our lives. When we emerge from the turmoil of divorce or final separation, we face a perilous moment of opportunity. We may discover creative possibilities and establish a more fulfilling relationship. Or we may wallow in depression, psychosomatic illnesses, and a bitterness that paralyzes our emotional growth and psychologically poisons our children.

It would appear that the risks of marriage are high. The United States has one of the highest divorce rates in the world. From a high of 50 percent in the 1990s, as of 2001 the divorce rate has fallen to 43 percent of those who marry. In *For Better or for Worse,* Mavis Hetherington's monumental summary of three decades of research on the long-term outcome of divorce, she speculates about the slight decline in the divorce rate. She attributes the decline to the fact that more people are living together and don't show up as part of the statistic. In addition, many people are staying married longer and divorcing later.

According to Hetherington, the major reasons cited by couples who are divorcing include "conflict, inability to resolve disagreements and lack of mutual supportiveness." Other factors include the lack of time spent together, difficulty in balancing dual careers with the needs of the family, and "inequities in the division of labor in the household".[1]

By the time separation occurs, the handwriting usually has been on the wall for some time. The seeds for a separation are sown long before the formal papers are filed. Often the roots of a breakup reach back to our relationships with our parents and even to their relationships with previous generations.

Just as the decision to break up a marriage or long-term partnership takes time to incubate, the period of recovery also can take months or years. Although each of us is unique, experts suggest that the period of intense crisis may last from several weeks to several months. This phase of being in shock is followed by a gradual period of readjustment that may take the better part of a year. For some, recovery may take one or more years.[2]

This chapter will show how dreams can provide insights, inner guidance, and confirmation of our feelings during the turbulent weeks and months of making the decision to separate, dealing with the sometimes devastating early impact on our identity and relationships and during the period of re-examining our priorities and gradually rebuilding our lives. Poignant vignettes of adult's and children's responses, show how remembering and exploring separation and divorce dreams offers:

* warnings about emotional impasses that we are facing at the end of a relationship or the beginning of a separation

* insights about issues from the past that are hampering our ability to accept the reality of the loss

* clarification of strong feelings such as grief, anger, and guilt, which we need to express and resolve

* awareness of our progress through the stages of grieving, emotional resolution, and rebuilding

* renewed hope and confidence by highlighting breakthroughs that we are achieving in our recovery from the separation

The Stages of Recovery from Separation and Divorce

Psychotherapists generally view recovery from divorce and separation as progressing through stages similar to those encountered in facing death or grieving the death of a loved one. The sequence of the stages may vary, but the psychological tasks that go with them are considered necessary for full recovery. Since four out of five divorced persons will remarry, it is essential to come to terms with the lessons of previous relationships or risk repeating the same mistakes.[3]

The process of recovery from divorce and separation can be seen as unfolding in three stages.

Stage One

The first stage is one of shock and denial. It often begins before we make the actual separation and continues until after the break. During this time, it's crucial for us to overcome a powerful tendency to hang onto the marriage and fantasize about reconciliation instead of accepting the reality of the separation.

Dreams in this period may include themes of being stuck, such as imprisonment and paralysis. Dreams of natural disasters such as earthquakes or tidal waves may occur, symbolizing the disastrous impact of the change. Other dream themes may include out-of-control events such as falling, cars going out of control, or losing valuables like a wallet or purse.

Stage Two

The second stage of the recovery process is one of anger, depression, and despair. Our culture tells us to be brave, to put aside our feelings and return to productive activities, so dealing with anger is an especially tricky dilemma. We feel hurt and abandoned and fear that we are unlovable. Blaming our villainous ex-spouse or assuming the victim role obscures our ability to resolve the emotional crisis of separation. We need to reach the point where we can express our anger nondestructively and take responsibility for our own shortcomings in the relationship.

Dreams in the second stage of transition may include themes of betrayal or rejection such as Sexual Rejection dreams or Left-Out dreams. They may also include dreams associated with depression in which we find ourselves feeling inadequate, self-destructive, or unable to cope with threatening forces. Other themes may include nakedness, symbolizing our vulnerability, or New Clothing dreams related to letting go of old roles. Dreams of anger or revenge are also likely to appear at this stage.

Stage Three

The final stage of recovery is one of hope and renewal. A new identity is forming. We reclaim our independence and rediscover the voice within us that goes back to the time before we were married, even to our childhood. In this final stage, we need to overcome our insecurity and self-doubt and take risks in building a new life.

As we move back into the world, we renew old ties and establish new friendships and interests. In this period we have what Judith Wallerstein called a "second chance": a window of opportunity to exorcise ghosts from childhood, achieve a more fulfilling marriage, and find deeper meaning in work and friendships.[4] And according to Hetherington's research, the majority of divorced parents and their children "are resilient and able to cope with the challenges in their postdivorce life. They emerge as reasonably, happy competent individuals".[5]

In this last stage, dreams of threat and struggle still occur but tend to end with greater resolution, like Nora's three dreams. In our dreams at this point, we may choose new outfits, find new rooms in houses, and discover unexpected valuables as we establish new roles and develop new parts of our personality. Unresolved issues from childhood or earlier relationships may also come to the surface and achieve resolution. We are beginning to thrive in the role of a single individual, and this is reflected in our dreams.

Dreams Foreshadowing Separation and Divorce

The stresses of balancing two careers, caring for children, and maintaining a household are enormous. A serious illness or death in the family, financial troubles, moving, pressures from in-laws, or traumatic events may tip the balance in a negative direction for a married couple.

The idea to separate or divorce may have been brewing in the mind of one or both partners for months or even years prior to the actual breakup. As the emotional knots tighten and hope dwindles, it is vitally important to decide whether the marriage is worth saving. For most of us this is an agonizing decision, especially if children are involved or our religious beliefs are strong.

Many people wait too long before seeking help when problems arise in their relationship. They are unable or unwilling to take advantage of family or friends who can provide support and guidance. Even if the necessity for professional help becomes clear, denial often causes couples to wait until the differences between them have escalated beyond repair.

Remembering and exploring dreams can help us to overcome denial and gain a crucial understanding of our unconscious reactions to a relationship impasse. Through our dreams we can gain a better understanding of what isn't working and be in a better position to seek help in repairing the marriage or in making the decision to leave a marriage that is emotionally destructive.

Adam, a successful bookstore owner, did not want to admit that things were not working in his second marriage, to Bev. His first marriage had ended unhappily seven years earlier. Because his first wife complained of feeling squelched, Adam was careful the second time around to choose someone who had her own professional identity. From the beginning, Adam had admired Bev's growing creativity and self-confidence as she became more successful as a fashion designer. As a result, however, she was working longer hours and traveling more frequently.

At forty, Adam was eager to have more children. He had wanted to be closer to his children in a way that had been impossible in his first marriage. At thirty-four, Bev didn't feel ready to have children. She felt her career was just getting launched. In fact, she was feeling less sure that she wanted children at all. After a series of bitter fights, Adam had a divorce foreshadowing dream that he feels changed the course of his life.

the faLLeN IDOL

> I am encouraging Bev to climb up on a stand that is something like a pedestal for a statue. She doesn't really want to, but she complies. I keep asking her to raise her arm higher, like the Statue of Liberty raising her torch. Suddenly she begins to teeter and fall off. I am terrified that she might get hurt or killed, but I'm paralyzed and can't do anything to stop her from falling.

As Adam related his dream to an old friend, he realized that he had put Bev on a pedestal. He had idealized her so much that he had been blinded to who she really was. Yes, she was creative, assertive, and successful, but she had been giving him a clear message for over a year: her career was more important than having a family or deepening their marriage. To his dismay, his idol had fallen.

The more Adam talked about his marital problems, the more he realized that Bev had been telling him the marriage wasn't working. She had withdrawn from him and invested herself in her career. Adam realized that if he really did want to have more children, he would have to leave her and find someone who shared his vision of family life.

Following this discussion, Adam sought individual psychotherapy. He realized that he needed to work out his tendency to idealize women and his fears of intimacy before he could achieve a successful marriage. Although he may have been on the verge of deciding to leave the marriage anyway, Adam credits his divorce foreshadowing dream for initiating the process that led him to separate from Bev.

When we are at an impasse in our relationship, dreams can help us understand where we are blocked. Knowing this, we can make a realistic decision about whether to repair the relationship or end it. In addition, dreams foreshadowing a separation give us clues to repetitive patterns in relationships, such as Adam's tendency to idealize women. Understanding these tendencies can help us avoid repeating the same mistakes in future relationships.

Sexual Rejections Dreams

Early adjustment to divorce is influenced by whether one is the person who leaves or the person who is left. The person who initiates a divorce generally feels more in control and suffers less distress in the immediate aftermath. The person who leaves may feel guilty but is less likely in the early stages of a divorce to feel the pain of abandonment and depression.[6]

In the weeks following a marital separation, Sexual Rejection dreams are common, especially for the person who has been left. A person who has experienced painful rejections and losses earlier in life is especially vulnerable to dreams of abandonment or betrayal. When one spouse is sexually unfaithful or leaves the marriage to be with another person, there is an even higher likelihood of feelings of abandonment taking the form of Sexual Rejection dreams.

For Sabina, the discovery of her husband's affair led to the breakup of their three-year marriage. The more she asked around, the more she discovered about Bob's philandering.

Sabina had repetitive Sexual Rejection dreams for months after their separation. In the first weeks many of her dreams had unresolved endings and, according to Sabina, distinct patterns. In some, she would feel lonely or longing for Bob. In others, he would either directly mention that he had been with another woman or she would find out the upsetting news from a friend. In the final pattern, she would be making love with him, and he would spitefully reject her plea for a committed relationship. One of Sabina's dreams combined all three of these themes into a series of degrading and enraging rebuffs from her ex-husband.

multiple rejections

I run into Bob at his office. He is telling me about an upcoming boating regatta. I want him to invite me but he doesn't. Then it seems like it is the next day at work, and one of my supervisors is telling me that she saw Bob in the building. I think he must have come to talk to me, but he goes around a corner without looking at me. Somehow, I hear that he is dating someone at the office. I go into the bathroom and there she is—wearing a bright yellow dress like one I used to have. I ask her point-blank if she is seeing him. She says she has been seeing him since October, which is before we broke up. I'm extremely upset that he would date someone so stupid. I'm looking for him again and catch a glimpse of him walking away, but he is gone. I go outside, furious. I start hitting cars with a baseball bat. I want to find him and tell him off, but he's nowhere to be seen.

Sabina's dream mirrors her inability to overcome her feeling of being deceived and abandoned. In this dream, the elusive Bob and his latest flame reject her, but she is still desperately seeking him.

Sabina's dreams indicate that she was bogged down in the shock and denial stage of adjustment to separation. Although the dream suggests rage and frustration in the final image of smashing cars with a baseball bat, she could not consciously accept her anger at Bob. Not only was she unable to banish him from her mind and go on with her life, but in reality she continued to seek him out for more inevitable rejections.

For Seth and Martha, there were no incidents of infidelity associated with their breakup. They had lived together for four years and then became engaged. Just before the invitations were to be sent out, Martha got cold feet and called off the wedding. Increasingly she became moody, found fault with Seth's behavior, and began to pick fights over minor issues. When pressed, Martha admitted to not being sure why she was alienating Seth. But she was increasingly convinced that they should split up.

After Martha left, Seth had great difficulty sleeping. Almost every night, he had nightmares of Martha rejecting him, going out with other guys and flaunting it. He was beginning to lose weight and found it hard to function at work.

Two weeks after Martha left, Seth had the following dream.

THE BABY THAT WILL NEVER BE

Martha and I have had a baby. It's two weeks old, but we haven't named it. We are distant. Martha seems especially aloof. I come home, and it seems like we have three houses. One isn't even furnished yet. She will be taking over one of them when we break up. I look all around to see where she is. I want to see the baby. When I see Martha, I tell myself that I'm no longer sexually attracted to her. But then I become nostalgic and do feel very attracted to her and start to touch her breasts in a sexual way. She responds but in a mechanical way, and I can see that she is no longer attracted to me or wanting to make love with me. The dream ends while I am wondering what to name the baby.

Seth awoke tearful. He had registered for a workshop on dreams and was eager to explore the meaning of his repetitive dreams of rejection. After describing his dream, he began to have a flood of associations. He felt that the two-week-old baby was more than just the baby that he would never have with Martha. It represented exactly the amount of time since they had broken up. *He* was the baby, and his dream represented his vulnerable new sense of self in the postseparation period. The fact that the baby was unnamed indicated that the separation was so new that he did not yet know who he was without Martha.

Seth wasn't sure about the meaning of the three houses, but another group member suggested that they symbolized the new house Martha had moved to, the house that Seth and Martha had lived in, and that same house (where Seth continued to live) in the post-Martha period. Seth remembered that he had been rearranging the furniture the previous day to make the house feel more his own. Seth also felt that the dream was telling him that he hadn't been able to detach himself from Martha yet. He tried to resist her but ended up making a sexual advance, only to be rejected.

When asked whether the dream reminded him of any events from the past, Seth recalled one of his earliest memories: his mother bringing home his baby sister when he was almost three years old. He remembered feeling upset that everyone was paying so much attention to the baby. His parents confirmed that he had had a bad case of jealousy of his sister and would tease her a lot when she was young.

Seth felt that discussing his Sexual Rejection dream helped him to understand the roots of his feelings of rejection that lay in his childhood and to lessen his preoccupation with feeling like a victim. Seth continued to keep careful records of his dreams. Although he had other Sexual Rejection dreams in the ensuing weeks, they became less frequent and less disturbing. Gradually his dreams changed. Occasionally, he would reject Martha in his dreams or meet other women who would accept his sexual advances. As time passed, the rejection theme became less frequent in his dreams as he recovered from the separation.

Dreams, Separation, and Depression

For over twenty-five years, Rosalind Cartwright, Ph.D., has been studying the dreams of people undergoing divorce and life crises and of those who are suffering depression. Funded by the United States National Institute of Mental Health and the National Science Foundation, her research projects were among the most comprehensive studies of dreams in the twentieth century. The implications of her research have illuminated important aspects of both the psychological and the biological function of dreaming during human adaptation to stressful life events. They have shown that dreaming is an essential part of how we cope with and recover from crises and from psychological depression.[7]

Cartwright, and her colleagues at Chicago's Rush Medical College, recruited hundreds of divorcing men and women. She interviewed them extensively, psychologically tested them, monitored their sleep, collected their dreams during a three-night stay in a sleep laboratory, and explored the meaning and content of their dreams. This was done immediately after separation with follow-up studies of dreams, depression, and coping a year later.[8]

Many of Cartwright's divorcing subjects were severely depressed. In one study, 39 percent of the women and 24 percent of the men were undergoing a severe depression at the time of separation, a percentage many times higher than the general population. According to Cartwright, many of the more seriously depressed people appeared to embody an intensely self-blaming attitude that "everything has gone wrong, and it's all my fault." Dreams featuring victimization, masochism, and abandonment themes were common in the early period following separation. Such dreamers had themes of drowning, having depleted resources such as a gas tank that couldn't be filled up, being totally alone, or being taken advantage of or threatened.[9]

Cartwright found that people who experienced normal grief, but not depression, had more disturbing dreams compared to those who were stuck in their depression. Although such dreams were very upsetting, the anxious and threatening elements were more often directed at others and not at themselves, compared to the dreams of women suffering from depression. The recovering women had dreams that harkened back to the past but also seemed directly connected to solving problems in the present and future. In other words, dreaming's problem-solving function appeared to be working in the recovering women and failing in the depressed women.[10]

Cartwright's results show that upsetting dreams may even be a prerequisite to emotional resolution of a turning point. Repressing bad dreams and distressing feelings may create an impasse in the necessary emotional tumult of working through a separation. This is consistent with Winget and Kapp's research discussed in chapter 4, which showed that pregnant women who had more dreams of threat and hostility had shorter labors and fewer complications.

Cartwright uncovered extraordinary patterns in the dream biology as well as the dream content of her subjects. She found that the dreamers who were not depressed, plus a large portion of those who were depressed but recovered quickly, had biological dreaming patterns that were unique. Physiologically, the nondepressed dreamers and dreamers who eventually recovered more rapidly began to dream very early in the nightly sleep cycle and had more dense bursts of rapid eye movements, which are characteristic of dreaming sleep. In other words, the recovering dreamers seemed to be having a more powerful and insistent physiological dream response as well as moderately upsetting dreams that they could tolerate remembering.

Those who were depressed but had abnormally early REM onset (a premature beginning of the first period of rapid eye movement sleep) were much less depressed one year later compared with those who were depressed but did not have premature initiation of REM. In addition, the divorcing people who were depressed and had dreams that featured a reference or appearance of their ex-spouse were doing better after a year. A later study of dream content and depression showed that those who had their most distressing dreams earlier in the night recovered more easily, and those who had bad dreams close to awakening remained depressed and sometimes carried anxiety from their bad dreams into an upset mood during the morning or the day after the dream.[11, 12]

This research suggests that during a crisis, we have a heightened need to dream. Disruptive and upsetting dreams and intensified dream physiology early in the sleep period are evidence of actively coping with conflicts related to the emotional upheaval of separation. This pattern is characteristic of a healthier emotional response to a turning point. Failure to recall any upsetting dreams is probably evidence of denial and an emotional impasse. In addition, very persistent nightmares that are unchanging, dwell upon the past, and always portray the dreamer as a victim are likely to be those of a depressed person who is frozen in unresolved grief and anger.

Some separation dreams can inspire us to investigate new avenues for resolving an impasse. Sabina, whose Sexual Rejection dream is mentioned above, had new insights through the following dream about her role as a victim in relationships. Two months after separating from Bob, she continued to fantasize about getting back with him and was unable to resolve her grief.

please help me find my old dog

I'm back in college studying hard for a final exam that I'm worried about. Then I am going to the exam with my old dog, Amber. Amber suddenly turns into a scraggly dog, contrary to what she was really like, and she runs away. Then my college boyfriend comes up to me. He was the one I was going out with when we got the dog. I ask him to help me find Amber. He refuses and is cold to me. I run out crying and upset.

Sabina explained that her dog, Amber, had died of old age one year earlier. At the time, Bob refused to go to the veterinarian's office when Amber had to be put to sleep. Sabina was very depressed after Amber's death and felt that Bob was unsupportive and insensitive. When she explored her dream, Sabina wondered why Amber had looked so scraggly and why her boyfriend had been so cruel and rejecting. She guessed that her old boyfriend represented Bob's cruelty to her.

For Sabina, the pathetic ghost of her dog represented her emotionally weary self. Being with Amber may have had to do with comforting her own depletion and depression. At first, Amber is a soothing presence during Sabina's big exam. The exam is probably symbolic of the emotional test that she is undergoing in facing the marital separation. As the dream progresses she loses touch with Amber, and her boyfriend coldly rejects her, paying no attention to her sense of loss or neediness.

Discussing her rejection dream helped Sabina realize how deeply she had sunk into her role as a victim and how her longing for Bob to become a loving partner was a false hope. It wasn't until weeks later that Sabina was able to see how her fruitless longings for a disinterested man were repeating a pattern from childhood with her father. (See her Caught in the Act dream below.)

If your dreams are filled with conflicts related to grief, anger, and rejection, and if over time these conflicts begin to show signs of gradual resolution, you are probably on the road to a healthy recovery even if your dreams are still upsetting or even nightmarish. On the other hand, if your dreams never achieve resolution and relentlessly portray you as a victim, or if they are bland and don't seem to focus at all on the separation, you may be at an impasse. It is vital to seek help from friends, family, or a psychotherapist as soon as you sense that your recovery may be stuck in the early stages of separation.

Clothing and Nudity Dreams

Many familiar roles are shed during a separation. For some this may feel like a relief, the necessary molting of an old, shriveled skin. For many others the change is more excruciating, like being stripped bare or having one's flesh torn away.

As old roles fall aside, we go through a period of flux and begin to experiment with new roles. Clothing and Nudity dreams may represent the phase of loss of identity, the naked sense of vulnerability, and experimentation with new roles and identities.

Rose's Clothing dream occurred shortly after her Riding a Unicycle dream, which is mentioned at the beginning of chapter 1. After a long period of contemplating the move, Rose left her husband of twenty-seven years and moved across the country to a city they had lived in ten years earlier.

Rose's unicycle dream took place just after her first meeting with her estranged husband, Leo, after five months of separation. In that dream she rides a unicycle, symbolic of the single life, when everyone around her is riding two-wheeled bikes, symbolic of married life. Although she feels alienated and clumsy, she is able to succeed and feel pride. The unicycle dream occurred just as she was beginning to shake the deep depression that had afflicted her prior to and immediately following the separation.

The following dream occurred two nights after her unicycle dream, one week after her meeting with Leo. The dream focuses on her attire or lack of it, and is further evidence of the awkwardness of the role changes that occur with divorce. As in the unicycle dream, Rose was beginning to achieve resolution about the identity change she was undergoing.

____ DRESSED IN AN OLD TOWEL AT THE COCKTAIL PARTY

I am at a cocktail party like the ones I used to go to for my husband's company. Everyone is dressed to the nines in furs and jewels. I realize that all I have on is a bath towel. It is kind of strange, but I don't really feel that weird. People start to look at me funny as if they are questioning or condemning what I was wearing. I can sense that all the people around me are not comfortable.

As she told her dream, I asked Rose to focus on the strongest feelings she was experiencing. She focused on the sense of being alienated from people. She said, "I have always felt that way a little bit, but my sense of not fitting in was especially strong with Leo and his business-oriented dinners and parties. The party in the dream reminds me of any number of real parties I used to go to in my other life with my husband. I hated those parties. They were so superficial, just like Leo. I never felt that I fit in."

The estrangement that Rose felt in her dream is characteristic of the unconscious and conscious experiences of the newly separated person. Rose's dream related to her sense of humiliation about being divorced, as well as to the financial hardships of separation.

In dreams, we often discover that details that seem trivial or mundane at first turn out to be rich with associations and meanings. For Rose the old bath towel was such an object. The towel reminded her of a set of towels she had bought years ago, before she married Leo. She smiled as she thought about them. Leo's mother had always hated them when she visited, but Rose kept them until they were torn and ratty. She realized that they were a symbol of the brief period of independence she had had before marriage.

In this dream, Rose is beginning to recover from her depression. One indication of this is that she's not alone and desolate in her dream. Although she is feeling inadequate, she is determined and able to weather the scorn of others at the party. In one of Cartwright's studies, 74 percent of depressed divorcing women had one or more dreams with no other person in them, as compared to 42 percent of the nondepressed divorcing women.[13]

Learning to accept loss or change in key relationships and adapting to the new status of being independent are crucial variables in getting over divorce or separation. Clothing and Nudity Dreams are among the ways our dreams express our reactions to our changing identity. Exploring these dreams can help us to clarify whether we are moving forward toward establishing a postseparation identity.[14]

Confronting Ghosts from the Past

Separation and divorce afford an opportunity to create a more healthy relationship with a new partner. In order to move forward and avoid repeating mistakes in relationships, it's vital that we learn from our own relationship history. We risk making the same or even worse choices if we fly forward into a new relationship without understanding our contribution to the demise of the one that just ended.

At turning points such as divorce, our dreams have an uncanny way of spotlighting issues and relationships from the past that are blocking us. A year after her separation from Leo, Rose had a Ghosts from the Past dream that helped her understand the roots of her difficulty in escaping her marriage. This dream, like the others, came around the time of a brief visit with Leo. She had only seen him twice since their separation, and she feared that the visit would make her revert back into depression. Although she was only planning to have lunch with him to discuss minor details of their final settlement, Rose was on the verge of canceling the meeting when she had the following dream.

UNStabLe GROUND

I am in the boathouse down by the lake where we used to spend summers when I was a kid. Instead of my father owning it, it seems to be my older brother's house. There is a big family party, and somehow the boathouse is different, larger. I am in a part of the house that had been added on. The house begins to undulate as if it wasn't stable. I keep struggling back to where the ground is more stable; my brother reassures me not to worry. The ground is still swaying dangerously under me. I am just able to struggle back to solid ground.

A year after her separation, Rose's dream was taking her farther back into her past, beyond Leo and back to her relationships with her father and brother. Rose recalled that the boathouse was not a place of happy memories. During the family's summer visits there, her father would drink and become verbally and occasionally physically abusive to her brothers. There were few other children in the neighborhood, and her older brother would tease her mercilessly.

Her dream of returning to the boathouse helped Rose see how she was still under the spell of the abuse. She associated her brother's reassurances in the dream with his denial of ever harassing her. She remembered that whenever she complained about the vicious teasing, her mother did nothing. Her family's lack of acknowledgment and protection had infused Rose with self-doubt and a self-defeating tendency that had influenced her whole life.

As she discussed her dream in therapy, Rose began to understand the incredible parallels between her relationships with her father, her brother, and her husband. Leo had been unexpressive and frequently criticized her. On three occasions he had undermined her attempts to go back to school and begin a career. He seemed to want a loyal wife who accepted her place.

For years, she told herself she was staying for the kids. But after they both went to college, it was another year before she could bring herself to leave. Through therapy and her own self-exploration, she understood that she had thought she deserved Leo's abuse and his constant sabotage of her autonomy.

The shaking of the ground under the boathouse symbolized the unstable period she had been going through. The dream helped her see that there could be no reassurance from her brother, her family, or Leo. She had to weather the earthquake she was experiencing and struggle back to solid ground alone.

In the dream, Rose discovers a new part of the boathouse. Dreams of discovering new rooms in a house and related images often occur at moments of personal growth when new aspects of our personality are emerging. Rose felt that she was trying to remake or rework her childhood, to find a room that would support her growing self-confidence and movements toward autonomy. Although the earth is swaying dangerously, the dream ends with Rose achieving a degree of resolution.

After discussing this ghosts from the past dream in therapy and with two close friends, Rose resolved to go ahead with the visit with Leo. She kept it brief and emerged from the meeting with a renewed confidence that Leo's spell on her—and that of her father and her brother—had been broken.

For Sabina, a dream five months after her separation shows that earlier conflicts with her father and mother remain unresolved and are still blocking her recovery.

caught in the act

I'm in my bedroom in my parents' home where I grew up. I can see the familiar yellow color of the walls. Suddenly I see Bob coming in through the window. He wants to come in my bed and have sex with me. I want to, but I'm afraid that my parents will find out. I go into the bathroom to put in my diaphragm. It is all wet in there, and it seems like my dad just finished taking a shower. Bob becomes impatient, so we start making love. A nun comes in ranting: "This is disgusting!" Then my mom comes in angry because of the nun screaming and because I'm in bed with Bob. I'm angry now also. I think they should get out and respect the fact that I had the door closed. I want to continue to make love with Bob, but all the interruptions seem to have ruined it and I'm disappointed.

In the dream, we again see Sabina's continuing desperation to be reunited sexually with Bob under any circumstance. The other elements of the dream made Sabina especially curious. As she recounted her dream, she was shocked by the graphic depiction of the sexual scene in her family home. It reminded her of constant fights she used to have with her parents when she was a teenager. They would yell at her and try to restrict her, but she was rebellious, shouting back and often defying them by going on dates with older guys.

Sabina thought the cameo appearance by the screaming nun was "weird." She wasn't Catholic. Why should a nun show up in her dream? At first she was sure that it related to her parents, especially her mother. When I suggested that the raging nun might represent a part of herself, Sabina became silent, and a sad look came over her face. Although she had been sexually active at an early age and had always prided herself on being liberated, maybe she did have fears and inhibitions after all. It would certainly make sense, given how negative her parents were about sex. Sabina guessed that some of her early sexual activity was the only way she could find to get love and attention.

Sabina became tearful as she thought more about how much mistreatment she had been willing to put up with when she was with Bob, yet how much urgency she still felt to win him back sexually. Her friends had been telling her that he was unkind and that she should give up on him. She knew they were right, but the advice just didn't sink in.

As she reviewed the dream, I asked her about the part in which she sensed that her father had just taken a shower. At first she remembered that her family only had one bathroom and that her father would take long showers, blocking anyone else from using the bathroom. As she thought more about this memory, she remembered that he was incredibly insensitive in other ways. "He was always critical. He never gave a compliment." Sabina remembered that in the period before her parents' divorce, when she was sixteen, her mother and father used to have shouting matches, and he would say incredibly nasty things to Sabina's mother.

Sabina began to make a link between the wet bathroom, her father, and her desperate need to make love to Bob at all costs. She had a strong sense that her difficulty in letting go of Bob concerned unresolved issues with her father. Bob was like her father in many ways, capable of being charming at times, but often selfish and temperamental.

Sabina's dream helped her to understand more about the addictive quality of her continuing preoccupation with Bob. Although her dream indicates that she is still at an impasse, her exploration of the dream helped her recognize her masochistic pattern with men and how it was connected to her unfulfilling relationship with her father.

Children's Postdivorce Dreams

After decades of research on the impact of divorce on children's personality and psychological adjustment, extensive insights have been achieved without full agreement among the principal researchers. In *The Unexpected Legacy of Divorce,* the research of Judith Wallerstein and her colleagues has highlighted the devastating and long-lasting emotional impact of divorce on children's well-being and even their attitudes and capacities for establishing intimate relationships in adulthood.[15] In contrast, Mavis Hetherington's conclusions, while not minimizing the impact of divorce, have highlighted children's resilience and capacity to recover from and creatively cope with the impact of their parents' divorce, even twenty-plus years after the fact.[16]

Nearly half of all children will experience divorce, and many will endure insecurity and stress before, during, and after the breakup. Subsequently, as both of their parents date and remarry, they may acquire new stepsiblings and half siblings. In some cases, the new family configuration may be more nurturing and harmonious than the one presided over by their birth parents. In other cases, children are caught in the crossfire of their parents' lingering animosity or are inadvertently neglected as their mothers and fathers undergo overwhelming emotional or financial stress.

Children of divorce are vulnerable to nightmares during the period immediately following the separation and later in response to acute divorce-related conflicts between their parents. Postdivorce dreams clearly reflect the nature of the child's adjustment to the emotional rigors of losing their original family and then changing all of the relationships they had counted on for security.

A widespread theme in these children's conscious thoughts, daydreams, and nocturnal dreams is the wish and hope that their parents might reunite. It is not surprising that this theme is a dominant one in younger children who have recently experienced divorce. However, even older teenagers whose parents have remarried or children whose parents are bitterly estranged have persistent dreams of reunions. Exploring these parental reunion and other divorce-related dreams will help parents understand that their child is struggling and gradually beginning to cope with massive insecurities.

In a second grade class, all of the students were asked to have their parents help them write down one dream on a particular night. Two-thirds of the students returned the next day with a recorded dream. Although the content of the dreams was fascinating, one theme stood out among the four students whose parents had divorced within the previous two years—a wished-for reunion of the parents. Two of these parental reunion dreams follow.

REUNION

My dream was about my mom *and* dad and that the divorce was all better, and they were happy again.

Lonely again

Everyone was sleeping in a big bed with me, my two older sisters, my mom *and* my dad. All of a sudden, I noticed that everyone went back to their own beds to go to sleep. I stayed under my blankets with my teddy bear. I was really feeling lonely.[17]

The first dream clearly fulfills the unconscious and probably conscious wish to undo the divorce's trauma, reunite the family, and heal the child's psyche. The second dream, "Lonely Again," has more complexity and shows a graphic image of reunification. It also replays the separation that follows each parental visit. Condensed in the dream are both memories of the warmth of his parents' love and an acute replay of the grief and loneliness of missing his mom or dad when he is with the other parent.

Parental Reunion dreams may provoke guilt and anxiety in a divorced parent who feels they have done everything they could think of to help their child. Parents should try to set aside their guilt, listen empathetically to the dreams, and use them as an indicator of feelings related to the divorce. Talking about the dream may be a safer way to communicate conflicted feelings, including grief, torn loyalty, and general anxieties.

Soon after a marital separation, children's insecurities run high. Ten-year-old Brian had always been sensitive to the plight of the disadvantaged. Despite his young age, he worried about homeless people, disaster victims, and people with HIV. Brian's precocious social concerns and his general anxieties increased when he learned that his father was moving out and divorcing his mother.

Brian may have sensed his parents' increasing estrangement as he began having worries and upsetting dreams even before the separation. His nightmares increased during the weeks following the separation when Brian and his brother, Jake, began spending weekends at his father's new home.[18]

One night, when his mother was tucking him in before sleep, Brian asked whether they could buy a rather expensive gift for one of his best friend's birthdays. Gina explained to her son that finances had become tighter due to the divorce. Brian immediately became nervous and wanted repeated reassurances from Gina that they would never become like the homeless people he had seen on the street. Even though Gina promised that that would never happen, Brian insisted that she couldn't guarantee it. Gina rephrased her offer to "do everything in my power to make sure we are never homeless." Brian finally began to calm down and eventually was able to fall asleep. His worries persisted, however, and were expressed in the following Left-Out dream that night.

Lost and crying

I am wandering around in a really old house with walls that are practically falling down on me. I keep looking everywhere for my mom and my brother and my dad, but no one answers. I start crying, and I feel like I am never going to find anyone, and finally I wake up, and I really am crying.

Gina comforted her son and wiped away his tears and her own. She too felt the loneliness and confusion that her son's dream so poignantly expressed. Having explored her own dreams for many years, Gina knew, however, that it was important to empathize with the dreamer's feelings. She responded by reflecting back to her son some of her own responses: "If that were my dream, I would feel really lonely and scared." Brian responded with more tears. "Yes, I miss Dad when he's not here, and I miss you when I am at his house. I'd rather just be in my own bed and have both of you here."

Remembering the previous night's discussion about homelessness, Gina knew that Brian would see right through any false promises. "I don't think Daddy and I are going to live together again, but we are going to try hard to stay friends, and neither of us would ever leave you alone like you were in the dream."

Brian reiterated how frightened he had been wandering around "that old house" and not finding anyone to help him. Gina suggested that Brian try to imagine that he was back in the dream so they could work together to think up new endings. Brian eagerly took his mother's invitation to fantasize and began describing an old house that was "all gross like in *The Addams Family*, with spiderwebs everywhere and squeaky floors." As if a lightbulb had gone off, he suddenly exclaimed, "I know! I'll find the phone and call your pager, and you can call 911, Mom!" Gina had gotten a pager after the separation, expressly for the purpose of allowing her sons to contact her in an emergency. This dream solution seemed immensely satisfying to Brian, who had indeed paged his mother in recent weeks just for a reassurance call.

This was not Brian's last postdivorce nightmare as many months of adjustment lay ahead for the whole family. However, Brian always came to his mother after a nightmare, eager to have her comfort him and brainstorm solutions to his dream dilemmas. And although Gina felt upset every time Brian had nightmares, she felt that their sessions discussing and rehearsing solutions to the dreams were not only enjoyable for both of them, they also helped her stay alert to Brian's divorce-related anxieties.

Whereas Brian's parents' separation was painful but relatively amicable, ten-year-old Alexander's parents had been squabbling for many years. He had two recurring nightmares that began shortly after the divorce, six years earlier.

Alexander's mother remarried a man with two older sons, and he and his younger brother got along well with his new stepbrothers. Alexander's father had not fared so well following the divorce. He had difficulty maintaining steady work and seemed to be in a constant rage against his ex-wife. He made it his mission in life to bad-mouth Alexander's mother and to fight for increased custody. He cursed at her, called her "a slut" and other derogatory names, and even threatened to take out a gun if Alexander's stepfather came to his house to pick him up.

Although the family court judge had reduced visits with his father to two overnight visits per month, Alexander would go through a cycle of tension and irritability for days before and after his visits with his father. He did not want to end the visits because he was afraid of both disappointing and angering his father whom he feared could hurt him or his mother.

Alexander's distress about the visits with his father became so acute that he began misbehaving at school. He refused to turn in assignments, was insolent to teachers, and had angry outbursts at home. He also began to have a horrible, repetitive nightmares about being trapped and paralyzed.

suffocation

It's the middle of the night, and I feel like I am pushed down on the bed. I can't breathe, and I can't wake up, and I can't endure it. I wake up right after that.[19]

Being trapped or paralyzed are universal nightmare themes. For Alexander, the Paralysis nightmares had become unbearable, and his hostility and antisocial behavior in school had resulted in two suspensions and the threat of expulsion from school. When Alexander was brought to me for psychotherapy, he was not enthusiastic about the idea and did not hide his resistance. He refused to talk about his visits with his father and was protective of any questions that even vaguely suggested any negative appraisal of his father's behavior. His defensiveness is typical of many children of divorce who feel torn apart by their loyalty to each of their divorced parents and unwilling to reveal any details that would hurt either parent.

When he learned, however, that dreams and nightmares could be part of the therapy, he became intrigued. He talked about his suffocation dreams and wanted to know why he was having them. He also recounted one other repetitive nightmare that he been having as far back as he could remember. He had had the dream again the night before the therapy session.

time bomb

I can hear this ticktock sound, and I can hear the footsteps. I am looking from the view of the guy with the bomb and hearing what he hears. The sounds are getting louder and louder, and all of a sudden it explodes.[20]

This explosion dream expresses Alexander's difficulty controlling his anger and his sense of loss of control related to his father's unquenchable rage toward his mother. He was both afraid of his father's anger and worried that he, too, might be unable to control his own anger.

The fact that the dream had occurred immediately after the visit to his father was of great interest to me and led me in some new and fruitful discussions with Alexander. He opened up and was able to discuss the distress he felt before, during, and after his visits with his father. This was a topic that he had refused to discuss prior to sharing the dream in therapy.

Exploring the dream helped Alexander feel more comfortable discussing his mixed feelings—the fact that he was frightened of his father's violent threats, swearing, and tendency to neglect him during their visits.

The following week, Alexander requested that his mother sit in on his therapy session, and he revealed more of his fears to her and asked whether it was possible to visit his father less often. Alexander told her that he was scared of his father's temper and had bad dreams right after the visits. He asked for shorter visits without sleeping over.

Over the next month, through a continuing series of discussions with Alexander and separately with his mother and stepfather, a plan was made to reduce visitation to two short visits per month. Within three months, Alexander's behavior problems at school had decreased dramatically. He was still occasionally defiant but was no longer facing suspensions and referrals to the principal. He no longer had dreams of bombs or paralysis but occasionally had nightmares of being trapped by a criminal.

Dreams reveal the valiant inner struggles that children are making to adjust as they form new images of family that will help them feel more secure. Exploring Paralysis and other anxiety-provoking dreams during these stressful periods will help diagnose the child's difficulties and can become part of the solution as you talk about the forbidden or difficult topics that dreams inevitably bring to our awareness.

Dreams and Recovery after Separation

Dreams provide a compass to navigate through the difficult passage of separation and divorce. Through our dreams we can understand where we are in our journey from being part of a couple to being a single person who may want to reconnect with a new partner.

In the early stages of breaking up, dreams and nightmares provide a gauge for viewing our confusion and our powerful feelings of grief, rage, and abandonment. Our dreams show us feeling out of control, threatened, exposed, and inadequate. At that stage our dreams can help us overcome our powerful tendency toward denial, bitterness, or clinging to the past.

Exploring our dreams also helps us to understand issues from the past that have contributed to the failure of our marriage and that may block intimacy in the future. During the crisis of separation, our dreams review events when we faced a similar loss or separation. Through dreams, the unconscious mind searches for times in the past when we solved a parallel emotional challenge. Our dreams can help us by picturing our crisis from many different angles and exaggerating it. We need to be able to see our predicament in a new way to make a change.

Rose's unicycle dream and Nora's art heist dreams show us how dreams are like rehearsals for crucial new behaviors and attitudes. Just as an expectant parent's dreams show a rehearsal of nurturing behaviors, divorcing people's dreams show a rehearsal of roles associated with a single life separate from a former spouse. If we are open to the messages of our dreams, we can use them to repair old wounds that prevent us from creating a fulfilling relationship.

6. WORK DREAMS RESOLVING CAREER CONFLICTS AND FINDING A MEANINGFUL JOB

Erica, age thirty-nine, had returned to graduate school after ten years of working as a waitress. She had completed her undergraduate degree at a top university with honors and was about to complete an M.B.A. At last she was ready to begin her career.

During her final round of job interviews, she began to experience bouts of anxiety. First she procrastinated in setting up the interviews. Then, although she performed reasonably well, she was terrified that her insecurity would be detected and she would not only be denied a job but would not make it in her new profession. During this period she had the following Career Breakthrough dream.

Leap of faith

I am on top of a mountain, being forced to jump from my mountain to the top of another mountain. There is a steep valley below so it is very dangerous. I know I have to take a chance. I imagine that I'm jumping and finally take a great leap and make it. I am aware of all my movements and how I'm breathing as I land.

Erica felt relieved when she awoke, as if a burden had been lifted. As she explored the elements of her dream, her first association was with her fear of heights. She was surprised that she would have climbed so high because in waking life she would have avoided such a mountain precipice.

The image of being on the top of the mountain also triggered associations for Erica about her career status. She was about to reach new heights in her career and was nervous about making the transition from graduate school to the business world. The image of the valley in her dream symbolized the lesser job she had worked in and the fact that she had come from a family of lower means.

Although it reminded her of dangers ahead, Erica's Career Breakthrough dream also gave her an image of confidence. In the dream she is able to jump from mountain to mountain, and she does make her final great leap. Remembering this part of the dream gave her a sense of confidence that she felt would help her persevere and succeed in her career transition.

During this same period Erica had another uncomfortable dream that she's had many times before while working as a waitress. After years of repetition, the dream took a more resolved form, again presenting a symbolic solution to her performance anxieties.

a new way of taking orders

I am waiting on tables at my restaurant. I am very nervous about confusing or forgetting the orders. I decide that I am going to try something new, and I give everyone a piece of paper to write down their orders. That way I don't have to risk getting their order wrong. I won't forget them, and I can correct them before I give them to the chef. I try it, and it seems to work.

For years, the dream had not included a new method of taking orders. It had been a purely apprehensive dream about ruining orders or being scolded by the customers or the chef for poor performance. The new ending provided a solution, indicating a sense of confidence that Erica could contain her anxiety and enjoy her work. In retrospect, Erica saw that she had never had complaints from the chef and rarely from customers because her anxiety caused her to be meticulous in her duties. Erica's dream solution paralleled a lessening of the anxiety that she felt in her job as a waitress. Her career breakthrough dreams also heralded a growing sense of esteem that allowed her to feel confident about returning to school and changing careers.

Career Change As a Turning Point

In this chapter we'll examine how dreams can guide us to find meaningful work that moves us closer to fulfilling our emotional, spiritual, and material needs. We'll see how dreams can help us navigate the many crises and transitions of our career. We'll explore dreams at each stage of the career cycle, focusing on the psychological issues and stages related to making a career transition.

During our thirty to fifty years of working, we face many turning points, some anticipated and manageable, others sudden and devastating. Most people can expect a number of job changes and one or more career changes. Even apparently positive events, such as receiving a promotion or a new job or getting an award, may cause serious work-related stress.

Virtually everyone experiences minor career conflicts and crises. Every so often, however, we experience profound career turning points that can alter our economic and social stability and even endanger our physical and emotional health. Turning points in the career cycle can be caused by external factors, internal psychological factors, or an interplay of the two.[1]

External situations that may precipitate turning points include being abused by insensitive supervisors or management; suffering a work-related injury; topping out or losing out on promotions; being demoted or losing a job; having to learn unfamiliar skills; dealing with boring, meaningless, or unrewarding tasks; lacking educational opportunities; and being subjected to discrimination because of race, gender, age, disabilities, or sexual orientation.

Common internal factors that contribute to career turning points include burnout, depression, authority conflicts, performance anxieties, fears of commitment, fears of success, reactions to stresses unrelated to work, and general dissatisfaction and loss of incentive.

There are distinct phases to the career cycle. As early as childhood we may begin to explore visions of our future work identity, idealizing our parents or movie stars, athletes, or teachers. This exploration phase may lead us to change majors in college or to experiment with different jobs to find ourselves. For some people, experimentation may be brief and decisive. For others, it may take them well into their twenties or even thirties and involve job changes and more schooling before they can settle on one path.[2]

Disengagement from a career or job is inevitable at retirement. We may also face the need to leave a job when dissatisfaction or adverse events make our work unbearable. At that point we need to decide whether to change jobs and start the career cycle again or find some way of adapting to our present job. Whether we change careers or revitalize our present job, we undergo a phase of exploration that can lead to breakthroughs in self-awareness.

Remembering and exploring our dreams can help us clarify internal and external factors that set off career turning points. Dreams can help us to:

* understand where we are in the stages of exploring, launching, establishing, reevaluating, revitalizing, or disengaging from a job or career

* acknowledge hidden emotional patterns and symptoms that get in the way of resolving career crises

* master work anxieties and enhance our ability to adapt to new challenges on the job

* discover new insights and solutions to conflicts in maintaining or changing careers

* renew a sense of meaning in our current job or discover a vision of a new path toward meaningful work

Launching a Career

When we begin working as young adults and later when we make a career change, dreams can help us find inspiration to choose a form of work that will be meaningful to us. Occasionally dreams will present specific ideas. More often our dreams help us focus on finding a way to express our talents and emotional needs through our work.

Kelly's career vision dream inspired an unexpected career choice. She had come from a poor family but had won a scholarship at an exclusive women's college and was finishing her sophomore year. Her parents, who both did clerical work, strongly encouraged her toward prelaw or premed studies. Kelly was debating between majoring in creative writing or psychology, but none of the courses inspired her. Although she was making above-average grades, she wondered where she was going and wanted to find out who she really was. While taking a course on psychology that referred to Freud and Jung, Kelly had a vivid dream that set off an amazing chain of events.

if i were a carpenter

I'm back in Louisiana, where I used to spend summers at my grandmother's house. I am out on a wooden pier on the river like the ones that were really there. I am building a new section of the pier, hammering and doing all the work. I've got a leather belt with tools hooked on it, and I am working away. My older sister, Lucy, comes over, and I am talking to her about her relationship with her husband. It's almost as if I am counseling her about her marriage. I felt really at ease listening to her.

When she awoke from her dream, Kelly had a sense of confidence that she'd rarely had before in her life. The dream stayed alive and active in her mind. Two days later when Kelly was at her work-study job at the school switchboard, someone told her about opportunities for women in trades. She needed a summer job and decided to enroll in a new preapprenticeship program for young women.

Within one week of her dream, she had taken a six-month leave from school and enrolled in the training program. She never returned to college. By age twenty-six, she had become a licensed contractor with a thriving cabinet-making and remodeling business.

As Kelly recounted her career vision dream to me ten years later, it was still as vivid as the day she had it. She wanted to understand how the dream had inspired such an unlikely career. She confided that prior to beginning her carpentry training, she had never built anything and her parents were not the fix-it type.

As she explored the imagery in her dream, Kelly focused on the setting, which felt especially important to her. The summers she had spent with her grandmother were "the happiest memories of my life. We played on the pier and would go fishing in the river in small wooden boats." She remembered how relaxed and cooperative the small community was. There were shared meals with fresh garden vegetables and fish. She remembered how the neighbors had collectively built her grandmother's pier. The summer world with her grandmother was earthy and had a joie de vivre that the rest of her life with her parents lacked.

Kelly's parents were stern, unemotional, conservative, and restrictive. They often discouraged her more independent ideas. Her closest sibling was eight years older, and Kelly was shy, isolated, and filled with self-doubt as a child and teenager. Getting the scholarship and leaving for college had been her first taste of freedom.

The part of the dream where she was counseling Lucy, her older sister, made Kelly think of how much Lucy was like her mother. It was almost like counseling her mother about her parents' marriage. Thinking about it in this way reminded Kelly of how much her father dominated her mother and never let her express her opinions openly or pursue her interests. This had infuriated Kelly for as long as she could remember. Perhaps the dream was part of her dawning awareness that she could become what her mother was never able to be—a woman who was competent and expressive, both physically and verbally.

Although Kelly didn't fully understand the meaning of her career vision dream at the time she had it, carpentry gave her an immediate sense of physical strength and emotional confidence that was an antidote to the restrictive life that her parents imposed. Being able to work for herself and create things reminded her of the freedom that she'd felt during those precious summers she had spent with her grandmother.

Not all dreams provide a direction as specific as Kelly's did. However, if we explore our dreams while we are searching for a career direction, we are likely to encounter feelings and ideas that will make our search more fruitful.

Recognizing a Career Impasse

When your work is filled with emotional conflicts, interpersonal tensions, or tasks that no longer bring you personal or financial satisfactions, your dreams can be a source of insight. Exploring career impasse dreams can help you recognize when you have reached an impasse in your career and can inspire you to begin a process of change to correct the imbalances in your work.

Lisa, age thirty-five, had given up a promising career in marketing in a large corporation to start a small restaurant. Using her training in marketing, Lisa had created an appealing environment for customers. Through strategic advertising, she had become moderately successful. Despite her success, Lisa was dissatisfied with her business. She'd developed an ulcer and had frequent migraine headaches. Although everything looked good on paper, she was increasingly unhappy with her business and was thinking about selling it. She had already begun to take courses in counseling to consider whether she wanted to change careers.

Although Lisa had rarely remembered her dreams, while she was participating in a course on dreams she found it easy to remember them. When asked to review all of the dreams she had recorded during a two-week period, Lisa was shocked to discover that all five dreams she had written in her journal included angry encounters between herself and her employees. In most of them she was victimized by her employees, who alternately stole from the cash register, screamed, and threw food at her. In two of her dreams she screamed back at her employees, but it didn't seem to have any effect on them.

too many chefs spoil the stew

I am talking to the chef at my restaurant. I want to ask him about making some changes in the menu. He's cooking something that looks strange, like a weird fish stew with live sea creatures in it. He's using a large old rounded pot that's rusty. I try to ask him politely what he is doing because it looks very unappetizing. He starts screaming at me in front of all my employees and even threatens to throw the soup at me.

Lisa had, in fact, been having difficulty confronting her chef. She tried unsuccessfully to work around his stubborn, opinionated style. The dream was a caricature of her relationship with him. He wasn't doing the kind of work of which she approved; she was being overly polite to him while he was somewhat abusive in return.

As she thought about the fish stew, it reminded her at first of a special dish the chef had created that hadn't turned out well. She had wanted to discontinue it immediately, but he insisted on trying it again. She didn't like it the second time, but he still wouldn't give up the idea of including it on the menu.

Further reflection made Lisa think of her ulcer. The rust in the pot made her think of the doctor's description of how the ulcer was eating away at the lining of her stomach. Although the ulcer was diagnosed before the present chef was hired, it had worsened since then. She became angry when she thought that his cooking and the way he was behaving were making her ulcer worse.

Lisa hadn't realized how much anger she had built up over the situation at work. She had prided herself on her easygoing management style. As a result she had been overly tolerant of poor performance from her chef and some of the other employees. Her Career Impasse dream series gave her undeniable evidence that she was not being assertive enough in setting and maintaining performance standards for her employees.

In some cases the symbolic language of our dreams gives us a visual image that will clarify a career impasse. Malcolm, a middle-aged man, complained of feeling directionless. His business as a real estate agent had been declining, and he was feeling disenchanted. Malcolm described a repetitive Career Impasse dream he had been having.

SPINNING my WHEELS

I'm in my car, but it's my old red Buick Riviera. I put my keys in the car and start the engine. At first nothing happens, and I am getting frustrated. Then it seems to start, but all I can hear are the wheels spinning. The car won't move. I keep trying the key over and over. I am very upset and feel powerless.

Malcolm was drawn to the image of the red Riviera. This was a car he had bought during a period when he was highly successful. It was a fashion statement at the time, as he had normally purchased more conservative-looking cars. The frustration of not being able to start the car was easy to link to waking feelings. He had been feeling low-energy and powerless.

When asked what he thought about spinning his wheels, he smiled. He hadn't caught the pun that his dream contained. He felt slightly embarrassed, but the phrase clicked for him. "I *am* spinning my wheels. I'm stuck, and I keep trying to turn the key in the same old way to get things started."

Malcolm began to talk about how he was stuck. The youngest of his four daughters had gone off to college two years earlier, and his wife had returned to work full time managing a clothing store. He felt lonelier and less important now that he was no longer the primary breadwinner. In part, Malcolm was a male victim of the empty-nest syndrome.

At work, his younger colleagues seemed to get all the new business, and many of them had surpassed him in sales. He hadn't been attending many of the clubs and civic organizations where he had drummed up business in the past. As his career was waning, his wife's was on the rise.

The image of revving that old Riviera and going nowhere both amused and fascinated Malcolm. He had lost the success of his thirties and forties. His car was no longer snazzy; he couldn't even get it running. The dream gave visual form to his career impasse. He couldn't keep turning the key in the same way. He had to try something new.

Inspired by this discussion, Malcolm decided to see his doctor to determine whether depression or any other health problem was depleting his energy and drive. Malcolm's wife was sympathetic to his new ideas and confided to him that she had been concerned about his depression for months. With her encouragement, he planned to rejoin some of the civic and church groups that had formerly been a source of social contact and business referrals for him.

In some cases dreams can help us discover or clarify inner resources that may be important in gaining the confidence we need to seek training in a new field. Psychologist Susan Knapp cites the case of a woman, whom we shall call Alexandra, who consistently worked in occupations that were far below her intellectual potential. She had always acted self-assured and nonchalant about her jobs, but this façade concealed a terror of failure that kept her from trying out new career possibilities.

Alexandra began preparing for the Graduate Record Exam to apply to graduate school. Both she and her husband dwelt on the emotionally catastrophic consequences of her failing to get in. Her husband went so far as to try to talk her out of taking the exam and applying altogether. After discussing her husband's attempts to block her career aspirations, she had the following dream.

finding my wisdom teeth

I dreamed that my teeth were falling out. Then the support system beneath them, which was made out of toothpicks, also fell out. But then underneath both the old teeth and the new toothpicks was a perfectly good set of new teeth.[3]

A dream of losing teeth is a universal theme and often symbolizes physical or emotional injury, maturing, growing older, or a loss of power or potency. In Alexandra's case, she appears to be losing her potency, which had been artificially propped up. This part of the dream probably refers to her fear of being powerless or of failing. But the dream shows an unusual twist. Rather than experiencing the upsetting, disfiguring loss of a whole set of teeth, she realizes that what she is losing is the false teeth that had covered her real molars. The new set of teeth represented the sense of power that she and her husband had conspired to ignore. This dream allowed Alexandra to understand the powerful resources that she had long denied and to move ahead with her career exploration.

Abby, age thirty, knew she wanted out of her job. She and her husband, Sandy, had both reached an impasse in their careers. They were commodity options traders at the Chicago exchange. There had been a period when they were flush with two incomes of six figures each, but Sandy had lost his job and suffered serious financial losses resulting in a huge debt. Now Abby was on the verge of quitting but was forced to continue working for a few more months to begin to pay off their debts while Sandy got established in another job.

Abby didn't think she could endure another day of aggressive male commodity traders screaming deals in her face on the exchange floor. They treated each other terribly and treated women even worse. She was sure the job wasn't worth the money. But as she prepared for the day when she would be able to give up her job, she found herself at a loss. She didn't know what else would interest her. She knew that she wanted something that was more rewarding and would be compatible with having children.

She considered teaching, counseling, and landscape architecture. She dabbled in some workshops but couldn't get any inspiration. When her mother and younger sister came to visit her for a week, she noticed that she felt very childish. She realized that she wanted her mother to give her some definitive motherly advice. But what her mother offered was familiar rewarmed advice and lots of criticism of Abby and her husband. That night Abby had a nightmare.

famiLy kiLLeR

Wendy, my oldest hometown friend, is telling me a terrible story. She seems very upset. She said that she and her husband, Todd, went camping, and the family in the next campsite had five bratty kids who were screaming and getting in trouble and running out of control. Wendy had just heard they had all been brutally murdered. She was getting very upset, and then we both realized that the murderer could still be nearby and might be listening to us. It's very dark in the forest, and we are running away from the murderer, who is now chasing us. He is about to kill us. We are desperately running away, but he is gaining on us.

Abby was haunted by the brutality of the murderer and the image of him threatening her. She rarely had nightmares, and this one was difficult to shake. As she thought about her dream, she connected it to the miserable time she'd been having at work. When I asked her whether it was linked to any recent events, she immediately recalled her mother's visit and the neediness and indecisiveness she'd felt at that time.

She wondered why Wendy was in her dream. Although Wendy had been her best friend in childhood, they had drifted apart, and Abby only saw her on yearly visits back to her hometown in New York. As we talked more about what Wendy was like, Abby described her as someone who never broke away from the influence of her mother and her family. She married a local man, who went into business with her father. In fact, Wendy was now friends with Abby's mother.

Abby began to have more insights about the meaning of her dream. Although she had moved far away and had had many fights with her mother in her teens and twenties, maybe she hadn't really broken away. Maybe she was, like Wendy, still psychologically close and dependent. Perhaps that dependence on her mother was keeping her from being able to make up her mind about a career change. At some level, she realized, she not only wanted her mother's approval but wanted her mother to tell her what to do.

Abby became animated as she thought about the murdered family and realized that there were five children in her family. Perhaps Wendy and her husband represented Abby and her husband or even Abby's parents. It was like her own family being murdered.

Abby felt that one way to look at the dream was that she was experiencing the death of some kind of psychological connection to her family. She longed for closeness with her mother, the kind of closeness Wendy or her younger sister had. But when she tried to be dependent on her mother, all she got was criticism and a deaf ear to her distress.

She felt that the dream had given her a clue about what was blocking her ability to be more decisive in choosing a new career direction. She hadn't established the ability to make independent decisions and was still locked into a cycle of needing her mother's direct advice and approval. Although Abby wasn't yet sure of her career direction, she felt that working on her Family Killer dream had clarified an important impasse that was holding her back.

A subsequent dream portrayed Abby feeling excited about moving to a smaller house with her husband. It was empty and was going to need a lot of work to fix it up, but she was looking forward to the process. With that dream, Abby felt that she had turned a corner. Her unconscious was beginning to picture a new identity, one that had not been clearly defined but would provide a workable challenge.

Exploring Options for Changing Careers

Donald was exploring options for a career change. As an attorney he had been highly successful in his work for a large law firm. Although he would have been a candidate to become a partner in two years, the seventy-hour work weeks and the adversarial battles in the courtroom had gotten to him. He wanted out. He took a leave of absence but knew in his heart that he could never return to a job like that.

Donald spent the summer traveling in Asia. In the back of his mind, he was considering going into international law or a business that would allow him to travel and not be confined to the law library and an office. When he returned from his travels, he began doing freelance legal work and decided to take an intensive course to become a travel agent and tour leader. He would be able to travel and meet interesting people and have a career that was more varied and relaxed.

Near the end of his travel course, Donald had an interview with a premier tour agency. They paid a high salary, gave in-depth training to their leaders, and had an outstanding reputation. The day of the interview, Donald noticed that he was uncharacteristically forgetful. Not only did he neglect to bring his résumé, he arrived late because he had forgotten the exact address. Despite those glitches, the interview went well, and he was offered a job leading his first tour in three weeks.

Donald was shocked at the speed of the process and requested the weekend to think it over. That night he had a career breakthrough dream.

if you travel you will unravel

I am thinking about going traveling. I'm not sure whether it's for work or pleasure. I am torn about going, and then it feels like some kind of legal argument with someone about the meaning of the word travel. I can't tell whether it's travel or travail. I can't justify which it is because travel would be for fun, but travail is work. As I wake up I hear a poem or a song with a silly tune saying over and over: If you travel you will unravel.

Donald was amused by his dream ditty. He knew it was connected to making a decision about taking the job but wasn't sure what to make of the dream. He was drawn first to the distinction between "travel" and "travail." He had always enjoyed knowing the meaning and etymology of words, but this argument seemed picayune. He wasn't even sure he was arguing with anyone, because there was no one else present in the dream.

The obsessive quality of the wordplay reminded him of how indecisive and obsessive he had been in debating every aspect of his career change. He could never make up his mind, and he always seemed to focus so much on details that he lost the big picture of what would be best for him emotionally.

In thinking about the dream song, his first thought was that unraveling meant being irresponsible. This puzzled him, and he was uncertain how to interpret it. Maybe he needed to be a little more irresponsible and a little less obsessive, a little more like someone who would sing silly songs instead of someone who would argue and ruminate on the meaning of a word.

Exploring his dream helped him see more clearly than before that he needed to balance his serious, obsessive side with a more fun-loving, relaxed side. He had thought that becoming a tour guide would accomplish that.

As he continued to contemplate his dream, however, he also realized that the final weeks of his travel course had given him an inkling that being a tour guide might not be so much fun. It could be a lot of travail—being available twenty-four hours a day, answering inane questions, and fretting over travel connections for a whole group. The word "unravel" had other associations for him as well. If he led tours, his authority and identity as a lawyer might disintegrate. He feared that loss of identity.

Through discussing his dream, Donald decided not to accept the plum job as a tour leader. He hadn't completely given up the idea of being a travel guide, but he was feeling more encouraged about searching for a position as a lawyer that might be less remunerative than his old job, but also less stressful and more emotionally rewarding. The real issue, he concluded, was changing and revitalizing his attitude, not starting a brand-new career.

Occasionally, vivid dreams help to crystallize a decision to change careers. For Shauna, two dreams were strongly linked to her decision to move and change careers. As a vocational rehabilitation counselor, she had her own business helping clients who suffered from industrial injuries. But Shauna was feeling burned-out and depressed. Over the last two years she'd become disillusioned with her work. Many of her clients were severely disabled and had great difficulty finding work. Others got unfairly low settlements from big employers. She was losing her idealism and enthusiasm. On top of that, a long-term relationship that she'd hoped would lead to marriage had broken up painfully.

In the midst of this period, she had the first of two intensely vivid Career Breakthrough dreams that motivated her to change her life.

the HILLS are alive

I am lying on a ledge or a cliff somewhere in the coastal hills of California. It's the end of summer, and the hills are all brown with grasses waving in the breeze. As I look at the hills, they suddenly begin to sprout, and they turn into mountain peaks that look like the mountains near Santa Fe, New Mexico. It is intensely alive and colorful.

Shauna was excited by this dream. She emphasized how real and compelling the image of the mountains was. Her brother and his family lived in New Mexico. They were the only relatives with whom she was emotionally close.

In the beginning of her dream, being on the mountain ledge symbolized her emotional state. She felt that she was on the edge of deeper depression and needed to make a change. Within six months she had decided to take a two-week trip to the Albuquerque–Santa Fe area to visit her brother and explore her options. A week before departing, she had another vivid dream that helped to confirm her decision to move.

INITIATION

Some members of an Indian tribe from the northern Midwest plains are standing before me. I'm taking part in a ceremony, and they say, "You are going to New Mexico." They come forward as a group and present themselves to me and tell me to carry something sacred. They say, "You are now qualified to carry the pipe for us." They hand me a medicine bag and tell me that I will have safe passage in a canoe. They also say something else, which is confusing: "Buffaloes are not at home in California."

Shauna felt convinced that she was making the right move with her upcoming trip. The Indian men in her dream reminded her of her interest in Native American spirituality and New Age practices. She wondered whether she would want to do vocational rehabilitation work with Indians if she moved to New Mexico. But she wasn't sure that was what the dream was telling her, since she wanted to change careers if she moved.

Remembering the part about safe passage in a canoe, she felt a surge of memories, and the presence of the Indians in her dream began to make sense. When she was young, she used to go on weeklong canoe trips in Canada with her father and brother. After her parents separated, when she was ten until she was fifteen, she was sent to a summer camp with Canadian Indian counselors. The long canoe trips with the Indian guides were her only positive memories during the miserable years of her parents' divorce and custody battles over her.

As Shauna thought more about this dream, she realized that the Indians didn't necessarily represent the specific type of work she might do, but rather the positive experiences of physical and emotional well-being. More lengthy exploration of this dream persuaded Shauna to search for some type of work that would give her the sense of adventure, camaraderie, and creativity that she had felt during her summer canoe journeys as a child.

Shauna's dreams gave her inspiration to continue a career search. Six months later, she was planning the move to New Mexico and taking courses in art and music therapy. Shauna felt that combining a desire to help people with an emphasis on creativity would make her work more emotionally rewarding. She hoped to work with children in hospitals or perhaps on the reservations in New Mexico. She was also intrigued by the possibility of combining her interest in New Age healing and Native American spirituality with future work as a creative arts therapist.

Lindsay had been working in sales for over fifteen years and was deeply discouraged with her work. She had been reading a variety of books on career transitions but hadn't found any inspiration that would help her make a change. After many months of dissatisfaction and searching, she had a "big dream" that affected her like a "bolt of lightning" and helped her begin to explore a new direction.

> There are several women friends meeting with me. I can see their faces, and they look familiar but are not anyone I really know. It's some sort of sales meeting, although I am not sure what the product is. We are talking in an animated way. They are dividing up the territory in the Bay Area, and we eventually spread out to California and the whole country. One woman had a computer system set up and says we will be connected by computer but also by our feelings. It has something to do with the group being all women. There is a feeling of synergy and excitement that is very strong.

Lindsay realized that she had always worked for male bosses and frequently differed with their management style. Now she wanted to take a quantum leap in her career and do something where she was no longer the employee, but part of management. She even considered starting her own business.

Inspired by the image of her dream team, Lindsay began to call other women she knew in sales and business with the idea of meeting as a support group to explore alternative forms of employment. Within a month the group had its first meeting. After six months the women were considering forming a company that would be run by women and would provide specialized professional services to other businesses owned or operated by women.

While Lindsay was exploring these career options, she changed jobs and was working for the first time with a woman, a noted entrepreneur. Lindsay was still unsure what direction her career transition would ultimately take, but she felt that dreams had given her the inspiration necessary to make the change.

Exploring career breakthrough dreams helps us find and pursue new career directions when we are searching for ways to revitalize our career or change jobs. Occasionally we may discover specific ideas or information that prove useful, such as Donald's dream warning about the travel business or Shauna's image of the California hills turning into the mountains of New Mexico. More often, our dreams spark insights that help us resolve issues that block us from achieving fulfillment in our present job or help us find the inspiration and motivation to make a change.

Confronting a Career Impasse

When we take concrete steps to change our job or make a career switch, we encounter both internal and external obstacles. External obstacles might include poor economic conditions, such as a recession or lack of demand for our skills. Internal obstacles include fears of failure, guilt about becoming successful, or a general fear of leaving a secure job and venturing into a new one with no guarantee of success. Exploring dreams can help us understand our reaction to external factors and inner conflicts that may block the success of a career transition.

Rusty had recently made a miraculous turnaround. Although he had a B.A. in English literature from Stanford, he'd been heavily involved in the drug culture of the late 1960s and early 1970s. His use of marijuana and LSD had initially been connected with radical politics, explorations of Eastern religions, and attempts at establishing a rural communal environment.

While living in a northern California commune, Rusty got involved with a group that was cultivating marijuana and smuggling various drugs for sale into Los Angeles. Although Rusty was not the ringleader, he delivered drugs to suppliers for about three years. During this time he had access to many drugs and became addicted to heroin.

Rusty was able to extricate himself from the drug ring, but his addiction to heroin continued. He was accepted at a prestigious law school but dropped out after the first month because of his addiction. He tried many jobs, but as his addiction worsened he was never able to hold them. Off and on he drove a cab, did construction work, and worked as a security guard. At times he would deal heroin or other drugs on a small scale to support his habit.

Although he was never arrested, Rusty encountered many dangerous situations because of his drug habit. Finally he was knifed by a drug-crazed customer who was attempting to rob him. Although the knife was aimed at his heart, he ducked it and it slashed his arm deeply, requiring many stitches.

The brush with death scared Rusty into changing his life. He entered a rehabilitation program, gave up heroin, and read every book he could find on changing careers. He entered psychotherapy and faithfully attended Narcotics Anonymous. He soon decided to seek certification as a drug counselor so he could help others overcome what had been so devastating for him. He enrolled in a certification program and volunteered with a local clinic. They liked his work so much, they promised him a job when he had obtained his certificate. While in school, he continued to drive a cab at night so he could attend classes during the day.

In the last month of his one-year program to become a drug counselor, Rusty noticed that he was getting feistier in all of his classes, openly disagreeing with his teachers. He began to have doubts about whether he wanted to go through with his career plans. He noticed that he was driving more recklessly. When he picked up customers in his cab whom he recognized as probable drug dealers, he began to feel temptations to use. He knew something was going wrong, but he wasn't sure what.

A week before graduation, he had a dream that affected him profoundly.

Lead me not into temptation

I pick up four people in my cab and drive them far out of town, down a logging road to a small cabin. I am invited inside and notice a small paper bag. I don't know what it is, but then I see that it is lots of pills, heroin, and a hundred new syringes. The people are grinding up the pills and preparing to shoot the drugs. The mixture is a bright pink color, which is very striking to me. They offer me free access to the drugs. I am extremely tempted by the offer. My whole body seems to want the drugs— just the way I used to feel when I needed a fix. I realize no one would ever know that I indulged. I fight the temptation for what seems like a long time. Finally I decide that I am not going to take the drugs or hang around those people. I leave the cabin and get back in my car to drive back to the city.

For Rusty the dream felt like an incredible triumph over the temptation to use drugs, defeat his recovery, and sabotage his career transition. He said, "Thinking about the dream gave me chills. I felt like I climbed over Mount Everest. It showed me that I do have the willpower to delay gratification."

Rusty described a chronic pattern of "opting out" in stressful situations and going on drug binges. He said that he had been able to hold to the dream's image of walking away from temptation; it had helped him settle down and get through his last week of classes.

Although the decisive moment of resisting temptation was the most powerful legacy, Rusty explored other aspects of this monumental dream. In particular, the bright pink color of the drugs fascinated him. Rusty thought of different medicines he had taken. When he was a child his mother used to put pink calamine lotion on his skin and occasionally gave him Pepto-Bismol. Later, in his twenties, he often took Pepto-Bismol for indigestion caused by drug use and poor nutrition. So the pink drug in his dream reminded him of substances that he had used to soothe himself over the years.

During recovery, many addicts and alcoholics have substance use dreams which may symbolize either falling off the wagon and returning to drug use or an internal affirmation that sobriety and recovery are solidifying. Fortunately for Rusty, his substance use dream was a confirmation that he was continuing on the road to recovery. He completed his certificate program, and three months later he passed his probationary period on his new job with excellent reviews. He was thinking of going to graduate school, perhaps to get a doctorate in English literature.

Changing careers involves many stresses that can trip us up. As we prepare to make a change in our job or career, our dreams highlight conflicts from the past and the present that may be holding us back.

Returning to a Career or Job after a Leave of Absence

Returning to a former career or job can provoke powerful conscious and unconscious reactions. Although many of the coworkers and job functions may be the same, some aspects of the job may have changed significantly. More important, most people returning from leave have just undergone an important turning point, such as a major illness or period of disability, the birth of a child, a long trip (on a sabbatical, for example), being rehired after a layoff, or returning to a job after attempting a career change (see Edward's dreams in chapter 7).

This scenario is especially relevant for women who return after a maternity leave. Leslie, age thirty-four, had been devoted to her career as an associate with an accounting firm in San Francisco. She worked long hours and had received steady promotions. She took pride in her work and had worked until the very day that she gave birth to her son, Brandon. She had expected to go back to work half-time when Brandon was six months old and full time when he was nine months.

A few weeks after the birth, she was enthralled by her son but still felt that she'd want to return to work full-time. She was surprised when she saw the grief and tears of other mothers who were forced by their employers or by economic necessity to return to work after three months. She didn't think that she would have that kind of reaction. She planned to be extremely cautious in selecting a day-care arrangement.

About six weeks prior to her return to work, Leslie began to have nightmares about her job. On different nights, she dreamed that her employers revoked her maternity leave, decided not to give her her job back, and reprimanded her for poor performance. She began to feel anxious about returning to work. She also began to feel nervous about leaving her son with a stranger. She paid close attention whenever she heard or read anything about child abuse.

On the day of her return to work, Leslie had a nightmare that recurred almost every night in a similar form for a week.

abandoned by my firm

It's my first day back to work. I'm getting off the subway and have to walk up a long staircase. It's longer than any I have ever seen, like one of those steep Aztec pyramids in Mexico. Then I have to go up an extra-long elevator, much taller than the office I work in, which is on the twelfth floor. When I get off the elevator, I find out that my firm has moved, and no one told me they moved or any details about where the new office was. I try to call from a nearby phone, but the number has been disconnected and there was no forwarding number. I feel like they had abandoned me, and I am very upset.

Leslie was very edgy that first day back in the office. Although everyone was polite and responsive, she couldn't stop thinking that she would be fired. And she was feeling naturally miserable about leaving her son with a stranger.

Leslie was still in an agitated state when she discussed this dream a week later. She knew that the dream was expressing her anxiety, but she was confused about the deeper message.

As she explored this Return to Work dream, many ideas came to her. The stairs looked just like the ones she had to climb every day to get to work. Leslie also had a phobia about stairs. Five years ago she'd fallen down a flight of stairs and broken her leg. The phobia had gotten so severe that she had sought treatment with a psychologist to help overcome it. Could the dream be evidence that the phobia was returning? When she'd been in Mexico recently, she was in fact unable to climb the steep steps of the pyramid and had watched while others ascended.

The stairs also reminded Leslie of the "corporate ladder." Leslie had made it partway up the ladder, but now she wondered whether there was going to be anything at the top for her when she resumed climbing. This confirmed thoughts that she'd had only recently—maybe the corporate ladder wasn't worth the effort. Her demanding job seemed incompatible with having a child.

The most powerful feeling in the dream was her sense at the end of being abandoned by her firm. They left no word, no forwarding number. At first she felt the feelings of betrayal were directed at the company. They were putting too much pressure on her; they weren't sensitive to working mothers. But as she continued to think about the word "abandonment," a strong association came to her mind: Brandon. She felt she was abandoning her son by going back to work. She began to cry and realized an important aspect of her dream: it was a reversal. She was being abandoned by her firm, but in reality she felt she was betraying and abandoning Brandon. It was Brandon who couldn't call if he had a problem.

Leslie's Return to Work dream helped her to acknowledge her grief and guilt about separating from her son. Exploring its meanings helped her to accept how challenging the role changes were, from corporate executive to mother and now working mother. Leslie was also worried about losing her job or missing the inside track on promotions because she no longer worked overtime. At the same time, she wondered whether her dream wasn't fulfilling a wish that she would like to abandon her old position and find a part-time job that would allow her to spend more time with her son.

After she had explored the feelings and issues that arose in her dream, Leslie's nightmares stopped and her stair phobia did not return. By acknowledging her hidden guilt and anxiety and focusing on the difficult role change she was going through, she was able to focus on realistic alternatives. She decided to investigate the possibility of permanent part-time status at her firm or at other companies. Leslie and her husband began to talk about how to balance two careers and a family.

When you return from a leave, the job may be the same, but you have changed. Exploring your dreams will help you understand and work through strong emotional reactions to the process of readjusting to your former occupation.

Using Dreams to Resolve Career Issues and Crises

Occasionally dreams inspire spontaneous solutions to an impasse at work or present new solutions for creative blocks. More often we must explore our dreams to gain guidance.[4] This can be done through journal work or other creative forms of dream exploration (see chapters 11 and 12), discussion with others, or psychotherapy.

Benjamin, a successful New York magazine publisher, emphasized to me the powerful impact of a dream on resolving a career impasse. He made a midlife career change from writing television documentaries to starting his own magazine. His magazine received critical success and was initially profitable. After five years he sold out to a large corporation but was to continue as publisher as part of the deal.

Because of decisions by the parent company and a changing magazine market, the circulation of Benjamin's magazine began to decline. He could see that it was facing a crisis. He was searching for a way to rekindle his magazine's spark and increase its public appeal. He had read about the problem-solving aspects of dreams and decided to incubate or request a dream that would help him find a new direction. He then had the following career breakthrough dream.

a message for the president

I am in a theater watching a football game on a large screen. Suddenly I realize that I am the president of a university, and I am dressed for that role in collegiate-style clothing. Although I know I am the president, it is strange because at the same time, I know I am myself. I walk out of the movie and toward the campus to a formal ceremony on the quadrangle. There is the traditional raised platform for the faculty, and everyone is dressed in academic regalia with students sitting on the grass in rows. I go with someone who is sneaking around the back of the platform to see how it is going. Someone who is there tells me emphatically, "You're not doing your job. You should be there more." These words stay with me, and soon I go to change my clothes.

Benjamin felt that his dream was an important response to his dream incubation question. He realized that he had become less involved and more complacent since he had sold the magazine. He wanted to get more involved again and decided to attempt to buy back the magazine from the parent company so he could revive it and take it in a new direction.

After lengthy negotiations, Benjamin succeeded in buying back his magazine. He implemented many changes, including a new format, and hired many new writers and editors. At first circulation did not rise, and the magazine was running at a loss. Gradually, however, the magazine achieved and surpassed its earlier level of success. This time, Benjamin followed the insights he had gained by exploring his dream and stayed more closely involved in guiding the magazine's management.

Dreams As a Source of Career Guidance

Exploring dreams can help us articulate our inner response to changes and problems at every stage of the career cycle. Paying attention to the messages of dreams and nightmares can help us find new directions and solutions to overcome both internal and external obstacles. When we listen for the guidance that dreams offer, we have a better chance of making our work more meaningful.

The venerable mythologist Joseph Campbell exhorted those of us interested in finding meaningful work "to follow our bliss"—that is, to pursue the activities and career that express our inner needs and bring meaning to our lives.[5] Exploring work-related dreams can help us resolve our career crises and transitions and discover our true calling in life.

7. mIDLIfe DReams
the tRaNSItION fROm OLD
IDeNtItIeS tO New ONes

Elena, a forty-year-old Mexican-American woman, lived the first half of her life in Mexico. She came to the United States at nineteen to attend college and then rose rapidly in a career until she became executive director of a large social service agency in San Francisco. She and her husband were financially successful, but the materialism and pressured lifestyle felt increasingly empty. She began to despair about the meaning and direction of her life. During a period of soul-searching, she had the following dream.

savING the cHILDReN

I am in a large office building like the one where I used to be the director. Just as I am walking in, there is a tremendous earthquake. I know this is the big one. I begin to rush for the exit. As I'm about to run through the doorway, I suddenly realize that the building is just a façade and that inside the modern building is an encampment or little pueblo of adobe houses like the ones my grandparents and cousins live in. I see lots of children in the huts. I know that I have to save them or they will be crushed. I rush into the little village and, using all my strength, I grab as many of the little children as I can carry. Holding all these children, I rush for the door and just make it outside into the sunlight as the brick building collapses behind me.

This rescue dream had a profound impact on Elena. It catalyzed her decision to make a major change in her career and living situation. Within months after this dream, she and her husband sold their home and moved to a rural area of northern California. Her husband bought a small restaurant, and Elena was student teaching at a rural public school attended by the children of migrant Mexican farmworkers. She was working toward an elementary teaching credential. She was also volunteering at a health clinic that served indigent pregnant women.

At a prenatal discussion group at the clinic where she worked as a translator and advocate for disadvantaged farmworkers, Elena recounted her rescue dream as if revealing a precious work of art or a cherished family secret.

Two other universal dream themes besides rescuing children were recognizable and crucial to the meaning and inspiration Elena discovered in her midlife dream—House dreams and Earthquake dreams.

Elena explored some of the dream's elements. She had only experienced minor tremors in her life, so the monumental earthquake in her dream didn't seem related to a memory. Rather, it felt clearly related to the inner shake-up she was experiencing. Earthquake and other Natural Disaster dreams are common and may relate to working out emotional reactions to a disaster. More often they symbolize the psychological reverberations of an impending or actual life-changing shift in identity, close relationships, or life circumstances.

The office building in the dream reminded Elena of the place where she used to work. Reflecting upon the discovery in the dream that the building was only a façade helped her understand why she felt her career success had felt like a psychological façade. It had not seemed genuine because it did not express the values of her native culture and her childhood.

A house or a building in a dream often represents an image of the self or the body. This rang true for Elena's house dream. The little Mexican village inside the modern-looking American building was a perfect metaphor for her identity. The dream helped Elena understand her need to balance her driven professional side (symbolized by the building) with the earthy, family-oriented part of herself (symbolized by the adobe village and the needy children). Her dream motivated her to escape before being crushed by the façade of her pressured lifestyle.

The theme of rescuing children was especially important for Elena. She had been unable to bear children herself, but her career had centered on administering social programs that served children. She had hoped earlier in her career that she could express her interest and concern by developing programs that benefited children, especially minority children. Recently, however, her duties had centered entirely on fund-raising and advocacy. In an era of cutbacks for children's services, she had become quite discouraged.

The dream helped her realize that she wanted to work directly with children, and ultimately she decided to get her teaching credential. She and her husband began to consider adopting a Central or South American child.

Saving wounded children or animals is a theme that often occurs in turning-point dreams. Although the meaning is unique for each individual, the theme often symbolizes the need to heal or attend to some emotional or physical wound. For Elena, the wound was the loss of some cherished aspects of her cultural and family heritage and the inability to reconcile the two sides of herself: the child who grew up in Mexico and the adult who lived in the United States. The dream showed her that she could draw on inner resources that were connected in her mind to her family's cultural values in Mexico.

Elena's Rescue dream gave her a vision that would guide her in undertaking an earthshaking midlife transition, a vision that helped her find a practical application of her mission of saving children. She would educate and advocate for them directly instead of being an administrator. Even more important, the dream gave Elena a lasting sense of confidence in pursuing a new career and lifestyle.

Understanding Midlife Crises

Carl Jung was the first twentieth-century theorist to focus on midlife as a time of crucial transition. He emphasized that the midlife crisis was a window of opportunity for self-awareness and personal growth, a time when we are able to become more individuated, to know ourselves better, and to make greater use of our inner resources. He based his formulation on his own wrenching midlife crisis, which led to a profound spiritual renewal and a sense of meaning that inspired much of his later work.

The popularity of Gail Sheehy's book, *Passages: Predictable Crises of Adult Life,* reflected a heightened awareness of an extended turning point that most of us undergo sometime between the ages of thirty-five and fifty. During this midlife phase, many of us go through a period of inner instability. We may question the most fundamental structures and relationships of our lives. Marital conflicts and breakups, career crises, or moves to a new area may occur. For some people, the outbreak of midlife angst is clearly connected to another turning point, such as an illness, loss of a job, or a divorce. For others, the origin of the midlife crisis may be invisible at first. It is like a silent alarm from an internal clock that was set years before to go off at midlife.

There is great individual variation as to when midlife transitions begin and which issues are most dominant. The state of certain issues in your life influences your midlife transition. These include the current status of your career or relationship, the ages of your children if any, and the incidence of destabilizing events such as losses or major stresses. These and other factors play a part in a complex and unpredictable formula that determines when and how your midlife crisis will begin.

There are also differences between men and women in the timing and psychological focus of the midlife transition. In his influential study of the psychology of men, *The Seasons of a Man's Life,* Daniel Levinson reported that the usual age of the onset of midlife crisis for men was forty to forty-one, with a range between thirty-eight and forty-three. For the men that Levinson and his colleagues studied, the average age for completing the transition was forty-five, with a range from forty-four to forty-seven.[1]

Some women enter midlife following a timetable similar to that described by Levinson for men. For those women who have not already experienced a midlife crisis, the onset of menopause may provide a milestone that initiates powerful psychological changes. Conflicts over how to balance career and family often create greater conflict in women than in men. But contrary to popular belief, the empty-nest phenomenon of children leaving the home may not be traumatic for all women and may in fact allow them to blossom in other areas when they're freed from parenting responsibilities.

Some researchers have questioned the universality of midlife crises, implying that such anxiety and painful soul-searching is a luxury of the middle and upper-middle classes and is less noticeable among people whose lives are economically unstable. Other researchers theorize that we go through continuous cycles of stability and instability, so midlife is as likely to contain a crisis as any other life phase.[2] In any case, a life crisis that occurs during the late thirties to early fifties will have its own unique flavor.

My clinical experience has given me strong evidence that people do go through a period of crisis during these years. Often I've observed that a midlife crisis is caused or accompanied by a chain reaction of events: divorce, the death of a parent, children leaving home, career dissatisfaction or conflict, or serious illness such as heart attack or cancer. Depression is a frequent complaint of people who consult with me during midlife.

If you have arrived at your forties unscathed, you may cautiously hope that you've evaded the anguish of a midlife crisis. Then suddenly, like an ambush, it strikes. You feel trapped by the structures you have created— career, marriage or relationship, family, and friends. An undercurrent of grief afflicts you as you approach the midpoint of your expected life span. You may feel bitterness about lost opportunities, roads not taken, and bright potentials that may never be fulfilled.

Media images of midlife crises tend to take a pejorative tone that mocks the sufferer's anguish. Men are pictured as behaving erratically, having affairs with younger women, buying flashy sports cars, and nursing hair transplants. Women are depicted as mourning the empty nest, being obsessed with physical signs of aging, and feeling exasperated with men who are emotionally distant. There is a pervasive fear that we will become trapped by foolish choices or indecision, left to spend our days depressed, divorced, or in a dead-end job.

We are vulnerable to many competing emotions and conflicts as well as to the negative effects of our erratic behavior. A passionate affair with a younger person, who seems to love us in all the ways our spouse doesn't, may help rekindle our dormant passion or at least stave off our fears of growing older. On the other hand, an affair may precipitate a divorce that will be followed by years of economic stress, loneliness, and custody battles.

Under optimal circumstances, a metamorphosis will have occurred as we emerge from midlife. We will have been able to grieve our lost youth, free ourselves of the inner constraints of our parents, master the emotional blocks lingering from childhood, discover new identities, and define ourself in new ways. We will have found new friends and new sources of fulfillment and will have revitalized our ability to be intimate in love and productive in our work.

In this chapter, we'll look at how we can use dreams to understand what triggers a midlife crisis, the stages and psychological tasks we must encounter and resolve, the emotional impasses of midlife, and ultimately the discovery of new directions, new identities, and a renewed sense of hope for the future. In particular we'll look at the following ways that dreams can be valuable:

* *Acknowledging and coming to terms with powerful emotional reactions that occur at midlife.* These may include grief over the loss of youth, bitterness about lost possibilities and past hurts, feelings of uselessness or hopelessness, an inability to accept the physical aging of our body, or any other reaction or emotion we have long suppressed.

* *Understanding the source of our anxieties,* including a fear of death, a panic about having limited time, and general insecurity about the unknown.

* *Getting an overview of the stages of midlife.* When we feel at sea without a map to guide us, our dreams can help us chart our progress through the stages of falling apart, groping for meaning, and finding solutions to midlife impasses.

* *Reducing our sense of isolation.* Through sharing our dreams we can feel more understood, less alone, and sense the deeper significance of the midlife passage. We can gain a vision of how the second half of life can be a new beginning and not a gradual deterioration.

* *Finding sources of emotional and spiritual renewal,* including inspirations for meaningful and productive new directions in work and revitalized relationships.

Entering Midlife: Confronting Our Own Mortality

Many midlife dreams feature an encounter with death. Vivid dreams of ourselves or those close to us being afflicted with mortal wounds or terminal illnesses symbolize the emergence of feelings of vulnerability and mortality. We face a growing realization that we won't live forever. We see gray hair, wrinkles, and other signs of aging. We grieve the loss of our youthful appearance, and the sense that the person we knew as ourself is dying.

In his autobiography, *Memories, Dreams, and Reflections,* C. G. Jung describes in detail the circumstances and dreams that marked the onset of his midlife crisis. At age thirty-seven, inspired by his dreams and conscious reflections, Jung broke away from his mentor, Sigmund Freud. He quit his university position, experienced a marital crisis, and entered a period of painful self-examination. During this time Jung felt depressed and profoundly disoriented, questioning his own sanity.

He felt that a series of Entering Midlife dreams with death references heralded the beginning of this dark period in his life. In one dream he was exploring a long row of tombs of figures from the distant past—crusaders, knights in armor, and other ancient beings. To his shock, the mummified corpses moved their hands one by one and came back to life. The death imagery was extremely upsetting to him. What was making these ancient souls rise from the dead? Would he soon die, or was he experiencing an emotional death? He searched through all of his childhood memories to comprehend what was happening to him.[3]

He could make no headway in understanding these disturbing dreams until he began to explore them by using painting, writing, and other creative techniques. Slowly he understood the emotional death and painful loss of identity that he was experiencing. Further dreams of death, destruction, and barren, frozen scenes confirmed this idea. And yet amidst the tombs there was something that might possibly be revived. This idea gave him hope that there was light at the end of the tunnel—or, in this case, the tomb.

Dreams of underworld beings—mummies, vampires, werewolves—may symbolize struggles with grief (see chapter 10), morbid aspects of depression, general anxieties similar to Creature Threat dreams (see chapter 2), or even responses to media or literary portrayal of ghouls or vampires.

Jung's dream, like others at midlife, contained imagery of tombs and mummies. When these dreams occur at midlife, the unconscious provides symbols that the person facing midlife has withdrawn from the outer world and is undergoing a painful inner process, a decaying and destruction of an old way of being.

Phoebe's midlife crisis came on the heels of numerous stressful events that occurred almost simultaneously. At age forty-five, she had finally decided to leave the hospital where she had worked for twenty-two years. She had been suffering from chronic back problems and over the past two years had become dissatisfied with her role as a nursing supervisor. Because she had planned to leave her job and had been training in a new career, she didn't anticipate that leaving the hospital would have a great impact on her. Soon after quitting, however, she became depressed, her back problems increased, and she had a disturbing nightmare.

my mother is dying

Someone comes and says that I have a phone call. When I get to the phone, I can hardly hear the caller. I think that it is my sister. She is telling me that my mom is sick, my mother is dying. I keep trying to find out more, but the voice keeps getting fainter, and the line is full of static. I try but can't reach her or get a better connection.

Phoebe's real mother was alive and healthy, so she took the dream as symbolic and not literal or predictive. In the language of her dream, the hospital was the mother that was dying. She had not only worked there, but she had been born there, went to nursing school there, and had her own children there. Leaving was truly the death of an era, an identity, a support network of friends and colleagues, and a second home. Her inability to make a call represented losing touch with a part of herself that had been so familiar. The (phone) connection with her mother was fading out; Phoebe was experiencing not only the loss of a job but the identity of her career and the first half of her life.

Reunions with the Dead dreams are discussed more fully in chapters 9 and 10. When there is no actual death impending for the dreamer's family and friends, these dreams frequently symbolize various forms and stages of psychological loss, change, and mourning. For Phoebe, an emotional death was occurring that would help her unload baggage from the past and experience a rebirth of new possibilities in her life.

Phoebe had kept a dream journal off and on for many years. Over the next few months of turmoil, she searched her dreams for clues to inner guidance and physical and emotional recovery. Her serious back injury gave her time to focus on herself in new ways since in previous years she had been working full time and raising four daughters. In addition to physical therapy, she began painting her feelings and dreams. Despite her injury, she took a course from a dance therapist. She wanted to understand any psychological basis for her back injury.

During this period, Phoebe began to have many important insights about unresolved conflicts in her previous close relationships. She felt that she was finally working out anger toward her ex-husband. At the same time, her current friendships were taking on new dimensions. She wasn't always the chronic giver but was allowing herself to receive; this was an important change.

Three months later, Phoebe was still reeling from the changes but felt she was beginning to turn a corner. On two consecutive nights she had Earthquake dreams, a theme that had been rare in her past dreams.

REBUILDING after the quake

I am in my own home. A large, rumbling, shaking earthquake comes. The house and its entire contents are lifted intact onto a green hillside above the lot. Only the cement foundation remains. I bring parts of the house back and try to reconstruct it. The pieces keep falling down. There may have been others helping, but it doesn't work.

the swaying elevator

I am in a freight elevator with an open iron door. When it moves, I can see out. An earthquake makes the elevator sway severely. The building is still. Only the elevator is swaying. There is a guard on one of the floor landings with his hand reached out to help me to safety. I just can't reach his fingertips. The movements stop, and I go down a flight of stairs and end up on the obstetrical unit of a hospital as if I am in labor.

As in Elena's case, the dream earthquakes that Phoebe experienced are evidence of the earthshaking changes that she was undergoing as she entered middle age. In Phoebe's first Earthquake dream, she felt that her house being ripped from its foundation was an apt metaphor for the loss of identity she had experienced. Although she was trying to rebuild with the help of others, she wasn't succeeding as yet in building on the old foundation.

In her elevator dream, Phoebe again was unable to benefit from the help that was offered to her in a moment of crisis. In dreams, the movement of an elevator between floors of a building is often taken to represent a transition between two states of consciousness or identity. That interpretation worked well for Phoebe. She saw the elevator as representing the transition from which she was not able to exit.

After the painful death and grieving for her old identity, Phoebe was especially intrigued at being transported to an obstetrics ward. This image gave her hope. Perhaps a rebirth was about to take place. Greater acceptance of her anger and increased ability to be intimate with friends made her feel that her midlife turmoil was on the verge of resolution. In the weeks that followed these Earthquake dreams, her back began to improve dramatically, she was less depressed, and she resumed taking courses to prepare for a career change.

For many, the entry into midlife may be punctuated by conscious and unconscious preoccupations with death, our own and others'. Heightened awareness of the inevitability of our own death gives the midlife period a special urgency. Dreams of death reflect awareness of our mortality and symbolize the painful loss of old identities as we enter midlife.

Crossing the Threshold: In the Throes of Midlife Passage

The central experience of midlife, according to Murray Stein, is that of liminality. This is an in-between state of suspended identity, during which we become a stranger to ourself, no longer at home in any of the familiar roles or feelings that we used in the past to define ourself. Deriving from the Latin root *limen,* meaning "threshold," the liminal stage is a twilight zone of identity confusion, fluctuating emotions, and erratic behavior. We are grieving the loss of our former self but have not yet discovered a new identity that feels comfortable or familiar.[4]

Judy, a forty-five-year-old divorced single mother, sought psychotherapy soon after her daughter, Corey, went away to college in a nearby city. Judy had been suffering from depression and had started drinking heavily on evenings and weekends. She was concerned about her drinking, which had never before been a problem. She also felt directionless, as if her life no longer had a purpose. After her first psychotherapy session, she had the following dream.

empty rooms

> I am in the small apartment that I lived in ten years ago just after my divorce when we sold the house. It feels very empty. There is no furniture, the paint is peeling, and the windows are dirty and have cobwebs. It doesn't seem like anyone else is even living in the building. I am searching desperately for my daughter, but she isn't there either.

Judy woke up from the dream feeling sad and lonely. As she told it again, the feelings intensified. Through her tears, she confessed that she hadn't expected her daughter's departure to be so upsetting. Judy was struck by the barrenness of the apartment and felt that it related to her own emptiness without Corey. Judy began to feel that the image of her daughter in the dream was a displaced image of her own younger self. Everyone had always commented on the striking resemblance between them. The idea that Judy was searching for images of herself from the past resonated deeply.

After her divorce, she had gone back to school and had become a paralegal. She also enjoyed her volunteer work with various political and social organizations, such as a group that provided legal assistance to battered women. Although she was quite attractive, Judy had avoided opportunities to meet men and had not gotten involved in any love relationships.

Through a lengthy exploration, Judy realized that besides being a dedicated mother, she had used her relationship with Corey to protect herself from men and from people in general. Although Corey had long protested her mother's overinvolvement and had even encouraged her to go out and meet men, it wasn't until Corey left that Judy felt the emptiness in her life.

The dream made her desolate feeling even more acute than she consciously admitted. Exploring the dream helped her to acknowledge her grief on a number of different levels. She realized that she had never worked out her feelings of rejection and grief from the divorce. Finally, alone at forty-five, she was grieving the loss of her youth, symbolized in the dream by her daughter.

Judy felt like the apartment in her dream, like an old building that needed fixing and redecorating. Her dream helped her see that she needed to find a new direction for her life now that Corey was gone. As a result of the insights she gained in exploring her Empty Rooms dream, Judy decided that in addition to her psychotherapy she would join a support group oriented toward women at midlife. She realized that hiding the wounds of her divorce had not healed them. It was vital that she decide whether to let people be close to her and whether to consider remarriage.

Reaching an emotional impasse, such as Judy's inability to resolve fears of rejection, may prevent us from moving across the threshold of midlife and emerging with new solutions. Paying attention to turning-point dreams can help us find ways to understand and correct unresolved issues and fears of change that can block our progress.

Men at Midlife

In Daniel Levinson's extended study of the seasons of men's lives, 80 percent of the men who participated underwent a turbulent period at midlife.[5] According to Levinson, the psychological distress is caused by wounds from the past that get reactivated as we try to close a chapter of our lives and begin anew. Depression, bitterness, nostalgia for youthful looks and vitality, feelings of uselessness and impotence, and a terror of facing death were all present. Although family and friends often viewed the men as upset or sick, Levinson concluded that this intense self-examination was a normal and necessary part of midlife, ultimately leading to emotional renewal. Levinson describes midlife as involving the following three stages.

1. *Reappraising the Past*
   In Levinson's midlife schema for men, the first stage is reappraising the past. As a man becomes disillusioned with the structures and relationships in his life, he instinctively looks to the past. He asks himself, What have I accomplished with my life? Am I living up to my potential? Have I allowed myself to open up and be close with my wife, friends, family, and children? Is this the life I want to continue, or do I need to make changes to have a more meaningful future?

2. *Planning and Experimenting*
   As issues from the past begin to get resolved, there is a stage of planning and experimenting. For some men, this involves dramatic external events such as changing careers, divorcing, remarrying, or moving. For others, the changes may be less visible but just as important, like becoming less preoccupied with work and more involved with family. Or the changes may mean becoming more concerned about making a contribution through creative, spiritual, or political pursuits, or guiding younger colleagues.

3. *Confronting and Resolving Emotional Polarities*
   At midlife men often discover that they possess a greater range of emotions than which they had previously been aware. When they are able to acknowledge these powerful feelings, they can enhance their close relationships at home and at work.[6]

Levinson emphasized four emotional polarities that men encounter and struggle with at midlife. The first is *youth versus aging,* which is a confrontation with mortality. Men experience a sense of confusion about still feeling young, yet finding themselves increasingly identified as middle-aged. In order to resolve this polarity, a man must confront mortality and make sense of being between youth and old age.

The second polarity is *destructive versus creative urges.* This includes coping with anger about lost opportunities, reconciling old emotional wounds and poor choices, and becoming more acutely aware of aggressive and malicious tendencies in himself and others. Resolving this polarity requires a greater acceptance of human tendencies toward destructiveness, without sinking into bitterness or cynicism. Instead, he must use the impetus of this conflict to discover new sources of creativity through work, hobbies, recreation, relationships, or socially useful endeavors.

The third polarity is acceptance of the *masculine versus feminine* parts of himself. This includes experiencing vulnerability, dependency, sadness, and warmth, which are feelings traditionally at odds with the stereotypical male image.

The fourth polarity is the tension between *attachment and separateness.* Resolving this issue involves finding a balance between his needs and those of family, friends, and society. A man needs to pay attention to his inner feelings and needs, and find out what is missing from his emotional life. Paradoxically, turning inward often does not lead to isolation. As he discovers his deeper feelings, he will often find new reserves of energy that lead to new and more passionate involvement with others.

For Larry, exploring and resolving impasses in his relationship with his father was the crucial stumbling block that had to be overcome. Larry, age forty-four, a psychologist, had given up his private practice three years earlier to undertake a real estate venture with his brother. After successfully completing one project, he was considering leaving his real estate job and reopening his psychotherapy practice. He began further training to refresh and enhance his skills but was still feeling uncertain about whether to continue in real estate or to return to psychology.

Distressed by his indecisiveness, Larry sought the counsel of friends and family members. In the throes of his confusion and depression, he had the following Self-Judgment dream.

awaiting court-martial

I'm in the army and know that I've killed someone. The authorities are on the way to arrest me. I feel incredibly guilty about what I might have done and terrified about being caught and tried.

Larry awoke feeling like he had indeed committed a horrible crime. But what was it? As we explored his dream, the term "court-martial" immediately clicked. Larry had become a conscientious objector during the Vietnam War. This had been a devastating disappointment for his father, a career military officer. Larry had always felt guilty about it and as a result had never broken away from his father's influence.

During his earlier years as a psychologist, Larry had chosen a mentor who was stern and critical—a lot like his father. Recently he had begun training with a new mentor who was much more encouraging and warm in his teaching style and in his therapy technique.

Larry felt that he was beginning to understand his dream "crimes." The murder was the death of his old self. He also felt he had murdered his loyalty to his father. He no longer had to submit himself to stern authorities to atone for his rebellion. And he no longer had to be afraid of being more successful than his father. He had finally begun to free himself from the inhibiting influence of his early paternal relationship.

The insights from this Self-Judgment dream inspired Larry to examine his relationship with male authority figures in general. Although the murder theme was repulsive, he realized that he was also confronting and working out his aggressive and destructive tendencies. Daniel Levinson asserts that resolving his destructive tendencies at midlife helps a man find new sources of creativity.[7]

Larry was encouraged by these insights but still feeling confused about whether he was doing the right thing in returning to psychology. Soon he had another dream.

i can't find the therapy room

I was back at the hospital ward, the first place that I worked as a therapist. I couldn't find a room to meet with patients, and I couldn't find my cotherapist to meet with the group or the family I was supposed to see. It was chaotic, yet I felt a sense of competence and some sense that it would work out.

In this dream, Larry remembered that he'd been very excited about that first job because it allowed him to be the coordinator of a treatment team involving nurses, social workers, and other professionals. For Larry, the dream was a snapshot of where he was in solving his midlife career crisis. Emerging from his confusion and disorientation was a sense of competence. The hospital job had been a rewarding experience that had helped him find a positive identity as a psychotherapist. He was again contemplating a new start in psychology and seeking a room or a place where he could feel he belonged.

Although he was still uncertain about his future, this dream confirmed that returning to work as a psychologist would be a positive step. The feelings of competence at the end of his dream gave Larry the impetus to face the confusing and difficult task of beginning anew at midlife.

Menopause: A Biological and Psychological Milestone

Psychological studies of menopause have suggested that a woman's midlife transition is strongly influenced by the biological event of ending her reproductive fertility. But menopause is not necessarily synonymous with a midlife crisis for all women. Some women undergo a premenopausal transition in their late thirties or early forties and have many reactions parallel to those described above for men. However, for many women, menopause does signal a profound period of psychological reorganization as well as biological change.

In her fascinating personal account, *Journey through Menopause: A Personal Rite of Passage,* religious studies professor Christine Downing describes a woman's life cycle as having three seasons: prior to puberty, the fertile period of menstruation, and the phase from menopause to death. With individual variations, the third season of a woman's life begins between forty-five and fifty, and menopause runs its course over a span of a few years.[8]

The physical changes that women may experience include hot flashes and sweats, headaches, dizziness, insomnia, fatigue, mood swings, and variations in sexual arousal. Some of these symptoms are induced by hormonal changes. Others may be generalized signs of aging or more likely are part of a psychologically induced change provoked by menopause.[9]

According to Downing, many women focus too much on the physical symptoms of menopause and neglect the psychological transformation. She feels that the symptoms that are most important are dreams, nightmares, fantasies, and visions. By attending to their inner reactions, women can understand distressing symptoms and find a deeper meaning in the changes that they are undergoing.

Themes of children, babies, fertility, and infertility are often prominent in the dreams of women undergoing a midlife crisis. One theme that appears often is that of searching for, rescuing, nurturing, or healing children, often sick or lost babies. For example, Elena's Saving the Children dream has a biological clock theme. Since Elena was infertile, she had to decide whether she would adopt a child or use her work with children as a substitute for childbearing. In Judy's Empty Rooms dream, the search for her daughter was related to the loss of her daughter and the loss of the childrearing phase of her life and identity.

At menopause, dreams often focus directly on fertility and childbearing issues. Christine Downing described a series of her own menopause dreams. A dream just before her fiftieth birthday, during a period of severe headaches, made her aware of the imminent onset of menopause.

PREGNANT WITH MY FATHERLESS CHILD

I am walking with my former husband among steeply sloping sand dunes like those I remember from my childhood. From time to time we could see the ocean, waves breaking high. The wind was blowing enough to make talking difficult; the dune grass cut into our calves; the sand shifted underfoot. We were intent on our walking, giving one another a hand now and then at a particularly tricky spot, thoroughly enjoying being together. At some point along the way, when we had slowed our pace a bit, I said, "You know dear, I think I'm pregnant again, and this time I don't even know who the father is." "Will we keep it?" he asked. "We always do, don't we?" I replied.[10]

As she thought about the dream, Christine realized that her period was several weeks overdue. She immediately connected the dream with a new stage in life, being pregnant with her menopausal self. Through exploration of this dream, Downing decided to devote attention to observing her reactions as the changes unfolded in her body and her psyche. To honor the importance of her dream, Downing elaborated fantasies about her dream child and created rituals to make the transition more special. As the stages of menopause unfolded, her dreams reflected other themes that highlighted the loss of biological fertility but pointed to the emergence of a new source of psychological generativity.

Not all of her dreams reflected positive expectations. Some revealed emotional turmoil, such as a dream about watching a decapitated dog actively search for its head. This grotesque image, she felt, was telling her that although her mind and body were feeling split, there was still vitality in her body.[11] Or perhaps the dream indicated that she was searching for a new mental representation of her body, a new identity for a body that still felt strong and vital but could no longer bear children.

In her book *Change of Life: A Psychological Study of Dreams and the Menopause,* Jungian analyst Ann Mankowitz offers an in-depth exploration of a dream series from a patient whom she calls Rachel. According to Mankowitz, exploring her dreams helped Rachel find guidance and strength through a difficult passage.

On the surface, life seemed normal for the fifty-one-year-old Rachel. She had been married for thirty years, had three grown children, and had gone back to school a decade earlier to train as a marriage counselor, which had become a rewarding career. But despite the appearance of stability and fulfillment, Rachel felt emptiness and a sense that her life lacked direction.

After a year of psychotherapy during which she reported few dreams, Rachel had a profound dream that helped her change her life. We'll look at one of the seven parts of this epic dream.

tHe BURNt House

I am walking around the house in the country, our family home where we all lived when my children were younger. It's burnt-out, destroyed by fire, a blackened empty shell. Part of it looks like dead petrified trees, some of it twisted like flames solidified, I am alone . . . utterly desolate. It's me, my insides, my womb . . . but not just that . . . my past life, my children . . . the whole way of life ended forever . . . but round at the back of the house there is new grass growing, and that gives me hope.[12]

Rachel's dream resembles Judy's Empty Rooms dream. In both dreams the image of a dwelling with a barren interior seems to be linked to the actual event of the children no longer living at home and to the psychological experience of having a womb that will soon be infertile.

In Rachel's dream the damage is more vivid. The interior is burned and petrified. Rachel was shocked by her dream. She associated the fire damage with the hot flashes she'd experienced and to feeling burned-out. Rachel felt that verbalizing her sense of desolation in this segment of the dream helped relieve the self-pity she had been feeling.

Exploring her dream series with her therapist helped Rachel grieve the loss of her youth and her identity as a childbearing woman. Images of botanical regeneration such as the green grass growing at the end of the Burnt House dream gave her hope. In the final segment of her epic dream, she is led by male guides to explore the illuminated foundation of a new house that is partially submerged in water. The new foundation suggested a rebuilding was underway as she moved toward resolving her midlife crisis.

Menopause requires mourning the loss of identity as a woman able to bear children. When a woman's grief can be expressed and resolved, a new birth occurs: the beginning of a new phase of life that offers the excitement and challenge of new roles and identities and new sources of fulfillment.

Return from Limbo: New Identities, New Directions

Carl Jung's midlife crisis lasted nearly seven years. At age forty-four, after long solitary hours making paintings based on his visions and dreams, examining his childhood memories, and writing in special journals, he had a Botanical Regeneration dream that signaled the end of his dark night of the soul. In this dream, Jung found himself traveling in the English city of Liverpool, which appeared as very sooty and dreary.

tHe BLoomiNg magNoLia tRee

While walking . . . we found a broad square dimly illuminated by street lights, into which many streets converged. The various quarters of the city were arranged radially around the square. In the center was a round pool, and in the middle of it a small island. While everything was obscured by rain, fog, smoke and dimly lit darkness, the little island blazed with sunlight. On it stood a single tree, a magnolia, in a shower of reddish blossoms. It was as though the tree stood in the sunlight and was at the same time the source of light. . . . I was carried away by the beauty of the flowering tree and the sunlit island.[13]

Jung felt that the dream represented his conscious situation at the time as well as providing a powerful image of future possibilities. He was still feeling gloomy, like the image of the industrial city of Liverpool. He hadn't yet been able to resolve the malaise of his midlife crisis.

He associated the name Liverpool, however, with a pool of life. His exquisite vision of the blooming magnolia on the island in the center of the pool gave Jung a feeling of having achieved the goal of his long exploration. The image of the central tree of life inspired him to develop his theory of the "self" as a part of the mind that, when activated, gives life meaning and purpose. Working with the dream centered him emotionally and gave him hope that something beautiful was emerging from his dark journey. In his autobiography, Jung repeatedly emphasizes that the agonies and ecstasies of his dreams and visions during his midlife crisis provided him with indelible insights into the mind's functioning that inspired all of his later writings.

After this dream, Jung gave up his intensive artistic exploration and embarked on a much more active schedule of writing, teaching, and traveling. He had resolved his midlife crisis and entered into a new phase of life.

Not every midlife transition ends in such a definitive fashion as Jung's. For some, the end of the transition may coincide with an event such as resolving a marital crisis, recovering from an illness, assuming a new job, or completing a creative project. More often the return from the threshold of midlife is gradual and not necessarily marked by one specific event or dream.

For Judy, her Empty Rooms dream came at the beginning of her midlife crisis and also at the beginning of her therapy. After three years of therapy, her life had changed dramatically. She had not succumbed to her depression or to drinking. She was still working part-time at her old job as a paralegal but had been accepted to a local law school's evening program. This fulfilled a long-held fantasy. She had been accepted to law school over twenty years earlier but had decided not to go because her husband's job had required them to move frequently. Judy had always done volunteer work in the past, and now she hoped to use her skills as a lawyer to work in a legal-aid clinic or in some kind of public-service position.

Her life was much fuller than in the days of her Empty Rooms dream. Although she was working hard, she had forced herself to develop more social contacts and become involved in a church group, where she had made many friends. Now that Judy had found other interests and friendships, she was putting less emphasis on her daughter, and their relationship had improved.

Near the end of her third year in therapy, Judy had a dream that helped her see how much her life had changed.

STAR STUDENT

I'm in one of my law school classes, and the professor calls on me to answer a very complicated question, something about discrimination, but I'm not exactly sure what he wants. I'm very nervous that I'll make a fool of myself. I look down and part of my blouse is transparent, so I'm afraid the class can see my breasts, though no one seems to notice. I start to talk and end up giving a very impressive answer. It's a topic that I know a lot about from my work as a paralegal. The professor compliments me on my answer, and all the students seem impressed, and no one notices my sheer blouse. People come up to me after class and want to meet me as if I could help them with their studies. One man who is about my age seems especially interested in talking, and I feel attracted to him.

Judy was somewhat embarrassed by her Nudity dream, especially the part about feeling exposed. She was puzzled by the image of the sheer blouse. When I asked what ideas she had about that, she thought the blouse in the dream looked like one she had recently purchased. It wasn't especially sexy but was very stylish. As her self-esteem had risen and her fears of rejection eased, Judy had begun to pay more attention to her appearance.

In any case, Judy thought there might be a sexual meaning to the dream. The man at the end of the dream was someone in whom she was interested. After talking to him casually a number of times, she'd recently gotten up the nerve to ask him out for coffee. She had begun to date sporadically, but he was someone in whom she might be more seriously interested.

The Star Student dream also helped Judy realize how she had minimized her intellectual abilities and her personal strengths in general. Judy proudly described how she had just received her final grades for the first year of law school and was the third highest in a class of over a hundred. She now felt ready to accept the praise and recognition of her professors and peers.

Judy felt that her Star Student dream was evidence that her self-esteem had significantly improved. She reflected on how anxious she had been while applying to school and during the first term. She had worried about flunking out or being ridiculed by professors. Both in her dream and in reality, though, she had become a star student. This was shocking to Judy, who had always been nervous about her abilities and had never been faced with a challenge as grueling as some of her law school classes.

Judy could see from this dream and from the events in her life that she had made significant changes both externally and internally. Her depression had lifted and her self-image was far more positive. She was excited about her career prospects and began to entertain the possibility of getting involved in a new relationship or even of remarriage.

Within three months, Judy had ended therapy feeling that she was well on the road to a new phase of her life. At this time she had not begun menopause, so her midlife transition had resolved itself prior to any biological changes.

For Judy, working with her dreams helped access her feelings and gauge her progress through the stages of her midlife journey. Her daughter's departure helped her understand how she had never resolved the rejection and grief that she'd suffered during her divorce. Through therapy and dream exploration, she was able to find unexpected fulfillments through a career change and the hope of greater ability to be intimate and find a loving relationship.

Discovering a New Midlife Identity

During a midlife crisis, a transformation of self occurs. We leave behind the roles, appearances, and infinite possibilities of our youth and enter an in-between period of inner turmoil during which we question many of the givens in our life.

Whether this crisis occurs in our late thirties, forties, or early fifties, its momentous effect shakes up our inner and outer worlds. Whether a midlife crisis is precipitated by a traumatic event, by biological changes, or by pervasive feelings that creep up and surround us, we are in for months and usually years of searching for new directions and structures in our life.

Because the midlife transition has only recently been considered important, there are few rituals and little information and support to guide us. Remembering and observing our dreams can alert us to the onset of a midlife crisis and help us navigate through the early stages of this difficult and confusing transition.

Resolving a midlife crisis requires turning inward, mourning the ending of the era of our youth, and finding new inspiration to guide us through the second half of life. Attending to our dreams helps us maintain a focus on our deeper feelings and can guide us to discover new directions and new sources of fulfillment during the midlife transition.

8. POSTTRAUMATIC NIGHTMARES
OUR INNER RESPONSE TO trauma, DISASTERS, AND TERRORISM

Catherine and Ron were on their honeymoon sailing in the Galapagos Islands with a small group of travelers. In the middle of the night, they were thrown out of their beds by a tremendous crash. A jagged rock had broken through the hull and into their cabin. Water began pouring in. Naked, they groped for the door and were slammed against the walls of the boat as it repeatedly smashed into the rocks. They barely made it to the upper deck. The boat continued to heave violently. Just as it capsized, Catherine and Ron jumped into the pitch-black waters, professing their love to each other and preparing to die.

Catherine was caught by a rope and drawn under the boat, emerging only after a desperate struggle. Then her body was knocked against the volcanic rocks. Ron and Catherine found each other and struggled up onto the slippery rocks that were lit only by the stars. When they called out to their fellow passengers and crew, miraculously all of them were on the rocks. None of the eighteen on board had been severely injured or killed. Catherine was bruised, had two broken toes, and was covered by spines of the sea urchins that lived on the rocks that had sunk their boat.

When the dawn broke, they could see the pieces of their vessel and debris of their belongings drifting in and out with the tide. Hours later, in shock and scorched by the heat of the equatorial sun, they were rescued.

For weeks, Ron and Catherine couldn't sleep through the night. They would wake up terrified by recurrent nightmares. For the first few nights, Ron jumped out of bed convinced that he was still in the boat and had to escape. He couldn't vanquish the terror that he felt. He began to remember the outlines of a dream that he would live with every single night for eight weeks.

the DROWNING waters

> I feel water rushing all around me. I'm totally disoriented and can't tell where I am or where I am going. There is no depth or dimension. I feel like I am going crazy or dying. I awake terrified.

With this Mortal Threat dream, Ron reexperienced the terror of the shipwreck. He would wake up in a cold sweat with his heart pounding. He couldn't make the memory or the dream go away. In fact, he felt the dream was making the memory worse. At times he wondered whether he was going insane. When his screams awakened Catherine, he told her his dreams. But he didn't want to disturb her too much because she was having her own nightmares.

Catherine's initial nightmares were similar to Ron's. For the first few weeks, she dreamed of water rushing over her, overwhelming her. Within a couple of weeks, her nightmares became more detailed.

a tidal wave breaches the sea walls

> I am sitting on a beach, and suddenly I see a tidal wave forming in the distance. It is rushing toward me at breakneck speed. I can see a series of walls that were built to hold back the tide. At first it seems like they will be able to hold back the water. But each time the water reaches a wall, I can see it surge relentlessly onward, getting closer and closer until it is just about to crash over me. I wake up panicked.

Although this disturbing dream came almost every night, it gave her some hope that she could overcome the terror that she had experienced in the shipwreck. Despite its repetition, the visual image of the walls in her Tidal Wave dream helped her feel she was beginning to develop some inner protection, some defense mechanism against the terror of drowning. At least there was something that temporarily held back the wave and gave her time to prepare, unlike the real night of the shipwreck.

Two months after the shipwreck, Catherine had a Rebirth dream that broke the pattern of drowning and tidal waves.

GRANDMA BECOMES A YOUNG BRIDE

My grandmother tells me that she is going to marry Don (my first boyfriend). Although I know she is very old, I'm confused because she looks regenerated as if she is a young woman with rosy cheeks. As she announces her engagement, I feel very happy for her but also confused because I thought she was old and close to death.

Catherine felt sad when she awoke and reflected on her dream. In reality, her eighty-eight-year-old grandmother was near death. Catherine had been extremely close to her. She grew up living in the same house with her. She had even been named after her.

Catherine knew that the dream was anticipating the loss of her grand-mother. Perhaps it represented a wish that her grandmother would find a fountain of youth that would allow her to escape death. But she also sensed that it had to do with her own recent marriage. Prior to the shipwreck, her courtship and engagement had made her feel younger and more innocent, as she had felt in her first love affair.

She shared her dream with Ron and explored it with her therapist. She began to think about how the accident had not only ruined her honeymoon but had abruptly ended the joy of her engagement and wedding celebration. She had been harboring a fear that something was lost that could never be regained. The beginning of her marriage had been marked with a terrifying ordeal that she wasn't sure she could erase. Like her grandmother, Catherine had been close to death. The dream of her grandmother's wedding was the first hint that the innocence and happiness of Catherine's engagement could be restored.

For Catherine, this dream marked a turning point in her recovery. She associated her exploration of this dream with an alleviation of the depression and lingering terror that had gripped her since the accident and the disrupted honeymoon. When her grandmother died a month later, Catherine used this dream as a positive image that she held with her through her mourning.

Catherine continued to have Tidal Wave nightmares, but they became less frequent and less overwhelming. Many of her dreams, moreover, seemed to refer to the shipwreck in symbolic ways as opposed to the raw terror of her drowning and Tidal Wave dreams. Slowly, she was recovering from the trauma.

Nightmares: Keys to Recovery

Exploring your posttraumatic nightmares can help heal the wounds of traumatic events. To show you how, this chapter will look at a variety of situations including accidents, crimes, natural disasters, combat experience, political terror, and torture. These situations may seem extreme if you or someone close to you has not experienced them. But you don't have to be a war veteran or an accident victim to apply the insights of this chapter. Our responses to other forms of trauma, both major and minor, tend to parallel those discussed here. This chapter will provide guidelines for understanding posttraumatic nightmares and using them for healing the emotional wounds of trauma and instilling a new sense of hope.

When we or those close to us experience an event that has lingering psychological side effects, we can expect nightmares within the first few weeks. Often the passage of time, emotional support from others, and our own inner resilience will get us on the road to recovery within a few weeks after a traumatic experience. In some cases, however, it can take months, even years, for the devastating memory and repetitive nightmares to loosen their grip.

It's important to recognize that the nightmares following a traumatic event are not necessarily a sign of pathology but are an unconscious reflection of our attempts to overcome the trauma. These posttraumatic nightmares are a vital source of information that can help us focus our recovery on the issues that have wounded us most deeply.

Posttraumatic Nightmares

When trauma victims reach an impasse in their recovery, they often suffer from persistent, unchanging nightmares that replay the event(s). In his book *The Nightmare: The Psychology and Biology of Terrifying Dreams,* Dr. Ernest Hartmann refers to the phenomenon of unchanging nightmares as *encapsulation.*[1] This is a condition whereby waking consciousness is unable to overcome the overwhelming feelings of vulnerability brought on by the trauma. This failure to cope is reflected in dreams that replay the trauma in an unmodified form. Hartmann likens the encapsulation of trauma in repetitive dreams to a physical abscess, a wound that doesn't heal because it is sealed off, with its infection eating away at us.

What Is Posttraumatic Stress Disorder?

Recurrent, unchanging nightmares are one of the most prevalent and characteristic symptoms of posttraumatic stress disorder (PTSD). This is a psychiatric syndrome that is common to people who have become emotionally devastated after being exposed to a traumatic event that "involved actual or threatened death or serious injury or a threat to the physical integrity of self or others."[2] People who suffer from this syndrome include victims of or witnesses to violence; for example, combat veterans, crime victims, battered wives, and children who are physically or sexually abused. It also may afflict the survivors of accidental or natural disasters such as car and plane crashes, terrorist attacks, fires, explosions, earthquakes, floods, and hurricanes. Besides insistent nightmares, the syndrome may include depression, withdrawal, insomnia, and other psychological symptoms.

People with PTSD may also experience severe anxiety, including flashbacks that cause them to remember and relive the terror. Intrusive memories usually come in the form of an involuntary mental preoccupation with the most dreaded and often violent aspects of the trauma. These insistent memories usually alternate with avoidance or denial of any feelings about the trauma.

Avoidance and denial are defense mechanisms that allow us to shut off memories that are overwhelming. Unfortunately, these unconscious mechanisms may protect us too well from our emotionally devastating memories. If our avoidance and denial are too strong, we are never able to face and resolve the emotional wounds caused by the trauma.

Recovering from PTSD

Why is it nearly impossible for some of us to overcome the alternating cycle of intrusive thoughts and denial? The magnitude of the trauma is an important factor. Experiences such as prolonged child abuse, frontline combat, being the victim of a crime or terrorist attack, or experiencing a life-threatening car accident may devastate even the most stable individual.

A crucial factor in the way we respond to and recover from traumatic events is whether we have suffered prior emotional wounds that are parallel. An example of a parallel emotional trauma would be a person who witnessed a murder or other violent crime as an adult and had also seen his father physically abuse his mother as a child. If he has not been able to work out the troubling emotions resulting from the childhood trauma, he will have a more difficult time working out the parallel emotional stumbling blocks caused by the adult trauma.

Another difficult stumbling block is what is known as survivor guilt. This syndrome occurs in people who survive a catastrophe in which other people perish or are seriously injured. The confusion about why we have survived when others close to us have died often leads to an unconscious belief that we deserve to suffer to make up for our good fortune. Survivor guilt can block our ability to recover from a trauma and can lead to depression, self-defeating behavior, or a tendency to be accident-prone.[3]

The inability to rebuild our lives after a trauma can also contribute to the persistence of PTSD. Ron and Catherine were able to return to their home and their careers and begin their marriage with the hope of happiness. On the other hand, a political refugee who was displaced by war in her homeland may never be able to return to her old way of life. She may spend many years facing poverty, discrimination, and culture shock in her new country. She will certainly have a more difficult time recovering and be more vulnerable to nightmares.

Many people who face death are able to make a greater commitment to personal change because of the sense of urgency triggered by their sudden awareness of the finiteness of life. For example, after the shipwreck, Ron decided to pursue a career change to a less pressured field so he'd be able to spend more time with his children than his father had spent with him.

How Posttraumatic Nightmares Can Be Beneficial

In this chapter we'll explore ways that you can break the spell of posttraumatic dreams and nightmares and use them in several constructive ways:

* *As a warning that you're still overwhelmed by the incident.* Dreams after a traumatic experience are normal and may even be a sign of unconscious attempts to master the trauma. But if profoundly disturbing nightmares persist in an unchanged form and are more like a memory than a dream, you may be suffering from an Acute Stress Disorder or PTSD and should seek help soon after the incident. This can help prevent the emotional wounds from becoming encapsulated and resulting in depression or self-defeating behavior.

* *As a way to understand what stage of recovery you have reached.* As you recover, your dreams may still be upsetting, but they'll often incorporate images and references from the present and from the pretrauma past. In addition, dreams marking recovery are more illogical and symbolic and include dreamlike imagery.

* *To help identify unresolved issues from the trauma and from your past.* Long-avoided conflicts from the past will often surface in dreams after a trauma. Dreams spotlight issues such as unresolved grief, survivor guilt, suppressed rage, and terrifying anxieties that must be acknowledged and worked through for healing to occur.

* *To help communicate the emotional magnitude of the traumatic experience and to feel more understood.* Sharing your emotions lessens the sense of isolation and prevents the distortions that may set in if you withdraw from friends and family.

Dreams after Natural Disasters

Disasters cause us to examine issues in new ways. They push us to deal with vital issues that we have been neglecting or denying. Earthquakes, hurricanes, floods, fires, and other natural disasters alter the lives of those who are injured, suffer property damage, lose their jobs, or are forced to move. For those who are catastrophically affected, severe, recurrent nightmares are common in the weeks and months after the disaster. Even for those who are less traumatized, the overwhelming force of nature and the close encounter with death can provoke strong emotional reactions.

On Sunday morning October 20, 1991, a small brush fire ignited high in the Oakland, California hills. Parched terrain, unseasonable heat, and hot Santa Ana winds were the perfect incubator for wildfire. Within minutes, a two thousand degree wall of fire, at times one hundred feet high, roared through the hills of Oakland and Berkeley. As the swirling inferno advanced deep into residential areas, many stunned residents were forced to run for their lives as they clutched family photos, jewelry, computer disks, or whatever they could hastily grab.[4]

Tens of thousands of people evacuated as the explosive flames threatened their homes, and later they watched live footage on network and local television of their neighborhoods burning. Dozens suffered burns, and twenty-five died in the hellish maelstrom, overcome by fumes, trapped in burning cars, or succumbing while trying to save others.[5]

Many of the evacuees did not learn the fate of their homes, and in some cases of their loved ones, for up to three days as the fire burned in areas cordoned off by officials. When they returned, they saw smoldering destruction comparable to wartime firebombing. Over three thousand homes were reduced to ash, and more than five thousand people were left homeless. For thousands of victims and hundreds of thousands of "lucky" survivors in Oakland and Berkeley, their basic trust in life was shattered, leaving the whole community vacillating between numbness, intrusive anxiety, and survivor guilt.[6,7]

Dream Journal Research

In the wake of the firestorm, I worked with colleagues Dr. Barbara Baer and Dr. Karen Muller to collect fire survivors' dream journals to analyze the patterns of their dreams and nightmares. We knew we had an unprecedented opportunity to understand the nature of posttraumatic nightmares and to learn how the psyche responds to a natural disaster. A further intention of our project was educational and therapeutic—to offer psychological assistance to the participants, and to provide education and guidance to the community of firestorm survivors. Results of the study were published in local and nationally syndicated news stories, aired on local and national radio and international television,[8] and were presented in a series of public forums at hospitals, clinics, and community centers.[9]

Two weeks after the Oakland Firestorm, we began recruiting volunteers and found forty-two participants for our study: twenty-eight who had lost their homes (fire survivors) and fourteen who had lived in the burn zone but whose homes were miraculously spared from destruction. (fire evacuees). A control group of eighteen individuals who lived outside the evacuation zone also participated in the study (control group).

All of our participants were given standardized instructions for completing a two-week dream journal (see chapter 12 for details). Most had never kept a dream journal. Each participant filled out depression and event stress questionnaires and participated in follow-up interviews reviewing their fire experiences and exploring their dreams.

Using established content analysis methods,[10] we compared 133 discrete dream themes to tap unconscious response patterns to natural disasters.[11] Comparing the groups, we looked at elements such as characters, settings, objects, architecture, disasters, death, sensory experience, heat and fire, natural disasters, injury and illness, instincts, character interactions, emotions, threat, masochism, ego mastery, food, shelter, clothing, finances, and common themes such as flying and falling.[12] The most frequently occurring themes were also subjected to qualitative analysis.[13]

The Hidden Wounds of the "Lucky Survivors"

A dramatic finding of our study was the profound and largely unacknowledged reactions of the fire evacuees—people who lived in the burn zone but whose homes were spared. Their unremitting survivor guilt, depression, intrusive thoughts, and nightmares were more distressing than those of the fire survivors. In addition, the fire evacuees' dreams were more focused on death, bodily injury, and disaster and had more manifest content references to the events of the firestorm than the dreams of the fire survivors who had actually lost property. The loss of property was not necessarily the firestorm's most devastating aspect. People perceived feelings of relief and celebration at the salvation of their homes as secondary. And apart from retaining their homes, the fire evacuees had parallel experiences during the fire: a terrifying brush with death, hours believing their homes had burned, and finding out that friends had suffered injury, death, or loss. In addition, they all faced living in a charred landscape for months to come.

This unexpected finding raised intriguing questions. Were the survivor guilt and the community denial of their invisible trauma so devastating to the fire evacuees as to result in morbid preoccupations? Or were the fire evacuees less traumatized and therefore more readily able to tolerate the recall of morbid themes? A further possibility is that fire evacuees who volunteered for the study were motivated by deeper distress than the fire survivors.

Andrea, a fire evacuee, fled the flames with her husband but returned to find that her intact home was the only standing structure left in her neighborhood. Her haunting Fire dream suggests both survivor's guilt and a residue of unresolved terror from the firestorm.

the fire seed

What I recall is an absolutely terrifying nightmare in which the fire had developed an organic consciousness. It was the embodiment of evil. It hid itself very well up on the hill in a pile of brush where it waited for all the fire departments to leave. Then it came back to get the houses it had missed. Somehow it had marked these houses with a fire seed, and all it had to do was pass by a fire seed for the house to ignite. I woke up screaming because I saw our fire seed begin to swell. In the dream, I was alone in the house.[14]

Depressed and wracked with survivor guilt, Andrea felt that she was marked by a fire seed, symbolizing in part her hidden posttraumatic wounds that could reignite at any moment. In Andrea's Survivor Guilt dream the mark of the fire seed signified the inevitability of retribution by nature—punishment for her home being spared.

Fire survivors who lost their homes had an external focus to their recovery requiring immediate activities. They had to find temporary shelter, purchase necessities, fight their insurance company, and plan and decide whether to rebuild. Despite their horrible fate, they had a map of external activities centering on establishing shelter and stability. They could deny or delay their inner anguish by immersing themselves in rebuilding their lives. Fire survivors also received sympathetic reactions from friends, family, and the general public.

In contrast, fire evacuees garnered no such sympathetic reaction. They were similarly traumatized during the fire; however, they had no map of activities to chart their recovery and distract them from their inner preoccupations. They believed they had no right to be upset. Their woes were not adequately validated by sympathetic reactions from friends and family. In this climate of denial, the fire evacuees felt that they had to shamefully conceal lingering reactions.

Results of our study suggested that special attention should be given to the hidden wounds of the "lucky" survivors of a trauma. They may not suffer injury or lose property, but they may require extended emotional support or professional help to resolve posttraumatic reactions. These findings also apply to survivors of natural disasters such as hurricanes, floods, or earthquakes who don't sustain losses or injury. Survivors of accidents and siblings of victims of violence and abuse may also bear these hidden wounds.

Impasse Dreams and Recovery Dreams in the Early Aftermath

Dreams recalled within the first few weeks after the firestorm proved to be excellent indicators of whether a person was fixated on the trauma or had turned the corner and moved onto a path of recovery. A favorable sign was dreams portraying a direct confrontation with the firestorm trauma (or its symbolic equivalents) and some attempts at mastering the threat within the dream narrative. This is consistent with Rosalind Cartwright's finding related to divorce dreams. Those who can tolerate remembering dreams about a traumatic event appear to fare better and recover more quickly. On the other hand, the dreams of fire survivors with past trauma or multiple life stresses at the time of the fire had meager evidence of mastering the threats in their nightmares and had more persistent and distressing dream images of violence, destruction, injury, and death.

One of the most haunting Firestorm dreams was that of Rebecca, a forty-year-old fire survivor. Her family home had burned down when she was a child of ten, and her mother-in-law, with whom she was close, died a week before the fire. She was emotionally devastated after the firestorm and immediately sought psychotherapy, troubled by repetitive dreams like the following one from her two-week dream journal.

BURNT aLive

I had an appointment with a psychiatrist that I used to see twenty years ago. I waited and waited. He finally left with a young man. I then was suddenly watching a woman burn alive in a building. I was watching her. There was nothing I or anyone else could do. She was terrified as she clutched the front of the charred building—flames all around her. She had blond hair. She couldn't scream—just looked out, terrified for help.[15]

There is little resolution here, only an image that would make a Munch painting seem tame. Rebecca was still unconsciously fixated on the trauma of the fire as well as on unresolved trauma and grief from the past and the present.

Rebecca's dream begins with a search for help. She returns to a psychiatrist that she saw briefly many years earlier. Her unconscious is perhaps seeking the understanding and compassion that she sensed with her old psychiatrist. But she is left waiting, unable to establish contact and then helplessly watching the grotesque incineration of the mute blond woman.

The dream's imagery appeared to reflect the recent and childhood traumas that she reported on her questionnaire and postfire interview. At a follow-up session, one year after the fire, Rebecca explored this dream and found roots deeper than the firestorm. To a small group, she revealed that she had been physically and sexually abused as a child. She had only remembered the details after the firestorm trauma painfully dissolved years of repression.

The nature of her grisly dream was, therefore, only partly explained by life stress before the fire, terrifying experiences during the fire, and adjustment problems related to loss of home and property. The firestorm and her dream opened a door to a black hole of childhood trauma. Fortunately, Rebecca sought the kind of help that was unavailable to her in childhood. Through her dreams and recovered memories, she was painfully engaged in confronting the double whammy of fire losses and the recovered memories of abuse.

In contrast, some fire survivors' Fire Disaster dreams showed early indications of emotional mastery of the trauma of the fire and losing their homes. Helen, a forty-nine-year-old teacher wrote the following vivid dream in her journal six weeks after the fire.

escaping the flames

I am in the Berkeley Hills with two women friends who were also burned out. We are in a condominium complex at the edge of the park and suddenly see gigantic flames coming rapidly toward us. Somehow we manage to escape and find ourselves in downtown San Francisco, where we can watch the flames with awe. We aren't afraid but are excited by the spectacle.[16]

Helen had little time to evacuate the day of the fire. Her family lost everything but a few photo albums, some artwork, and some jewelry. In her dream, she experienced the terror of the swift and deadly flames but succeeded in eluding the flames and getting a visual and emotional perspective on her harrowing escape.

A tamer, but thematically related Emotional Mastery dream occurred at the end of her two-week dream journal. In this dream, while on a camping trip, Helen was exhilarated when she managed to turn off some hot water at a campground. She experienced the camping trip setting as an activity that requires self-sufficiency while exposed to the elements. She saw this as a metaphor for her homeless status after the fire, staying with friends and living out of suitcases. This later dream depicts a less direct confrontation with mortally dangerous flames—the water's heat is less wild and more decisively controlled than the actual firestorm that burned her house.

At the end of her two-week dream journal, Helen's dreams showed intermittent signs of emotional recovery that reflected favorable waking life circumstances—full insurance, supportive friends, and strengthened family bonds. The fire had not shattered her life nor touched any emotional nerves from the past.

It should be emphasized that not all of Helen's dreams were uplifting or hopeful. An analysis of the ten dreams recorded in her two-week dream journal revealed themes of grief—a friend's father dying, melancholy images of her long dead father and grandmother, and a dream of being homeless.

In contrast, though, other images did include joy at becoming unexpectedly pregnant and finding many green sprouts in her charred garden. The alternation of hopeful images with persistent struggles to overcome the trauma is a typical configuration early in recovery. This mixture points to the need for exploring a series of dreams rather than relying on one dream to assess recovery from a trauma.

Nine months after the firestorm, while her house was being rebuilt, Helen had recurring dreams of discovering new rooms "much larger than I expected, almost like a hotel" and having parties with friends to celebrate the new house. Three days before the one-year anniversary of the fire, she dreamed that she was traveling in Hawaii and found "a beautiful place to live, surrounded by flowers, with orchids lining the path." Botanical Regeneration dreams were common for other survivors who were beginning to recover emotionally from the trauma.

On the one-year anniversary of the firestorm, in her follow-up questionnaire, Helen rated her adjustment in all areas of her life as better than before the fire. A painter in her spare time, she had lost most of her own artwork in the fire, but she had engaged in painting again after the fire to master her lingering anxieties. At the anniversary follow-up meeting, she was excited about an exhibition of her recent oil paintings based on photographs of the fire.

Body Integrity Dreams

Dreams depicting physical injury to the dreamer or others or disability expressed attempts to master the unexpected mortal threat that the fire posed and the disorganizing impact of the experience. Dream characters suddenly contracting fatal illnesses, especially AIDS, and dreams of physical injuries or losing teeth all speak directly to unresolved concerns about both the physical threat and the grave emotional injuries that the dreamer is attempting to resolve. Susan, a forty-four-year-old woman, had smelled smoke and run for her life within fifteen minutes, had the following Losing Teeth nightmare six weeks after the firestorm.

I Lose my weakest tooth

I see the wrong dentist. He makes a mistake and accidentally knocks out my weakest tooth. I am devastated! I weep and then feel grim and angry.[17]

The dentist reminded Susan of the insurance adjustor who was trying to extract more money from her settlement. Dreams of lost or crumbling teeth frequently symbolize physical injury, narcissistic wounds, or impotence. The loss of the aggressive, cutting power of a tooth for this survivor was a debilitating dream injury symbolizing an inner sense of being psychologically damaged and powerless.

Resolving Natural Disaster Nightmares

Natural disaster themes occurred significantly more often in the dreams of the combined fire survivor and fire evacuee groups than in the control group. Specific images included heat and fire damage as well as floods, mudslides, and other disasters.

Disaster dreams with apocalyptic themes were reported by a number of participants in the early days after the fire. Three weeks after the fire, Michael, a fire evacuee whose house had been miraculously spared from certain destruction by air-dropped fire retardant, dreamed of a flood of biblical proportions.

the great flood recedes

I am in my house watching the flood waters rise. Soon I look out the window, and the ocean waters are coming right up to the edge of the house. I start getting worried. Ultimately the waves start splashing against the house, and water starts leaking in. I take my computer, unplug it, and start to carry it upstairs. More water starts to leak in. I tell my wife that we may get flooded, and she gets worried. Then as I watch out the window, the flood recedes like in the movie *The Ten Commandments*. Mary, a friend who has suffered bad fire damage, is wet and upset. I quickly receive two tennis warm-up jackets from friends to help me recover.[18]

Images of flood waters and mudslides represented the destructive violence of the firestorm in some fire survivors' dreams. Michael's Apocalyptic dream reflected what felt like a divine reprieve from destruction. Just when the dream flood waters were about to destroy his house and drown him, he is saved. The tennis jackets represented the warmth of friends, and he felt that his wet, burned-out friend Mary may represent the emotional damage he suffered, despite his house being saved.

Tidal waves and floods in dreams are often connected to overwhelming and out-of-control emotions that the dreamer is facing in waking reality. For Michael, the flood also symbolized severe anxiety symptoms that flooded him the day of the fire when his house appeared doomed and for weeks afterward.

In the flood dream, Michael, a fire evacuee, is passively saved from the apocalypse that threatened his house. Ten months after the fire, he had a dream that suggested more active mastery over a group of environmental terrorists threatening the forests in his neighborhood.

fighting the destruction of my neighborhood

I am returning to my house in a huge wooded area with other houses on large lots. As I approach, I see hundreds of backhoes tearing down the forest around my house. I can hear their engines throttling. It reminds me of pictures of the destruction of the Amazon rain forest. I run up to the foreman and shout at him, "You are destroying my house and my whole neighborhood." I was outraged and started ringing all my neighbors' doors, urging them to join me in fighting back. I organized a protest group to sit in front of the bulldozer. I was pissed off to the point of violence. The police came to break it up, but it became violent, and they began chasing and beating people. Finally the cops agreed to stop the destruction of trees and houses. I felt satisfied.[19]

In this dream, Michael is more active in confronting the destruction of his neighborhood. In reality, his immediate neighborhood had been virtually destroyed, with houses burned on three sides of his lot. He was living daily with the construction noises of rebuilding and a barren landscape that had been lush before the fire.

At the time of the dream, he had begun to master his postfire anxieties, and his life was stabilizing. His active role in mastering the destructive threat in this dream echoed his increasingly conscious sense of mastery over his firestorm anxieties.

Of all the factors shaping coping and recovery, one invisible dimension of the fire survivors' and fire evacuees' experience was dominant—the lingering emotional impact of earlier losses, traumas, and deprivations. Those people with more trauma and loss in their backgrounds were more severely impacted and slower to recover. Their dreams after the fire and at the anniversary of the fire frequently used the metaphor of their earlier traumas to depict reactions to the firestorm and its aftermath.

Remembering dreams opens a window for observing the evolution of recovery from a natural disaster. For disaster survivors, remembering and exploring their dreams provides access to earlier emotional wounds that shape posttraumatic response patterns. Finding linkages between the present trauma and its emotional roots in the past can stimulate vital insights that may promote the resolution of both present and past traumas.

Where mental health resources are limited after a disaster, dream journals can serve as a self-help tool and a focus for support group discussions. Disrupted sleep and recurrent nightmares are part of the psyche's normal response to trauma.

Dream images are sensitive indicators of impasses in recovery from a trauma. Survivors who suffer from repetitive nightmares or frequent dreams of undisguised brutality may need immediate psychological help to resolve the posttraumatic syndrome before it becomes entrenched. Nightmares are a cardinal feature of posttraumatic stress disorder, and when repetitive dreams dwell on a disaster for months afterward there is a danger of fixating on the trauma.

Most of the participants in our study felt that keeping the two-week dream journal and participating in individual and group meetings to discuss their dreams and link them to fire experiences was therapeutic. There was an expectation of being helped by the ritual of remembering, sharing, and exploring their dreams. There was also an emotional catharsis and a sense of reassurance that their nightmares, grief, and guilt were legitimate and human rather than shameful, bizarre, or pathological.

A disaster survivor will see and experience images evoking hope and recovery as more dreams emerge with themes indicating the beginning of emotional recovery such as rebuilding, rebirth, new discoveries, or botanical growth. A series of such dreams often shows progression toward resolving the trauma. Nightmares that are like graphic memories of the trauma gradually fade, giving way to dreams that are less focused on the trauma and more mixed with other concerns.[20]

For months and years afterward, disaster survivors continue to be hypersensitive to subsequent life crises and stresses. Anniversary reactions, episodic regressions, and other delayed posttraumatic reactions were not uncommon. For some people, emotional regressions occurred after substantial progress had been made, signalling a breakthrough in their ability to face their most abhorrent memories and emotions of the firestorm. Continued exploration of dreams can transform disaster survivors' nightmares into powerful vehicles for personal insight and resolution of posttraumatic reactions.

The Terror of Nightmares after September 11

In the aftermath of the tragic events of September 11, 2001, an epidemic of nightmares broke out, not just in lower Manhattan but in New York, throughout the United States, and all over the world. The media exposure of repeatedly watching the planes collide with the World Trade Center Towers and images of the buildings collapsing into an explosive wave of debris triggered some of the nightmares as did insecurity about future attacks and the preparations for and a protracted battle against terrorism.

A May 2002 survey by the New York Academy of Medicine estimated that approximately 425,000 New Yorkers had suffered clinical symptoms of posttraumatic stress disorder, which included "symptoms of nightmares, anxiety, irritability and outbursts of anger." An additional half million New York residents had suffered a serious episode of depression after the September 2001 attacks, with half of those estimated to be directly related to the WTC events.[21] But the impact was felt far beyond the Hudson River. A Pew Research Center poll in late September 2001 indicated that one-third of Americans had difficulty sleeping through the night as a result of the attacks.[22]

In early October 2001, I was asked to appear on NBC's *Today Show* to provide both reassurance and information about the nature of posttraumatic nightmares. People from all over the world emailed nightmares related to September 11 in response to a posting on the MSNBC website on October 4, 2001, inviting people to send their dreams.

Of those people who emailed their dreams, residents of the greater New York area reported very graphic dreams, such as a man from Long Island, whose repetitive nightmares were of "screaming people jumping from the windows." Occasionally it was "me inside the burning building, not able to get out." A woman from Brooklyn had recurring dreams of explosions and falling airplanes as well as many nightmares of being "separated from her family by a river with no way of getting to them." Neither of these dreamers knew anyone who died or was injured in the destruction of the World Trade Center Towers, and both wondered why they were having such graphic nightmares since they had not lost anyone directly.

Sleep disturbances and increases in anxiety and depression were not limited to the New York area either. Many people who were vulnerable to nightmares and sleep disorders and to anxiety and depression observed a dramatic increase in those difficulties. In the emails, many reported extreme desperation connected to their nightmares. Some people reported praying for relief from both their fears and their nightmares.

Allison, a young mother from Miami, lamented a recurring explosion nightmare she had "that never ends and never gets resolved."

the tragedy of the teddy bear kids

I am sitting in a mall food court surrounded by hundreds of children holding teddy bears. We are about to start singing a song when a bomb-carrying school bus suddenly rips into the food court and explodes.

This Mortal Threat dream is typical of many posttraumatic dreams that focus directly on the upsetting event but disguise or combine the upset with other important life events and concerns. For Allison, the events of September 11 provoked fear and insecurity about her own young children. For many children (and even some adults), teddy bears are the ultimate source of comfort and security. Food courts in malls usually offer a wide variety of comfort food choices. In the dream, neither the stuffed animals nor the comfort food could protect the vulnerable children. Early in the aftermath, Allison's insecurities were persistent and unresolved.

There are many stories of heroism connected to the aftermath of the World Trade Center destruction. Many dedicated professional firefighters, doctors, clergy, and mental health workers as well as hundreds of nonprofessionals volunteered vast amounts of time to help the survivors heal.

One such hero was Kuuipo Ordway, who was a veteran of rescue work from Hurricane Hugo and other disasters. She was also a doctoral candidate in psychology, one of the students in my graduate course "Understanding Your Dreams" at Alliant University's California School of Professional Psychology. Under the auspices of the Adventist Community Services, she traveled to Manhattan on September 16, 2001, to offer free counseling services to the survivors. Working long hours without pay, she and sixty other volunteers offered group and individual counseling and support groups to over eighteen hundred people. Working with the Red Cross and other groups from a staging area near Union Station, she conducted daily psychological support groups and individual counseling sessions for deeply distressed survivors. Many people found out about the groups when they were aimlessly wandering the streets, searching for survivors or appearing numb in a zombie-like state of emotional paralysis.

Although the focus of the groups was not specifically nightmares, many of the participants found immediate solace in sharing their fears and dreams with others. This corresponds to what psychiatrist Judith Herman describes as the first stage of treating trauma survivors, which is the "establishment of safety."[23] In her book *Trauma and Recovery: The Aftermath of Violence—from Domestic Abuse to Political Terror,* Herman asserts that "a supportive response from other people may mitigate the impact of the event."[24] The second stage on Herman's map of recovery from trauma is remembrance and mourning, and the third stage is restoring social contacts and reconnecting with everyday life.

The following vignettes document a dream series of one survivor who barely made it out of the South Tower alive. During a two-week period of participating in group therapy and discussing his nightmares, he went from isolation and terror to safety and remembrance through sharing and exploring his nightmares.

Nathan, a financial analyst in his early thirties, had been working in the South Tower for over nine years and had survived the basement bombing of the World Trade Center in 1993. On the morning of September 11, 2001, when the first hijacked plane hit the North Tower, chaos broke out in his office with people running around to alert each other. The Port Authority was trying to reassure the workers to stay or return to their offices, deciding that the damage was in the other tower. Having survived the 1993 bombing, Nathan's instincts took over. He ignored the Port Authority reassurance and headed for the elevator banks. As it turned out, he was on the last elevator that made it safely down from the South Tower upper floors. He ran out of the building as quickly as he could and made it to safety. In the grim aftermath, he counted over ninety colleagues and friends that he lost that day.

At the support group's second meeting, he revealed a recurrent Tidal Wave dream that had occurred each night since September 11 and was deeply upsetting.

screaming heads

It's a beautiful day, and I am out sailing with my friends who are in many boats. Everything seems perfect. There is a gentle breeze, just strong enough for sailing. Everyone's laughing and having a great time. Suddenly, the waves begin to churn and the sky fills with dark, angry clouds. It starts pouring rain, and the waves grow larger and larger until a huge wave crashes down on all of us. All that's left are splinters of the boats. I see all the friends that I lost from the WTC. They are just heads with no bodies! Even though it's just their heads, they are still alive, and they're all terrified and screaming. I keep turning around in the water looking for someone who is alive and a whole body, but I'm just surrounded by the screaming heads of my friends. I wake up terrified.

Nathan had always been an avid sailor and yachtsman. He had been a Sea Scout as a teen and had served in the naval reserve. He loved to sail and kayak and would frequently invite his friends from work to sail with him on weekends.

In his screaming heads dream, yachting, the activity he loved so dearly, is converted into a massacre with the floating heads of his friends forming a ghastly floating graveyard. He could not shake the visual images nor the haunting wails of his disembodied friends.

After sharing the dream with the group, he was visibly relieved and expressed a sense of comfort that the group members seemed to understand and empathize with his distress. The next night, his dream seemed to respond to the dream work he had done with the group. The beginning of the next nightmare is very similar to the repetitive one he had been having. A beautiful day of sailing with friends is interrupted by a sudden devastating storm that builds to a crescendo with the arrival of a huge, deadly wave. This time, within the dream, he senses what will happen.

talking heads

The huge wave is coming again, and I am feeling even more anxious because I know, even within the dream, that it's going to get worse, that this huge killer wave is coming. I watch the giant wave crush everybody. I am choking and bobbing in the water. I wish I had been drowned because I don't want to look up to see their faces again. But I can't stop myself from looking at all my friends' heads floating in the water. This time they are alive but speaking to me rather than screaming. They keep telling me to get to safety, to swim to shore, to keep kicking, and to stay above water. The clouds begin to fade, and I can see land. I start sobbing while looking at my lost friends' faces. I wake up remembering them telling me to swim to shore.

After telling his second dream, Nathan appeared somewhat relieved and seemed eager to remember further dreams and to receive additional counseling. After the meeting, he requested an individual session for the following day. At that time, he revealed another Reunion with the Dead dream. While still very painful, the dream seemed to mark his transition to Judith Herman's second stage of recovery.

remembering and mourning my friends

The dream started with the waves crashing all over me. The boat was turning over and tossing me into the sea when the killer wave arrived, crushing every boat including mine. I'm barely treading water. This time I don't just see the heads but see my friends' sad faces. I don't want to look away because I think another wave might swallow them and I'd never see them again. I begin to cry and swim toward them, but another big wave comes along, and I get carried away with it. I keep trying to look for my friends, but I'm being pulled underwater and the next thing I know I'm lying on the shore choking and coughing up water. On the shore, there is a miniature altar with Mary and Jesus on it laying only a few feet from me. I crawl to it and collapse, holding on to it while I sob. I don't know exactly why I'm sobbing. I just keep sobbing so hard that it wakes me up.

Nathan stressed that he felt it was crucial for him to remember the faces of his friends from his dream because he did not have a chance to say good-bye to any of them. He also mentioned that he had talked to his mother and grandmother the previous night, and they had lit candles for him to thank God for keeping him safe and to bless the memory of his deceased friends and coworkers.

On the last night of the two-week group, Nathan stopped in early to say he was starting to sleep more soundly and the nightmares had diminished in frequency and intensity. He was no longer seeing the screaming or crying faces in his dreams but he did have one more dream that he was eager to describe.

saved from the killer wave

The dream again started in the middle of the storm, with the killer wave crushing everything. Another big wave comes right behind it, and I find myself swept up in it and start swimming as hard as I can. As the wave begins to crest, I see the shore and it is sunny. I don't understand how this could be, but I just keep swimming until the wave dumps me on the beach. I'm slammed onto the sand, and my clothes are all torn, and everybody on the beach is just looking at me at first, and then they rush to help me. As they speak, I keep hearing whispering. I know the whispering I'm hearing is the voices of my friends, but as I look around I can't see them. Somehow I know they're not on the beach. I look out to the ocean, and I can't even see a sign of a storm having been there.

Nathan did not feel as haunted by the voices of his friends as he talked about this dream. He felt that hearing the voices gave him a way of remembering and staying connected with the friends who had perished. Twice he repeated, "I think I need the voices so I won't feel so alone." He had just started back to work that day for the same company at another location. It was painful, but he felt that being at work was helping him feel more normal.

Although he was still in the early stages of recovery, there was evidence that with the help of the support group and dream sharing, Nathan was progressing into the stage of remembrance and mourning. Returning to work helped him take his first step into the final stage of recovery, reconnecting with everyday life.

Nathan was both vulnerable and highly receptive. During a relatively short period of intense group counseling, his chilling dream series began to evolve. Exploring the images in a supportive setting accelerated his recovery process and altered the content and severity of his nightmares. The screaming heads became talking faces, then sad faces, then whispering friends who were both sad and comforting. The killer waves went from cataclysmically destructive to a tide of deliverance that brought him battered but safe into the supportive arms of helpers and rescuers. Finally, his dreams moved from inconsolable social isolation to rescue and connection with helpers and healers.

Although directly impacted by the destruction of the WTC, Nathan's nightmares had no fires, no hijacked planes, no crashing buildings, and no people jumping. In contrast, the dreamers from outside New York, who did not suffer any direct losses, had dreams filled with fire, explosions, planes, and more direct references to the hijackings and destruction of the WTC.

In many cases, the dreams are more disguised for disaster survivors who are closer to the impact zone or who witness horrors, narrowly escape death, or suffer direct losses. We saw this in the firestorm survivors' dreams as well as in post–September 11th dreams and it applies to survivors of accidents, crime, war, and other disasters. Those who are more indirectly impacted often dream of symbolism more directly related to the disaster. This seems counterintuitive. However, it is explained by the fact that dreams may camouflage extremely upsetting events to protect us from being overwhelmed in the early stages of recovery. This unique characteristic of posttraumatic nightmares allows a slow but steady recovery by disguising the dream content to gradually allow us to emotionally process very devastating experiences.

For survivors of the World Trade Center and other disasters, nightmares are one of the most upsetting and repetitive outcomes. Even when the symbolism does not overtly or directly refer to the traumatic event, bringing nightmares into the light of day can relieve the terror and get the cycle of recovery moving forward. Survivors who share nightmares frequently feel less alone and more understood—not to mention feeling relieved about having fewer bad dreams!

Crime Victims' Dreams, Nightmares, and Sleep Disorders

Nightmares and sleep disorders disrupt the slumber of those recovering from acts of violence. Barry Krakow, M.D., is a pioneer in understanding and treating the sleep and dream disorders of crime victims. He has received government funding, which has allowed him to develop and pilot innovative treatment strategies to heal the nighttime suffering of survivors of violence.

Krakow and his colleagues have designed a nightmare treatment program based on dream imagery rehearsal and behavioral strategies for soothing insomnia. Using cognitive behavioral therapy, he has demonstrated that treating the symptoms of nightmares and insomnia also triggers improvements in anxiety, depression, sleep disorders, and posttraumatic stress disorder symptoms.

In one of Krakow's studies, the nightmare sufferers who improved with imagery rehearsal had had posttraumatic stress disorder symptoms and recurrent nightmares for an average of thirteen years. This is additional evidence that nightmares are both a key to analyzing symptoms and an entry point for successful psychological treatment of crime survivors. It is important for crime survivors to receive treatment that focuses on both waking anxieties and devastatingly painful nightmares.[25]

Case studies featuring the dreams of rape survivors have been documented by a number of authors. Jungian-oriented psychologist and trauma specialist Karen Muller, Ph.D., described the dreams of Jasmine, a woman who was violently abused as a child and also suffered a gang rape when she was twenty. Exploring her dreams in psychotherapy helped Jasmine dramatically, but her full recovery was equivocal due to the massive traumas she had suffered, both as a child and as an adult.[26]

Psychoanalytic authors Marquis Wallace and Howard Parad described a more full recovery of a rape victim whom they call Hilda. She was treated with a form of crisis-oriented therapy that utilized dreams as the central focus of discussion. Their approach to crisis therapy seeks to help the client not only to return to her former level of functioning but to use the turning point as an impetus for personal growth.[27]

Hilda, a twenty-five-year-old nursing student, sought therapy two weeks after being raped. She couldn't stop crying and was having severe difficulties concentrating on her studies. She said that her self-esteem was "about one on a scale of ten." Her boyfriend broke up with her a week after the rape; she was emotionally estranged from her parents, who lived a hundred miles away. In her first session, she tearfully reported two recurrent Left-Out dreams.

seeing my grave

I am there, but not there. I see my grave. I wonder what it would feel like not to exist. I am afraid of being by myself.

i'm invisible to them

I am on a country road. I see a beautiful wheat field. My mother and brother and I are there. We stop at the top of a hill. It seems that my mother and brother—and father, who suddenly shows up—don't even know that I'm there. I wake up with my mouth open. I am lonely. I have the strange feeling that it is easy for them to leave.[28]

Hilda expressed loneliness and anger toward her boyfriend who had rejected her in a moment of need. She also dwelt upon the feeling of being invisible and realized that her parents had not paid much attention to her as a child. Her sadness alternated with anger at her parents as she explored her long-standing sense of emotional neglect.

Over the course of twenty therapy sessions, Hilda realized that the rapist's brutality had set off painful memories of insensitive and neglectful treatment by her parents, especially by her stern, alcoholic father. Exploring her dreams not only helped her to express and work out her emotional reaction to the rape, it also accelerated her ability to resolve the sense of being invisible.

The "invisible" dreams, plus others that depicted her father interchanged with her ex-boyfriend, helped Hilda realize that she got involved with men in an attempt to win her father's love. Although she would cling to them, they often treated her poorly. By the end of the therapy she had begun a relationship that had a different quality.

During the course of the therapy, Hilda testified against the rapist at a preliminary hearing. Before, during, and after her testimony, she had nightmares that renewed the terror and invisibility that she felt during the rape. After testifying, she dreamed that she reexperienced the rape but was able to run away. Although she was still reliving the trauma, there was now evidence of emotional mastery of the trauma of the rape. Apparently the assertion of testifying, along with the therapist's continuing support, had altered her dreams. Experiencing the trauma with a new, partially resolved ending is a typical sign that recovery is occurring.

Ultimately, the rapist confessed. After he was sentenced, Hilda felt more secure but continued to have an occasional terrifying dream, such as the following Creature Threat dream:

attacked by a ferocious bear

A ferocious bear was trying to get me. It attacked. I tried to counterattack but was helpless. I am close to getting eaten, and someone is trying to help me. The bear claws at me all night, over and over again. It reminds me of frog and spider dreams that I used to have.[29]

The image of the bear provoked incredible feelings of rage in Hilda. She was angry at her father. Then she became ferociously angry at the rapist, expressing murderous fantasies toward him. When the therapist suggested that the bear might represent her own anger as well as an image of the rapist, Hilda responded positively. She realized that she had always denied her own anger and had made excuses for people who treated her poorly. The dream allowed her a sense of catharsis and a chance to awaken her assertive side, which had always been dormant.

At first glance, the image of the ferocious bear would seem to contradict the idea that Hilda was making progress in her recovery. But often when we've taken a significant step toward mastering a trauma, we feel safe to release and work through more powerful feelings that had previously been inaccessible. The renewal of nightmares was not a regression but a sign of a greater ability to tolerate and master the very feelings that previously had been overwhelming.

Dreams and War

A combat-related stress syndrome has been recognized for centuries. In the American Civil War, the term *soldier's heart* was used, and the severe symptoms were ascribed to coronary malfunctions. In World War I, the term *shell shock* was indicative of the prevalent belief that brain trauma was the source of the anxiety and nightmares. In World War II, vast numbers of traumatized soldiers precipitated study of the symptoms.[30]

It was the acute public reaction to the problems of a large number of alienated Vietnam veterans in the 1970s that led to the inclusion of posttraumatic stress disorder as an official psychiatric diagnosis in 1979. Although organic causes have not been ruled out, the prevailing wisdom is that PTSD is a psychologically induced syndrome that occurs in survivors of severe trauma. For Vietnam veterans, the emotional wounds were compounded by the scorn they received upon their arrival home from a war that the United States had lost and would have preferred to forget.

In the dreams of combat veterans, we find abundant evidence of how the human psyche copes with overwhelming trauma. Jungian analyst Harry Wilmer has worked extensively with Vietnam combat veterans and conducted a study of 359 dreams from 103 veterans. Recurrent dreams were counted only once; therefore, the 359 recorded dreams represent thousands more actual dreams.[31]

Wilmer found many consistent themes in the veterans' dreams. The most common motifs included killing, being killed, death, dying, being wounded, and committing atrocities. General themes such as being chased, threatened by animals, and looming danger took on the characteristics of war scenes. Themes portraying the cycle of service in Vietnam were also common. These included dreams emphasizing approaching combat, direct engagement, returning home, and longing to return to Vietnam.

Out of his research, Wilmer observed three stages or categories of impasse and resolution in the dreams that coincided closely with the actual stages of recovery that the veterans had reached.[32]

Stage-One Dreams

Wilmer's stage-one dreams were characteristic of the men who suffered the most severe symptoms of PTSD. These dreams were more realistic and less dreamlike. They tended to replay horrific events that the dreamer had witnessed, and the content had little to do with the dreamer's past or present life. Stage-one dreams accounted for 53 percent of the total dreams in the study.[33]

A gruesome example was that of a veteran who had been confined to a foxhole for four days with one buddy. They couldn't even get out to stretch their legs because of the sniper fire. The Posttraumatic nightmare replays an actual memory in an unchanged form.

MY BUDDY GETS BLOWN AWAY

I am talking with my buddy. It is dark. He lights a cigarette, and all of a sudden his head blows off. His brains come out all over me. I wake up screaming.

Wilmer's descriptions of the graphic and grotesque stage-one nightmares of the most vulnerable combat survivors were corroborated by the findings of nightmare researcher Ernest Hartmann. Hartmann believes that soldiers who lose a person with whom they were extremely close are the most vulnerable to the psychologically disabling impact of PTSD. Soldiers who were younger, less mature, or had an insecure sense of self were even more at risk because their adult identities had not been fully formed. Often the nightmares would not begin for these men until months or years later, when a subsequent loss, rejection, or trauma would trigger the painful memories that had never been dealt with.[34]

Stage-Two Dreams

Wilmer found that in the veterans that he treated or in those who recovered spontaneously, the imagery in their dreams began to transform as the therapy progressed. In what he describes as the second stage, the nightmares still focus on catastrophic memories, but the content begins to be mixed with events from the present or from other eras of the person's life. This indicates that they have begun to resolve their fixation on the terrible events of the past and are dealing more realistically with other pressing issues of their current life.

Dream mastery of trauma usually is characterized by matching those emotional challenges with parallel incidents from the past. These stage-two dreams reveal the psyche's attempts to transform the trauma into a more symbolic form that can be mastered. These dreams accounted for 21 percent of the total from the study.

Stage-Three Dreams

Wilmer's stage-three dreams are more like ordinary nightmares, but they tend to have Vietnam as the setting. More metaphorical and dreamlike, they mix in many images of the present and combine them in new ways. There are often the dreamer's attempts to fight back or overcome the dilemmas faced in the dream.

According to Wilmer, the emergence of a stage-three dream after prolonged unchanging nightmares is an important part of the healing process. Observing the lessening or ending of their brutal repetitive nightmares helps the veterans to feel understood and to see their inner response to the therapy and the healing process. As an example of what he calls "the healing nightmare," Wilmer presents a number of cases of veterans who experienced a transformation in their dream life that correlated with general improvements in their condition.

Jim, age thirty-six, had a stage-one nightmare for twelve years before beginning therapy. It was always the same: a reliving of an actual ambush in which he led seventeen newly arrived soldiers to their death. Nothing could stop the dream. The incident had forced him to resort to excessive use of alcohol and drugs in an attempt to blot out the memory. After two months of twice-a-week therapy, his dreams suddenly transformed to stage three— to the shock of Jim and Dr. Wilmer.

RESCUING the wounded HeaLeR

Everyone is getting killed. Harry [Dr. Wilmer], they got you in the center of the ravine bleeding from gunshot wounds. You are leaning against a tree and crying for help. . . . Now I am standing on top of the ravine and a nurse is with me. She and I slip into the ravine. I hit the Viet Cong over the head with the butt of my rifle, and she dresses your wounds. I carry you out on my back. Sometimes in the dream, your hands are tied. When I pull you out, I wake up in tears.[35]

In the past, Jim had always awakened from his nightmares in a cold sweat, never in tears. It appeared that he had broken free of his nightly ambush and was beginning to work through his grief. Although still a nightmare, his Rescuing the Wounded Healer dream reveals a transformation of his inner life.

The discussion and other therapeutic work with Dr. Wilmer was impacting his dreams. Jim's relationship with his "healer" was reversed in the dream. Instead of depicting his doctor as helping him, Jim became the rescuing hero. He was determined to give his doctor, bleeding and crying in a ravine, the desperately needed treatment for his wounds. He would even risk his life to carry his doctor out on his back. This scene was emotionally parallel to the positive effects Jim was feeling from Wilmer's determination to heal his emotional wounds.

In addition, saving a man from a combat zone is exactly what Jim had been unable to do during the ambush. The success of his dream rescue mission suggests that he was finally overcoming the terrible guilt and achieving a sense of mastery over the incident that had occurred a dozen years earlier.

Jim's example is what Wilmer calls a healing nightmare, a dream that results in an emotional breakthrough. In the process of exploring it, Jim gained evidence that he was deeply engaged in a positive working relationship with his therapist. He became aware of the emerging grief that he would have to deal with—a grief that he had never allowed himself to admit until that moment.

Jim was finally able to allow himself to be taken care of, to accept nursing and doctoring just as he had provided in the dream. The exploration of his Rescuing the Wounded Healer dream gave him a feeling that he was regaining control over his waking life as well as his dream life. This renewed sense of control and hope for the future was a crucial building block in his continued recovery.

Refugees' Nightmares

The posttraumatic nightmares of refugees reveal the emotional scars of political repression, terrorist threats and attacks, and psychological or physical torture. Many refugees are haunted by persistent nightmares of being threatened or attacked by murderous troops. Others are plagued by dreams of wounded children crying out in pain, images of mutilated bodies, and terrible scenes of destruction.

Psychologist Adrianne Aron has worked extensively with Salvadoran refugees living in the San Francisco Bay Area, especially with those who sought political asylum after threats against their lives. Almost three-fourths of the subjects she interviewed spontaneously reported nightmares, and over two-thirds of those were plagued by nightmares of men trying to kill them. In many cases these dreams were based upon actual experiences of armed threat or harassment.

One Salvadoran woman, Blanca, had been apolitical. She was picked up on a Monday and informed that she would be killed on Friday. She was blindfolded, isolated, and starved for four days. She heard others being tortured and shot and fully expected that she too would be murdered. Miraculously her family was able to bribe a guard to secure her release. Soon she escaped to the United States, carrying with her the searing memory of her torture. Shortly after her release from detention, she began having a recurrent Mortal Threat nightmare that would plague her for years to come.

MURDERERS PURSUING me

There are armed men coming after me. I am running, and they are getting closer. I don't know what they look like, but I can feel them behind me, preparing to kill me. I feel the heat of the blood running down my back, and I realize that I have been shot. Then I wake up.[36]

The dream depicts Blanca reliving the horrific days when she fully expected to be murdered. Her unconscious is frozen in a state of terrified expectation, and she is actually shot in the dream. Blanca awakened screaming from this dream almost daily for her first two years in the United States. The content and frequency of her dream are typical of the dreams of other political refugees. In fact, the nightmares of refugees are so similar that Aron has identified a two-part pattern that is almost universal.

In the typical first scene of the dream, the victims are usually being chased by armed men, who are often faceless or unidentified. The dreamers feel the ominous presence gradually overtaking them and preparing to kill them. In the second scene, the victims are shot, beaten, or subjected to other forms of deadly violence. They may respond by fighting back or trying to disarm the assailant, but they usually fail; a gun may misfire, or they are paralyzed or overwhelmed by superior forces.

Many refugees are unable to gain political asylum or secure residency status in a new country. Further, they may face deportation and the threat of torture or death if they are returned to their homeland. The United States grants asylum to only about 3 percent of Salvadoran refugees. Until they obtain residency or establish a stable life in their new country, the night-mares and posttraumatic stress disorder may continue.

Eventually Blanca married an American citizen, gained legal status, and began to feel more secure. Six years after leaving her country, she continues to have this nightmare when other events in her life are stressful, but the frequency has been reduced to once a month.

Even when refugees gain residency, they must confront grief and rage over the loss of their family, friends, and career. In addition to the loss of their old way of life, they face overwhelming new problems of acculturation. Many require psychological treatment to shake their nightmares and anxiety.

Julio, a nineteen-year-old Salvadoran, was also apolitical. When every male in his family was murdered, he knew that his days were numbered. He fled to the mountains and escaped to the United States. Four times a week for over six years, he was plagued by a repetitive nightmare so upsetting that he rarely slept more than two hours at a time. It was only when he suc-ceeded in winning political asylum in the United States that his nightmares abated and his psychological condition improved.

Armando served in the Salvadoran air force and continued to work at a military armory in a civilian status after his discharge. The national guard falsely accused him of stealing weapons and collaborating with the guerrillas. Although he maintained his innocence, he was mercilessly tortured by being burned, shocked, hanged, and beaten.

Armando's most distressing nightmare, like Blanca's, was an endless replay of being pursued. However, the response to the murderers in the second part of his dream was different. It begins with armed men chasing him with deadly intent. And then . . .

trying to fight back

. . . I stop, because I have a gun. I turn and take aim and shoot at them. But the gun misfires. I wake up.[37]

Although Armando's dream gun is impotent, at least he wields it in a desperate albeit futile fight. In reality, Armando fiercely maintained his innocence and his belief that some justice or law would prevail in his favor. In the dreams of many persecuted refugees, they are unable to rearm themselves or fight back. Armando's fighting suggested some degree of resilience in his spirit. A number of times Armando has had Apocalyptic nightmares like the following.

the eve of destruction

I know the world is going to end because I see the firmament breaking into pieces, floating in an enormous sea. Everywhere, I see people falling into the void. I am standing precariously on a little island.[38]

The dream reflects Armando's perception that his world was being shattered. The island represents a stubborn assertion of innocence in the face of his world's destruction. Some related dreams portray the Savior's presence at the end of the world. The dreams may reflect Armando's inner struggle to give a religious meaning to the horrendous torture he was suffering.

Armando's Apocalyptic nightmares gradually became less frequent in the year after he fled his homeland. He dreamed that the Savior appeared and abolished all evil from the world. He was eventually able to achieve political asylum, which gave him some hope that his nightmares would diminish and his life could begin again.

Healing the Wounds of Trauma

The wounds of trauma are slow to heal. When you become victimized by violence, abuse, accidents, or natural disasters, you need empathetic ears to hear your feelings, assist you in rebuilding your life, and help you ease the terror of your nightmares and other anxieties.

It is important not to feel ashamed about seeking help after suffering a trauma. Early intervention that includes individual or group discussion of the traumatic events can head off the development of posttraumatic stress disorder and put you on the road to recovery from your emotional wounds.

Exploring posttraumatic nightmares allows you to gain access to the hidden wounds that paralyze you. As you review your traumatic memories, their grip upon you is loosened. Dreams also provide vital information about what stage of recovery you have reached and whether you are at an impasse in getting over the trauma.

When you listen to the dreams of someone else who has suffered a traumatic experience, remember that you need not feel compelled to offer a sophisticated explanation or analysis. Often having someone willing to listen and try to understand the victim's troubling feelings will help break the spell of posttraumatic nightmares.

9. HEALING DREAMS RECOVERING from INJURY AND ILLNESS OR NEARING DEATH

When we're injured or ill, our dreams express our deepest fears and help us understand the full range of our emotional reactions. Dreams give us symbolic pictures of the stages of our illness. They can help us participate more actively in selecting the nature of our treatment, and they may even help us improve our response to it. And sharing our dreams allows us to build supportive connections with friends and family at a time when we are especially vulnerable.

Breast cancer struck Susan in the prime of life. At thirty-five, she had finally recovered from an emotionally devastating divorce five years earlier. She had also just completed her doctorate in psychology after having made a career change from nursing.

During the first six months of recovering from her mastectomy and going through chemotherapy, Susan began to reach out more to friends for emotional support. She had contemplated joining a support group for women with breast cancer but had been afraid to talk with others for fear of making her own situation feel more real and upsetting. While debating whether to enter the support group, Susan had the following dream.

WHY am I DOING tHIS aLONe?

I am with a group of women who have been kidnapped and sent to the USSR. A guard is telling us that we have to have special shoes. But I defy him and walk with the other women. The other women go ahead, and I fall behind. I suddenly realize that I can catch up and walk with them, and I ask myself, "Why am I doing this alone?" I call out to another woman and ask to walk with her. Later, we are all in Gorbachev's office, and he is talking to Bush and negotiating our release. I am with the other women, and we are told that we'll all be let go, and I start hugging the translator and jumping up and down with joy.

Susan's dream helped resolve her immediate dilemma of whether to join the support group. At a deeper level, however, her dream depicted a resolution of old fears about dependence versus independence. Susan was especially moved by the question in her dream, "Why am I doing this alone?" She had always been ready to give aid to others. As the oldest child, she took care of her younger siblings. As a nurse, she was extremely dedicated to her patients. In her marriage, she had always put her ex-husband's needs before her own. In fact, she had been very dependent on him and had grown to resent his dominance. Until her husband left her, she took no steps to develop her more assertive side. Now the cancer and her dreams were pushing her to develop her sense of independence.

She no longer viewed marriage as a threat to her autonomy and began to feel open to the idea of marrying again. Although she was continuing to work in a helping profession, she felt more balanced and less like she needed to be a superwoman in her work with clients and her relationships with friends. In fact, the illness had made her acutely aware of how precious her family and friends were.

The joy that Susan experienced at the end of the dream was associated with the ending of chemotherapy. After five months of treatment, she was pronounced cancer free. Susan had minimized the importance of the end of her treatment, but the dream helped her acknowledge how great a burden had been lifted when she received a positive prognosis.

Although Susan still experienced bouts of depression and anxieties about the recurrence of the cancer, her dreams helped her see that she was actively coping with her fears and reaching new dimensions in her personal and professional life.

Making the Connection between Dreams and Illness

Like other turning points, an encounter with serious illness produces recurring dream images as we respond to the emotional challenges of sickness. Clocks and references to limited time, for example, are common in the dreams of people who have been diagnosed with a terminal illness. Acute awareness of time in dreams relates to our internal sense of how much time we have left. One person who was given a terminal diagnosis dreamed that he was told it was 11 P.M., indicating that his death was imminent, but when he checked his watch in the dream, it was only 9:15. His Limited Time dream indicated that his internal clock still had time on it, and he ended up living longer than expected.[1]

Out-of-Control Forces dreams tend to be associated with the physical characteristics of a particular episode of illness. For example, people with cancer often dream of cars going out of control and crashing—symbolizing the deadly, out-of-control growth of cancerous cells. Epileptics sometimes dream of explosions, which may symbolize the sense of fragmentation that they feel during a seizure. Women may dream of water spilling out of containers prior to or at the onset of a miscarriage.

In his book *Dreaming with an AIDS Patient*, Jungian analyst Robert Bosnak chronicles the long dream series of a man suffering from AIDS. In the period when his patient was approaching death, the man's repetitive dreams of polluted water seemed to symbolize that his inner fluids were contaminated and his condition was deteriorating.[2]

Other patients with AIDS and cancer dreamed of spreading wildfire, symbolizing the consuming destructive power of the disease process. A colleague recorded a dream of William, a Protestant minister suffering from AIDS. William had left the ministry to pursue a secular career in the social services. After contracting AIDS and suffering a near-fatal bout of pneumonia, he had the following Out-of-Control Forces dream during a period of remission.

WILDfiRe IN tHe CHURCH

I am in a church that is on fire. The fire is raging out of control, and everyone is fleeing the terrible danger. I look for a place to hide and go up to the pulpit and stand behind the cross thinking that I will be safe from the fire there.

This dream inspired William to renew his faith. He decided to halt his other career plans and return to the church. He expressed the hope that his spiritual renewal would help him stave off or recover from AIDS. Unfortunately, the fire had spread too far; William died within a few weeks.[3]

In this chapter, we'll explore how to use our dreams during periods of illness to help us overcome barriers to reaching out to others, work out the emotional impasses that arise at times of serious illness, find a sense of meaning during demoralizing phases of an illness, and transform periods of suffering into opportunities for personal growth.

We'll consider key dreams in various stages of confrontation with life-threatening illness, chronic ailments, injuries, and surgery. In our exploration, we'll look at dreams that:

* occur shortly before the onset of illness and appear to foreshadow the arrival of the illness

* coincide with the onset or immediate aftermath of an illness, injury, or surgery

* portray symbolic or direct references to the injured or ill body

* play a role in triggering episodes of certain disorders such as asthma, epilepsy, heart attack, or miscarriage

* depict resolution of emotional blocks related to illness

* illustrate stages of recovery or deterioration

* indicate the imminence of death in terminal patients

Dreams Foreshadowing Illness

On the verge of serious illness, a compelling nightmare may foreshadow our imminent physical danger. Many people I've worked with have associated a particular dream to the period just before they became aware of their illness. In psychological literature, there are many examples of troubling nightmares in the weeks before the onset of a serious or fatal disease. There is even some scientific evidence that dream content alters dramatically in the weeks prior to the outbreak of a severe illness.

Six weeks prior to her cancer diagnosis, Susan dreamed of a terrible earthquake shaking her house down. Although Earthquake and House dreams are not uncommon—especially for people living in the San Francisco Bay Area, as Susan does—this dream stayed in her mind, troubling her for weeks.

my House is crumbling all around me

> I am in my bed, and my house begins to shake. I am not worried at first, but the shaking gets stronger and stronger. I am horrified as I see parts of my house falling down all around me. Despite my terror and the destruction that occurs, I end up being safe.

Susan tried to reassure herself. What could be wrong? She'd had a mammogram and a full physical just a few months earlier. She had never felt better and was taking care of herself—not overworking, eating a healthy diet, exercising, and feeling fulfilled with her new career.

In the days following her diagnosis and surgery, Susan's Earthquake dream kept coming back to her. She knew there was no way of proving it, but it seemed to have predicted a disaster about to strike her.

As she progressed in her recovery from cancer, Susan thought about this dream many times. She thought that the house represented her body. In the dream as in reality, she couldn't believe that the disaster could really be happening. Just as parts of her house broke off, a part of her body had to be removed. The one element of the dream that Susan began to draw solace from was the ending, where she survives despite the destruction. In her more optimistic moments, Susan imagined that she would survive the destructive influence of cancer just as she had survived the earthquake in her dream.

Susan also saw the crumbling house as a metaphor for the upheaval in the stability and structure of her life that was about to occur. During her recovery, she felt that she was rebuilding her life on a firmer foundation.

Natalie, like Susan, had no reason to suspect that a cancer was growing inside her. At thirty-two, she had made a successful documentary film and was studying for her doctorate in sociology. She had a steady relationship and was feeling that she had begun to break free from her mother's stifling influence.

Four months before receiving the shocking diagnosis of malignant cervical cancer, she had a dream that upset her deeply.

the evil magician

> I'm leading a little girl into an auditorium, and somehow she gets lost. As I try to find her, a young man dressed in black leads in an older evil-looking magician also dressed in black and has him lie on a couch. Suddenly I can sense which room the little girl is in. I realize to my horror that the magician has annihilated the girl whom I am responsible for. I attack his left arm and touch a green spot on it. I realize that I too am contaminated with the evil power of taking someone's soul, and I'm left with the feeling of being evil.

Dream themes of contamination and poisoning are common in people with cancer and other serious ailments. For Natalie, the Contamination dream didn't make sense until after her cervical cancer was diagnosed. Like Susan and others, Natalie later viewed this as a prodromal dream. The term *pro-dromal* refers to a symptom that appears before the outbreak of a disease that gives some clue to the nature and severity of the illness to come.[4] Pro-dromal dreams often reveal an internal physiological condition before there is conscious awareness of the illness.[5]

Death and the threat of death may be represented by the intrusion of a stranger and at times by the color black, although this varies in different cultures and with different individuals. Natalie's evil, murderous magician may have been a personification of the cancer that was growing within her. Later Natalie came to feel that the magician and the poisonous green spot had other important meanings besides the cancer. They represented her dark side, the part of us that Jung called the shadow, the unacceptable and scorned attributes of our personality. Part of the courageous struggle that Natalie would wage in her fight against cancer would be to overcome the deadly aspect of the poison and to find the green or life-giving aspect of herself.

Dr. Robert Smith of the Department of Psychiatry at Michigan State University has been researching the relationship of dream content to recovery from heart disease and other serious ailments. He has found that men who had dreams featuring death themes and women who dreamed of separation themes recovered more poorly and had a higher death rate than others who suffered heart attacks.[6]

Other researchers have found a recurrent theme of heat in dreams of people suffering from thyroid disorders.[7] Cancer surgeon Bernie Siegel, in his book *Peace, Love and Healing,* described a journalist who had a prodro-mal dream about being tortured by hot coals placed on his throat, searing his larynx. Simultaneously, his girlfriend dreamed that the two of them were in a bed that was filling up with blood. When they discussed their dreams, he found himself blurting out that he had throat cancer, though no such con-dition had been diagnosed. Soon he had another dream that featured a group of medicine men circling around him and sticking hypodermics into what they were calling his "neck brain."[8]

A few months later he began having symptoms and went to see a doctor. Upon initial evaluation, all of his tests were normal, and the doctor expressed skepticism about the dream-inspired self-diagnosis. When pressed, the doctor reluctantly scheduled further tests. When they were completed, a diagnosis of thyroid cancer was confirmed.

C. G. Jung and other Jungian analysts have observed that afflicted animals in dreams may predict illness and also may provide an indication of the recovery process. Jung and his colleague Marie-Louise von Franz have written about horse symbolism in dreams as an archetypal or universal symbol of the unconscious or animal life of the body, connected to our instincts and aliveness.

Jung was consulted in the case of Marie, a seventeen-year-old girl whom one specialist had been diagnosed as suffering from a disease of progressive muscle atrophy and another had diagnosed as suffering from hysteria. When Jung inquired about her dreams, Marie said that she'd been plagued by nightmares. Her recent dreams included one in which her mother was hanged and another about a frightened horse that jumped out a fourth-floor window and ended up mangled in the street below.

In mythology, horses have heralded death, and in reality, horses are subject to stampede behavior. For Jung, the panicked self-destructive horse was a symbol of out-of-control biological forces at work in the girl's body—forces that she was not consciously aware of. Jung felt that the morbid symbolism was forecasting a more serious diagnosis; in fact, her doctors later confirmed a fatal prognosis.[9]

Von Franz reported another horse dream in a sixty-one-year-old cavalry officer who died unexpectedly of heart failure four weeks after having the following dream, the setting of which was his days in officer training school thirty years earlier.

DISCOVERING THE HORSE IN THE LEAD COFFIN

An old corporal, who in reality had the meaningful name of "Adam," appeared and said to him, "Mr. Lieutenant, I must show you something." He led the lieutenant down into the cellar of the barracks and opened a door—made of lead! The dreamer recoiled with a shudder. In front of him, the carcass of a horse lay on its back, completely decomposed and emanating an awful smell.[10]

For von Franz, the horse in the dream took on further dimensions because it was intimately connected to the officer's lifework as a mounted soldier. In his dream, the horse may have symbolized the instrument of his work as well as his life force. The dream's setting, back at the beginning of his career, and his horse's death suggested that his career cycle was ending.

The value of exploring such afflicted animal dreams is not in making concrete predictions. Dreaming of a dead horse or an earthquake does not mean that we are doomed or will soon be afflicted with a life-threatening illness! But our dreams may reflect processes in our body of which we are not yet consciously aware. This is especially true if those changes impact our physical survival. Disturbing dreams are an inner warning when we face both emotional and physical crises.

Heeding these warnings is not as simple as looking at a thermometer. Rather than using our dreams to make concrete predictions, we can consider the cues we receive and explore whether there is some aspect of our physical health that we need to evaluate. This may help us to discover a health problem through intuitive and emotional reactions to our dreams.

Our Inner Response to Illness

When we are stricken with an illness or injury, when we receive a diagnosis of a life-threatening ailment, or when we go through surgery, our dreams express uncensored emotional reactions to the dangerous physical situation that we are enduring. Dreams contain important messages that can guide the emotional healing that complements any medical treatments we receive.

In some cultures, dreams at the onset of illness are believed to contain crucial information about the healing rituals that are necessary for a cure. For example, according to anthropologist Jackson Lincoln, the Navajo believe that some dreams are the cause of illness either through their content or by their effect on the dreamer.[11] They believe that illness emanates from the spirits of dead men or animals who enter dreams and afflict people.[12]

The Navajo also believe that dreams prescribe specific curing rituals, such as herbal treatments, songs, or ceremonial dances. They refer to specific dream symbols when selecting from the repertoire of possible healing techniques. For example, dreams of death (of oneself, neighbors, or others) and dreams of teeth falling out were considered particularly ominous and required a special chant. Other dream symbols called for chants or dances that involved other tribal members and served to increase emotional support for the dreamer.[13]

Western medicine needs to pay more careful attention to dreams in diagnosis and treatment planning as the Navajo do. We would be wise to include a closer look at dreams as part of our approach to treating and healing people during bouts of serious illness.

A dramatic feature of dreams at the onset of illness is that they contain graphic images of biological reactions to the dangers the dreamer is facing. In many instances these images are transparent references to the specific disease. For example, one dreamer with multiple sclerosis, a disease that withers the nervous system, dreamed that she stepped on and paralyzed a tarantula.[14]

In my work with cancer patients, I found evidence that specific types of cancer may be represented in dreams by recurrent images related to the site of the cancer and the meaning of the illness to that person. This is consistent with the research of psychologists Meredith Sabini and Valerie Maffly, indicating that some forms of cancer may be symbolically linked to unresolved grief and other deep psychological conflicts.[15]

Two of the women that I interviewed who suffered from cervical cancer had Contamination dreams about their mouths and lips at the onset of their awareness of being ill. Ruth had her dream the night before going to visit her gynecologist to get the results of a Pap smear that was part of a routine physical. She didn't consciously anticipate that she would be receiving a diagnosis of cervical cancer.

my DIRty moutH

I am riding in a bus to see my former gynecologist. The bus driver says, "You are disgusting." I realize that my mouth is dirty and there are sores on my skin around my lips and in my mouth. I notice that I am sitting in a section of the bus reserved for handicapped elderly people.

Ruth was shocked and angry when she received her diagnosis and a recommendation that she undergo a hysterectomy. The images in her dream came to her repeatedly in the days that followed.

At first her dirty mouth dream felt like a prediction or even a metaphoric description of her reactions to her illness. She felt that the diseased lips and inside of her mouth were symbolic of the lips of her vagina and the interior of her womb. The reference to the elderly section of the bus related to the stigma of feeling ill and old, perhaps even close to death. She also felt humiliated by the bus driver's cruel remarks and frustrated that she was relegated to the disabled section. This reminded her of the difficulties that she had experienced with her ex-husband and other men.

Ruth had always been a strong proponent of women's rights. As a journalist, she'd written stories that had exposed the way women experienced discrimination in the workplace and in relationships. For Ruth, being yelled at by a cruel male driver and forced to sit separately reminded her of the oppression that she felt as a woman and campaigned against in her professional work.

Ruth wondered why the doctor in her Contamination dream was her former gynecologist and not her present one. As she thought about this, she remembered that he had left traditional medicine and now practiced a form of alternative medicine that involved the use of imagery and other New Age healing techniques. This part of the dream intrigued Ruth and helped her decide to refuse the hysterectomy and pursue various forms of psychological and alternative treatments.

Natalie was also shocked and overwhelmed when she learned of her malignant cervical cancer. She found herself denying that it was true. After a second opinion, the reality began to set in. "I felt wounded and ashamed, and I felt betrayed that this could have happened to me, especially at the high point of my life." Natalie was fiercely determined not to have a hysterectomy despite the opinion of three doctors and her friends and family. Shortly after being diagnosed, she had the following dream.

oral birth of my cat's kittens

My cat, Celeste, is having kittens, and I suddenly become her, with my own face. My lips become very sensitive and swollen. Out of my mouth comes a gray sac, and I see myself giving birth to my cat's kittens.

Natalie felt that her oral birth dream was a diagnosis dream that described her condition at the onset of her illness. The swollen lips in her dream seemed to describe her physical state and her need for a hysterectomy (the removal of the gray sac). As Natalie explored her dream, it took on meanings that went beyond a mere physical description of the nature and site of her illness. The dream had a malevolent feeling. The oral birth seemed unnatural. Natalie saw herself as unexpressive emotionally, so she was shocked that her mouth would produce something as incredible as the birth of kittens.

Although the dream was frightening, it affected Natalie deeply in a positive way. She realized that something was changing inside her psyche. She became convinced that she wanted to marry and have a child. She realized that a good part of her motivation in refusing or delaying the hysterectomy was that she didn't want to foreclose the option of childbirth, even if it meant running the risk of death if the cancer spread quickly.

Like Ruth, Natalie saw this initial dream as revealing crucial psychological blocks that she felt may even have contributed to her illness. She wasn't sure whether emotional conflicts could cause cancer, but she was convinced that awareness of her illness was giving her a powerful impetus to heal emotional wounds that she had never before felt the strength to face.

Susan, whose dreams we examined earlier, had a series of important dreams just after undergoing a modified radical mastectomy. On the second day after her surgery, Susan had a Left-Out dream that related to her struggle to adjust to her new body image and to keep up hope in the face of her sudden life-threatening illness. The dreams in this series always featured images of bathing in hot tubs and swimming pools.

the otHeR womeN's BRutaL staRes

> I am with my best friend and am changing into a bathing suit so we can go in a hot tub. I am changing into a one-piece bathing suit that is low cut. I feel great, and I'm excited to be there. We get in the circular hot tub. There are a few others seated around the edge. Each of them is pushing water in unison with their feet. Two women are staring at me and looking at me funny. I look down at my chest and realize that I only have one breast. I'm frightened and run away. I meet an older woman who reassures me not to pay any attention to their critical stares.

Susan woke up sobbing hysterically. She felt that her dream was exaggerating her loss. She was now different from the other women in the hot tub with normal bodies. The terrible loss of her breast seemed hard to bear.

As she explored the different parts of her dream, she began to see it in different ways. The first part of the dream seemed to portray the period just prior to the diagnosis, a time of excitement about her life and possibilities. In the middle of that happy period, the cancer and mastectomy devastated her emotionally.

It was difficult for Susan to break the spell of this nightmare. But as she read it over again and talked about it, she began to think about the end of the dream, when an older woman reassured her and told her not to be swayed by the intolerance of other women or the sense of being different. This Inner Mentor dream theme can be linked to what Jung might have called "The Old Wise Woman," a personification of the feminine aspect of the inner guide or healer within us. Susan was able to receive and be comforted by the inner guidance of the wise old woman in her dream. In reality, Susan was learning to reach out to her friends and rely on them during dark moments of hopelessness.

Susan began to take some comfort from the ending of her brutal stares dream. As in her Prodromal dream of surviving a cataclysmic earthquake, there is a concluding hopeful note that helped bolster Susan's sense of optimism.

Dreams and Psychosomatic Illness

There is some evidence that dreams may be implicated in triggering physiological crises in people who are prone to suffer certain ailments, such as asthma, arthritis, miscarriage, and posttraumatic stress disorder (see chapter 8). In most of these cases, it's impossible to distinguish whether the dream triggers the episode of illness or whether the dream portrays the biological distress at the moment it occurs.

Psychiatrist Harold Levitan has conducted extensive research on the prodromal dreams of psychosomatic patients and has identified fascinating patterns in the dreams of people who suffer from asthma and arthritis. Levitan believes that, for those people who are predisposed to illnesses that may be exacerbated by stress, dreams may trigger an incident of illness.[16]

Levitan focused one of his studies on the dream patterns of people suffering from acute asthma. He identified four highly repetitive themes in the dreams immediately preceding a nocturnal asthma attack. The themes included being violently attacked by others, attacking or victimizing someone else, active or passive involvement in incest, and powerful emotions experienced by someone other than the dreamer in the dream.

For asthmatics and others who suffer from psychosomatic illnesses, the dream state may be a time of particular vulnerability, a nocturnal Achilles heel. Levitan believes this is because of the emotional impact of how we experience traumatic events in dreams. We are much more likely to witness a brutal attack or even a murder in a dream than we are in waking life. People with psychosomatic disorders tend to be less able to cope with strong emotions such as rage or grief in waking life and are even more overwhelmed by emotion in the sensitive arena of dreams. According to Levitan, an especially violent dream in an asthmatic may actually create a physical reaction that sets an asthma attack in motion.[17]

If you or a friend suffer from asthma, rheumatoid arthritis, hypertension, or other psychosomatic disorders, exploring your prodromal nightmares may be difficult, but they can give you important clues about underlying emotional issues that may trigger an episode of illness. When the nightmares are especially violent and seem to worsen your physical condition, it would be advisable to seek treatment from a mental health professional who can coordinate your treatment with the physician who treats your physical disorder.

Obstacles and Breakthroughs: Dreams and the Stages of Illness

Monitoring our dreams during bouts of serious illness can provide us with important sources of information. We can see the unfolding stages of our reaction to illness and get a sense of whether we are recovering or have reached an impasse. Occasionally, treatment strategies are inspired by or explicitly suggested in dreams.

Toward the end of five months of chemotherapy, Susan was feeling a stronger sense of hope that the treatments would prevent a recurrence.

Periodically, however, she had dreams that frightened her and nearly cata-
pulted her into a pit of depression. She dreamed once of a group of women
being massacred and another time of women being hanged. She would try
to save them but would fail. In one dream she was barely able to resuscitate
her sister, who had become unconscious while taking a bath. Just before
learning the outcome of her chemotherapy, she had the following Car
Crash dream.

THE MIRACLE OF THE CAR CRASH

I am buying some plants to give to a friend for his birthday. I get into a
long line to pay. The clerk is cleaning up a lot of blood on the counter
from a woman who had an abortion. The clerk is sympathetic to the
woman. In my left hand, I am horrified to see a bloody towel with the
head of the fetus that was aborted. Then the scene switches, and I see a
guy who I used to go out with. He seems very infatuated with me in an
aggressive way. He keeps insisting on a relationship. I feel frustrated and
annoyed and ask one of the clerks to call the police. I wait for the police
to take me home, but I'm still afraid the guy will come back and hurt me.
I finally see the police car arrive. Out of the darkness, a bright orange car
appears. It is totally out of control and smashes into the garage at high
speed. I was shocked by it all. The man from the store goes to check on
the driver, who I think must be dead. They come back with a baby, who
it turns out is unharmed. Everyone is cheering that the baby was healthy.

Susan woke up feeling incredibly relieved. Although some of the imagery was
horrifying, she felt that it was a recovery and rebirth dream, confirming what
she knew—that she had survived the fearful "accident" of being hit by cancer.

As Susan explored her dream, she focused on the image of the bloody
aborted fetus. It seemed to symbolize the blood and guts of her surgery and
her fear that it would have been abortive. The man insisting on a relationship reminded her of her ex-husband and other men who had dominated
her. Her relationships with men were a crucial psychological issue that the
cancer had inspired her to focus on. The dream suggested to Susan that she
had made progress in dealing with pushy men. She would no longer tolerate
their insensitive advances and would seek help in dealing with this issue. In
the dream, the authority she sought was the police. In waking life, she was
finding an inner sense of authoritativeness.

The car crash and its miraculous aftermath were the most vivid features
of the dream. Dream images of cars going out of control have been associated with the growth of cancer cells. Susan associated the bright orange car

smashing into her garage with the shock of the cancer invading her body. She viewed the driver who is presumed to be dead as her own fears of death. The miraculous transformation of the bloody fetus into an unharmed baby at the end of the dream is a magical reversal of doom. Despite the dream's gory aspects, the happy ending gave her hope and reassurance that her own recovery would continue.

John Prendergast's research on dreams of people with life-threatening illnesses revealed that rebirth imagery is common in people who have experienced a remission. It is less common in terminal patients or in those who are entirely well. Dreams of rebirth, miraculous recovery, and renovation projects in those recovering from life-threatening illness symbolize a sense of relief, creative renewal, and triumph over adversity.[18]

After being diagnosed with cervical cancer, Natalie had a dream that strongly influenced her decision to forgo surgery and pursue nontraditional treatment approaches.

fINDINg my pLace IN tHe wave

I am diving into waves, going back and forth from the water to the beach. I dive into a very large wave in slow motion and sink to the bottom. I find it very peaceful on the bottom of the wave. It feels like I will be able to withstand the immersion until I come out of the wave.

At the beginning of the dream, her flexibility of going in and out of the water struck Natalie as out of character. Before her cancer, she had been more rigid personally, and the dream portrayed a new image of who she was becoming. Natalie was especially impressed by the image of the wave. She felt that it represented her cancer. It seemed overwhelming, but somehow she was able to slow down the motion, submerge, and trust that she would be able to survive.

Her wave dream gave Natalie a sense that it would be safe to take the risk of delaying a hysterectomy until she was sure that it would be right for her. Because of her refusal to follow the recommendation for surgery, Natalie had great difficulty in finding a doctor who would treat her medically because the doctors feared malpractice suits if her cancer worsened.

Natalie felt that her cervical cancer was "a wound of the feminine," related to the trauma she had experienced growing up with her mother. The belief that a cancer can be related to particular psychological conflicts is controversial. However, it is interesting to note that Natalie, Ruth, and other women have linked wounds in their relationship with their mother as causative factors in their cervical cancer.

Jungian analysts have emphasized that there may be a link between a cancer's site and profound losses. Using evidence from dreams and psychotherapy sessions, they have speculated that the development of cancer may result in part from old emotional wounds such as the death, desertion, or emotional unavailability of a parent.[19] Whether these speculations will prove true remains to be seen. One thing is clear from my own research on cancer patients' dreams: the dreamer often feels a strong subjective sense that the nature of the cancer has a psychological meaning.

In any case, resolving her troubled maternal relationship was a crucial dimension of Natalie's psychological recovery. She realized that this conflict had held her back from wanting to have children. She hadn't wanted to risk perpetrating on anyone else the emotional neglect that she had suffered. She felt that some of the rigidities in her personality and her inability to express herself were linked to her mother's insensitivity.

As time passed, Natalie spent many hours grieving the loss of her grand-mother, who had died when she was ten. This grandmother had been much warmer and more loving than Natalie's mother. Natalie had internal fantasy dialogues with her grandmother about whether or not surgery was the right decision. A crucial turning point occurred for Natalie after she had the following dream.

Leaving my mother and grandmother behind

My mother, my grandmother, and I were all taking my grandmother to a college where she will be studying. We are looking for her dorm room, and I want to make sure she will be OK. We find the room and all say good-byes. As it turns out, I say good-bye to both my mother and my grandmother and leave.

For Natalie, this dream was pivotal in helping her understand the need to resolve her relationship with her mother and grandmother. The college setting reminded her of when she left home for the first time. For Natalie, the separation from her grandmother in the dream felt more like an incorporation of her love and support. Leaving her mother, however, symbolized breaking free of the deprivation and rejection that she suffered during childhood.

Two years after her initial diagnosis, Natalie married and gave birth to a daughter. The oral birth dream took on a new level of meaning. She not only learned to express her feelings, she felt ready to accept the challenge of loving and caring for her daughter in a way that would be different from the pattern with her own mother.

She ultimately did choose to undergo a hysterectomy when her daughter was four months old. Almost eleven years after her initial diagnosis, she hasn't had a recurrence of cancer. Through a confrontation with death, Natalie learned to live by the guidance of her dreams. In so doing, she discovered unexpected new dimensions in her ability to love herself and express love for others.

Dreams of People Approaching Death

Recurrent symbols and themes seem to appear in the dreams of people who are approaching death. Some are inspiring images. Others are more disturbing or confusing. Most of the dreams suggest an inner struggle to acknowledge and accept what the dreamer knows is about to happen. Even when the dreamer is consciously denying or fighting the inevitable, the images reveal the psyche's attempt to prepare for a transformative experience.

Carl Jung's last reported dream, just days before his death, featured an image of a mandala (a Hindu magic circle) that was similar to the symbolic patterns he had observed in his patients during periods of psychological and spiritual growth and change.

THE STONE OF WHOLENESS

There was a "great round stone in a high place, a barren square, and on it were engraved the words: 'And this shall be a sign unto you of Wholeness and Oneness.'" There were also "many vessels to the right in an open square and a quadrangle of trees whose roots reached around the earth and enveloped him and among the roots, golden threads were glittering."[20]

The image of the gilded tree of life carved on a stone for eternity suggests that Jung had reached an acceptance of his imminent death. His mandala dream reveals a final sense of fulfillment about his lifelong work with the healing power of imagery in dreams, mythology, mysticism, and the arts.

Threshold of Death Dreams

Dying peoples' dreams contain fewer characters and a greater degree of separation and aloneness than in other periods of life. There is often a sense of loss that is not resolved at the end of the dream. In some cases, death appears as a stranger approaching or stalking the dreamer. The dreamer frequently is a target of violence or a victim of cataclysmic events such as tidal waves and earthquakes, which are symbolic of the overwhelming natural force that is about to overtake them.[21]

A dramatic and recurrent theme is that of clocks and the limitations of time. Jungian analyst Marie-Louise von Franz cites the following Limited Time dream of a man on the verge of death.

the end of time

He sees the clock on the mantelpiece; the hands have been moving but now they stop; as they stop, a window opens behind the mantelpiece clock and a bright light shines through. The opening widens into a door and the light becomes a brilliant path. He walks out on the path of light and disappears.[22]

Von Franz associates the window with an alchemical term, *fenestra aeternitatis,* Latin for "window into eternity."[23] The dream appears to be picturing not only the sense that time has run out, but a view and a pathway into an afterlife or other reality.

Despite the alluring light of possible afterlife in the dream above, imagery of rebirth is common in people recovering from serious illness but not in those who are dying.[24]

Life-threatening illnesses can offer us a heightened opportunity for psychological growth and awareness. The sense that death is near may stimulate the desire to resolve important relationships and to express hidden feelings before it's too late. Discussing and exploring our dreams can be very valuable, especially in the days and weeks prior to death. Dream sharing helps the dreamer to process his or her emotional reactions to the imminence of death, to overcome denial, and to find the energy to finish old business in the outer and inner worlds.

Dr. Susan Fair related the following dream series of a man dying of AIDS. She was therapist to Earl, a thirty-year-old black man who had worked for the post office as a supervising clerk for twelve years. At their second meeting, Earl asked Dr. Fair whether she was going to write a book about him. He encouraged her to do so in order for others to benefit from understanding "my awful disease." Earl's story and his dreams are presented here with his permission, as his dying gift to others who suffer from AIDS and to their families and friends.

Earl had been in and out of the hospital for a variety of serious ailments related to AIDS. Early in his therapy with Dr. Fair, Earl's illness worsened and he became bitter and suspicious of everyone who tried to help him. One day he screamed at Dr. Fair and railed at the unfairness of life.

Their work became more intensive when Earl was hospitalized for the final time, two weeks before he died. They met for short periods two or more times a day. Earl began to sense that he was failing and said that he had "no more reserves to fight the battle." At times it was difficult for him to speak. He asked Dr. Fair to read to him and suggested *The Wizard of Oz,* which had been a childhood favorite. He wanted her to read only a little bit each time—apparently so she wouldn't reach the end of the story.

A week before his death, he requested that he be taken off all medication except for pain pills. The next day he made a point of telling her about a vivid dream that took him to the edge of the realm of death.

CRAWLING TO FREEDOM

I am crawling on the dirt floor of a cabin. I have to crawl through it to escape. It reminds me of slaves in the South escaping to freedom through the Underground Railroad.

Earl was frightened by his dream but curious about what it meant. He seemed to perk up as if he had saved up his alertness and strength to tell his dream and explore its meaning. The reference to slaves puzzled him. It reminded him of stories he had read about slaves who made dangerous but successful escapes to freedom with the help of others as they fled the South. For Earl, the metaphor of escape from slavery revealed his sense that he was near death and that the freedom he was seeking might be a release from the slavery of his terribly sick body. He felt that the dirt floor represented the poverty of his childhood and his enslaved ancestors as well as the basic level of existence he was left with.

The crawling escape was scary for Earl. Dr. Fair suggested that it might be an image of dying—going through the feared transition out of the house of his physical being. At the end of their meeting, Earl seemed comforted by both the fears he had expressed and the sense of hope that remained after discussing the issue of slavery.

Three days before death, Earl's body was deteriorating fast. He was incontinent and could not get out of bed. But he perked up once again and reported the following dream with a sense of urgency.

A CAGED ANIMAL

I am in a zoo instead of a hospital. The same people are around me, the nurses and doctors and patients, but it is a zoo cage instead of a hospital room. It feels very strange that I am in the cage and they are outside. I feel a strong desire to get out and demand that they let me out. They ask me where I would go, and I say I don't know. I just want to get out.

Dr. Fair suggested to Earl that his Trapped dreams were pictures of his feelings. He said, "I guess I must really feel trapped." Taking the cue from Earl, Dr. Fair further suggested that he might feel that it was hard to watch life going on all around him and see all the people watching him who couldn't help. He said this made sense. He talked about his frustration at being weak and no longer able to make his body do what he wanted.

The evening before he died, Earl again became alert when Dr. Fair entered the room. This time he reported what she surmised was a hallucination.

a feast of CHINese fooD

I am wide awake, and I look at the hospital table, and there is lots of delicious food there—Chinese food like fried rice and pot stickers—my favorite dishes. I can even smell it.

Dr. Fair reassured him that he was probably having a hallucination due to a lack of oxygen. He asked her if the food was really there. She said it wasn't, but that he should enjoy it anyway. He smiled weakly and said that he had always loved Chinese food. She continued her reading of *The Wizard of Oz*. Earl never got to hear the end of the story. He died peacefully the next morning.

What Dreams Can Teach Us During Illnesses

Illness forces us to face the finiteness of our physical existence. Our unconscious becomes sensitized to the physical threat that illness represents. When we sense that we may have less time left, we become concerned with resolving deep conflicts. In this way serious illness can spark a psychological turning point that inspires personal growth.

Dreams can help us turn the suffering of an illness into an opportunity for becoming more fully alive. As we work out solutions to problems from the past and present, we may discover new sources of hope that can influence our ability to recover our physical well-being.

Dreams allow us to monitor vital information (in the form of images and symbols) that can help us understand the emotional factors that influence the onset of and recovery from an illness. They may occasionally foreshadow illness, picturing physical changes in our health that we aren't yet aware of. And they can help us see what stage we have reached in our response to an illness.

It is important to keep in mind that most dreams are symbolic and should not be taken literally. However, when we use the images, stories, and feelings from our dreams as a jumping-off point for further exploration, we can take advantage of their healing power. Exploring our dreams helps us to tune in to the vital resources of our own intuition, allowing us to be more actively engaged in whatever form of medical treatment we seek.

When we or our family members approach death, sharing and listening to dreams can help us overcome denial, resolve lingering issues, and find new sources of meaning even in the final weeks of life.

Listening to the dreams of those who are injured, ill, or dying can enhance the lives of those of us who are well. We can connect more deeply with our friends and relatives at a time of crisis, feel rewarded by our efforts to help, understand our own reactions to illness and death, and witness the drama of emotional healing that may accompany the experience of illness.

Listening to the dreams of the dying doesn't require fancy interpretations. Through our empathic listening, the dying person can feel reassured and understood at a crucial time of fear and confusion.

10. grief dreams
resolving the loss
of a loved one

Doug's father died just six weeks after being diagnosed with pancreatic cancer. In the weeks following his father's death, Doug experienced a terrible case of insomnia. He was waking up and remembering three and four dreams each night. Many of them were nightmares that left him in a cold sweat and terrified to go back to sleep. He said he was "feeling open and raw, as if I had lost a protective coating."

Soon after his father received the terminal diagnosis, Doug had a terrifying dream in which he was trying to erect defenses to shelter his home and his family from imminent nuclear war. At the end of this Apocalyptic dream, he heard on the radio that missiles had been launched, and he lay on the floor bracing for the explosion. He wasn't sure whether his house would withstand the blast. When he explored this dream, Doug felt that the inevitability of the nuclear attack related to anticipating the pain of losing his father. The house and its defense represented him and his own psychological defenses, which were threatened by the news of his father's grave illness.

After his father had undergone a final unsuccessful operation just prior to his death, Doug dreamed that he was attacked by menacing thieves and stabbed with spears. Although the spears went through him, he was somehow able to survive. Doug immediately associated the spears with the surgery. In his dream he was empathizing with his father's suffering, being sliced by the surgeon's knife and barely surviving.

Doug's empathy with his father continued in a powerful dream one month after his father's death. In this dream, which took him to the threshold of death, Doug's relationship with his young daughter paralleled his relationship with his own father.

CROSSING INTO THE LIGHT WITHOUT MY DAUGHTER

I'm standing in a hallway with my one-year-old daughter in my arms. I'm facing a couple of double-swinging hospital doors made of aluminum. I know that I have to go through the doors into the room beyond. There are small windows in the swinging doors so I can get a feel for the other room. It is very light in there, like a gymnasium. I am scared to go through the doors because I'm afraid that something will attack me, like some kind of demon that will be very dangerous and that I can't subject my daughter to. She is upset and crying for me and not wanting me to put her down. I know I have to go through the doors, and I can't bring her with me. I am broken up but can't take her. I go through the doors to the brightest place that I have ever been to in my life. It opens expansively and is blindingly light. I sense that my deepest fear is there, but don't know how it will materialize. I hear my daughter crying on the other side, and I'm terrified. I wake up in a cold sweat.

His Threshold of Death dream was excruciating. For Doug, the blinding intensity of the room he had entered and the demonic forces lurking there represented death—the world beyond, where his father had gone. He was troubled by the fact that his dream appeared to portray his own symbolic death. Was it telling him that he too would soon die, leaving his infant daughter fatherless?

As Doug explored his dream, he realized that it had to do with his grief, not any physical danger or illness that he was facing. Through his unconscious empathy with his father, his dreams were allowing him to go in his father's place, to suffer the spears of surgery and the atomic blast of death and ultimately to enter the world of the dead with its mystical blazing light.

As he continued to explore his Threshold of Death dream, Doug was most upset about having to leave his daughter behind. Although he had been extremely happy to become a father for the first time at age forty, his dream left him preoccupied with the thought that someday he would have to say good-bye to his daughter, abandon her, and travel to the world of death, just as his father had done to him. Doug realized that his daughter's tears and separation anxiety in the dream symbolized his own sadness. He felt that his dreams helped him understand not only his attachment to his father but also the significance of his relationship with his daughter.

Three months after his father's death, Doug continued to have some disturbing dreams about his father, but they were less frequent and their impact did not linger. His insomnia improved, and he began to have a series of dreams about remodeling his house—adding rooms, redesigning his study, and fixing up the interior walls. The room with the bright light that represented death in his earlier dreams was beginning to take on a new form, representing growth in his own personality that had been stimulated by his father's death.

Threshold of Death dreams depict characters at death's door or crossing over to the realm of the dead. Doug's grief dream paradoxically portrayed both raw terror and a white light so blinding it could only be compared to the visions of religious mystics. Threshold of Death dreams are often associated with dreamers who are grieving, close to death, or close to someone who has died or come close to death. At life's turning points these dreams may symbolize grieving other losses, painfully shedding old identities, changes in cherished relationships, physical transformations related to aging, or other issues the dreamer may be grieving. For the bereaved, when time has passed, dream visits to the realm of death and dying may be a prelude to a rebirth of the spirit, a lifting of depression, or a resolution of grief.

Resolving Grief through Dreams

When someone close to us dies, we begin a process of grieving that may last for months or years. Because our culture tends to deny the profound psychological impact of death and we lack adequate rituals to guide us through this turning point, we are often at risk during the stages of mourning. If our grieving does not progress, we may succumb to its dark, depressive pull and become paralyzed. We may be unable to accept the loss or restore a sense of hope and continuity in our life. On the other hand, suffering a loss can become a transformative experience that leads to a deeper resolution of our relationship with the person who has died.

The focus of this chapter is on understanding the patterns in dreams during the grieving process. We will look at how exploring dreams can help us recover from the emotional devastation of loss and transform it into a new beginning. We'll also examine the symbolic meaning of death and dead people in dreams.

During the grieving process, our dreams give us access to the emotions that we endure—sadness, anger, fear. They also help us to see whether we are caught in the common impasses of grief, such as denial, depression, withdrawal, and substance abuse. Our dreams help us to see the slow evolution of our reactions to death and loss through acceptance, catharsis, detachment, and finding new involvements and relationships.

Reunion with the Dead Dreams

Dreams provide crucial guidance in the vulnerable period of adapting to the death of a loved one at any stage of the grieving process. If we pay attention to our dreams, we can observe vivid appearances of the deceased person. They may be calling out to us in pain or sadness or appearing serene in otherworldly surroundings, suggesting that they've made it to a heavenly place of repose.

Early in the grieving process, the appearance of the deceased person in a dream is disturbing. When we awaken, the contrast between the dream and the fact of the person's death is jarring. The person seems so real in our dreams, more alive than ever. Many cultures accept the notion that through dreams, we have our greatest opportunity to achieve real contact with the spirits of the dead.

In some cultures, events during dreaming are considered to be a crucial part of the grieving process. Bereaved members of the Negrito tribe of the Philippines do not hold a funeral feast until the dead person appears in several of their close relatives' dreams.[1]

In contemporary urban Thailand, after a death, family members discuss their dreams together to hold on to their connection with the deceased. Even the children learn to share their dreams and search for references to the dead person. This informal ritual of dream sharing promotes emotional sharing and facilitates the resolution of grief.[2]

For those people whose religious beliefs include an afterlife and the possibility of true contact with dead spirits, these Reunion with the Dead dreams offer a way to work out their unresolved issues with the dead person before their spirit fades. In Thai culture, if one dreams of a relative immediately after his or her death, the dreamer pays the clergy homage to ensure that the relative reaches a safe sanctuary.

Whether we view the appearance of dead relatives as a psychological manifestation or actual communication with the dead, dreams can be helpful in many ways during the grieving process. Reunion with the Dead dreams may occur for months or even years after the death of a close relative or friend. They are perhaps the most easily recognizable and common grief-related dream theme because of the overt appearance of the deceased. Dreams are more often painful in the early stages of grief. As grieving progresses, Grief dreams may continue to be intermittently distressing but frequently become less anguishing and more reassuring and meaningful as time passes and the impact of the loss is slowly emotionally digested.

The Benefits of Exploring Grief Dreams

We don't have to wait for the deceased person to make an appearance in our dreams to benefit from the wisdom of our dreams. Deeper exploration of almost any of our dreams during a period of acute grief will help us to:

* overcome denial, acknowledge the loss, and mourn more openly

* express and resolve troubling feelings stemming from the death, such as rage, abandonment, or even relief

* recognize when we are afflicted with grief-related depression or suicidal urges

* relieve guilt and self-reproach connected to the death

* honor our attachment to the deceased person by reviewing memories and beginning to integrate positive aspects of our relationship with the deceased

* acknowledge the spiritual dimension of grief

* confront our own mortality

How Dreams Reveal the Stages of Grieving

Psychological studies of bereavement support the notion that reactions to a death unfold in stages. Elisabeth Kübler-Ross popularized the notion of the stages of grief in her book *On Death and Dying*. She proposed five stages of reacting to the inevitability of one's own death, which are also applicable to facing the death of a loved one. The stages are denial, rage, bargaining, depression, and acceptance.[3] Another valuable way to conceptualize the evolution of grieving is as a three-part process that involves (1) overcoming denial and accepting the reality of the loss, (2) letting go of emotional ties to the dead person, and (3) becoming ready to form new relationships and move forward in life.[4]

Different conceptualizations of the stages of grief can give us helpful lenses to view and compare our experiences as we grieve. However, many years of experience as a clinical psychologist have convinced me that not everyone goes through all the stages, and they may occur in a different order for some people.

Although the map of the stages may vary by individual and in different cultures, there is definitely an evolutionary process that can be seen in the dreams of the bereaved. At first there may be an increase in the number of dreams and nightmares that are recalled. However, in some cases, the dream spigot turns off, and the bereaved dreamer is frozen in an impasse without the ability to access dreams.

When grief dreams begin to flow, especially early in the grieving process, denial is a major theme. This early denial is not necessarily a sign of pathology or abnormal grieving. It is the way the psyche protects us from being over-whelmed and a chronicle of our struggle to gradually come to grips with a gut-wrenching loss. Denial of Grief dreams take many forms.

For those who do recall dreams in the initial grieving period, denial is a major theme. In many Denial of Grief dreams the dead person upsets or even taunts the dreamer and provokes a painful confusion about whether the death has really occurred. This theme is related to the struggle to over-come denial and accept the reality of the loss.

In other Denial of Grief dreams, life is back to normal or there is a return to the time prior to the deceased person's illness or demise. These dreams may be pleasant during the dream but are jarring when the bereaved dreamer awakens.

Based on her extensive collection of grief dreams, Patricia Garfield con-cluded that dreams featuring denials of death are extremely common early in the stages of grief. In these dreams, the deceased person appears, and the dreamer is surprised to see them or may not realize that they are, in fact, dead. These dreams can be excruciating as the reality of the loss becomes acute upon waking.[5]

Dream references to either the dreamer or the dead person undergoing separation, aloneness, or suffering are also common in the early stage of adjustment. For example, shortly after her mother's death, Padma, a physician who was raised in India, had repetitive dreams of seeing her mother dressed in black and appearing forlorn. She was worried about her mother, who had never liked to be alone while she was alive. In the dreams she tried to express her concerns, but her mother was unable to hear her.

Common dream themes in the middle stages of mourning include strug-gling to communicate with the dead person and expressing unresolved feel-ings of grief, anger, or guilt. Memories of past losses, such as previous deaths of people who were important to us, may surface. Evidence of loneliness, depression, and self-destructiveness may also appear.

Six years after her mother's death, Padma had a Rebirth dream that helped her see that she had finally worked out her grief about her mother's death. It was the first dream in which she experienced a clear resolution.

I can see my mother from a distance. It looks like the place where we used to spend our summer vacation. She seems younger and sprightlier, like she appeared before she became ill. I have a sense that all her karma had been paid for, and she was going to be reborn into a new life.

Like my own dream long after my grandfather's death (see the introduction, "In the Orange Grove with My Grandfather"), Padma's Rebirth dream gave her evidence that she had worked out long-standing conflicts about her loss.

Dreams can help us to confirm when a resolution is reached in the process of letting go of our attachment to a loved one. Dreams that herald this breakthrough may include some of the following themes:[6]

* peaceful images of the dead person from an earlier era, usually prior to their illness or aging

* appearances of the dead person as an angel, benevolent ghost, or spiritual being from a realm apart from the living

* words of comfort from the dead person or a sense of reassurance from the circumstances that the dead person appears in

* a focus on some positive quality of the dreamer's relationship with the dead person

* forgiveness emanating from the deceased person or from the dreamer

* receiving a gift or specific reassuring message from the dead person

Resolving the Loss of a Parent or Grandparent

The death of a parent or other close relative is usually the first major death-related loss that we experience. Our grieving is influenced by the nature of our relationship with the parent or grandparent, whether the loss was expected, the depth of our emotional support network, and the way we have coped with other losses in the past.

Whenever we suffer a loss, our reactions extend beyond the actual loss of visits, phone calls, and letters to and from the person. There are symbolic losses that are crucial to face if we are to transform a period of darkness into one of growth.

With a parent's death, we lose the sense of security that a parent will always be there to protect us and be an emotional or financial safety net.

With a parent's death, we confront our own mortality in a concrete way. Our illusions of immortality are shattered as we are thrust into the role of an elder in our family. There is awareness that ours will be the next generation to face death.

In the extended period of grieving, we must learn to cherish the memory of what our parents gave us. We also must learn to heal wounds from occasions when they failed us by not giving us the quality of empathy, attention, and love that we needed. I have observed that many adults in psychotherapy are caught up in a quest to win the approval and love from their parents that they were denied in childhood as a result of a divorce, severe economic stress, the birth of a sibling, or a parent's substance abuse or other psychological problems. When a parent dies, we must let go of the hidden hope that he or she will someday fill those needs. Facing those unresolved desires may provide a crucial opportunity for psychological growth—to mourn the lost love and find constructive ways to meet our needs in the present.

Desperately Searching Dreams

Terri felt a numbness following her father's death from cancer. She was depressed, empty, and barely able to maintain her responsibilities at work. Her grieving was at an impasse.

When Terri called to make an appointment to be interviewed, she could not remember a single dream from the two months since her father's death. On the following three nights, however, she had a series of dreams that she did remember. At the beginning of our first meeting, she said that the act of writing and sharing these dreams with her husband had made her more hopeful that she could overcome her grief and depression.

On the first night, Terri dreamed of her father's car, not his recent car but the one he had when she was ten years old in the period after her parents divorced.

SEARCHING THE TRUNK OF MY FATHER'S CAR

I am at my father's house, outside, looking in the trunk of his car. The stuff in the car is there for me to take. I'm gathering up things that I could carry out of the trunk: his golf clubs, his satchel, and his golf shoes. I am feeling in the dream that I had better take it now because he is going to be gone. But every time I pick anything up, it disappears.

The image of her father's old white Cadillac convertible with tall, pointed fins brought back a flood of memories for Terri. It was in that car that she used to spend part of her weekly Sunday visits with her father. He would take her to the golf course, then take her with him in his golf cart despite the rules against it. She even learned to enjoy playing golf with him as she grew older.

The car reminded Terri of the traumatic divorce. After the divorce, the car would always be filled with dirty and clean laundry, golf clubs, and files from his business. It always smelled like cigar smoke. She used to spend a lot of time sobbing in the backseat without her father knowing. She felt caught between her parents' animosity. Her mother constantly expressed hatred toward her father, refusing to speak to him for ten years after the divorce.

Although her father faithfully kept up his visits and did have a great sense of humor, he was never able to express any warmth or love for Terri directly. He always seemed to have a word of criticism about her weight or appearance. In recent years he had been incredibly stingy with her. In his will he gave all his money to his second wife. Toward the end, when Terri begged for some special mementos from him, he refused, as if he had some odd mental block about being generous to her. Before he died, Terri had wanted him to give her a special antique set of golf clubs. He gave them instead to a friend. He did give his current golf clubs to Terri's husband. On the day of her father's death, Terri spoke with him and told him she loved him. His response from the delirium of his deathbed was to inquire about her husband's recent golf scores.

For Terri, the disappearing goods in her father's car represented the golf clubs and the many other things that her father never gave her. At another level, they represented the direct expression of love and acceptance that he was never able to give.

The next night, Terri again dreamed about her father's old Cadillac. This time it was a more painful image.

Last CHANCE to get anything from my fatHER's CAR

My father's car is moving. The trunk is open, but there were fewer things in it, just his golf shoes and clubs and some clothes. I have a sense that this is the last time I'll be able to get anything from the trunk. The car is moving slowly, but I have to run faster and faster to try and catch it. I get my hands on some things but end up dropping them and falling behind the car as it moves away. As the dream ends, I have a strong desire to get something, anything, from the car.

Through discussing this Desperately Searching dream, Terri could feel her numbness lifting. The deprivation was feeling more acute and the memories more clear. The dream was telling her that her father's old car and its goods were no longer in her grasp. He was gone.

In her third dream, Terri's father appeared to her from the world beyond.

my fatHeR caLLINg my Name

I hear my father calling me by name . . . Terri, Terri, Terri. I can see his face now. It sounds so familiar, so real. I'm trying to find out where he was calling from. It seems like it is heaven or somewhere high up. I answer, "Dad, how are you?" And he says, "I'm OK. I think that it is harder for Peggy [his current wife] than it is for you." What he seems to mean is that he is in heaven and not suffering pain and grief, but we are. He seems to be living with some peace. I feel like I'm not!

Terri grew angry as she thought more about the end of her dream. Her father was worried about his second wife but not about her. He had been generous with his wife but not with Terri. Ultimately, Terri realized that the reason it had been difficult for her to mourn was that she was angry at him. She had been the one who was always supposed to take care of him and put out the raging fires of her parents' hatred for each other. She had never expressed that anger directly when he was alive, and since his death she had been afraid to stir up old wounds or to break the taboo against being angry at a dead person.

A month after her three-dream series, Terri had a further dream that focused even more clearly on the past. In this dream, she was trying to tell her father what she needed to hear him say before he died. She appeared as a young child pleading with him to say that he loved her.

Focusing on her dreams helped Terri to accelerate her stalled process of grieving. Her dreams precipitated feelings of loss and anger, crystallizing images of what was missing in her relationship with her father. By reexperiencing the lingering pain of her parents' divorce and her father's emotional shortcomings, she began to heal old wounds.

Adam, whose divorce dreams were explored in chapter 5, had two powerful dreams after his father's death. Adam's father and younger uncle were successful dentists who practiced together and were very close. Although it had been hidden and denied for many years, both men were addicted to drugs that were available through their practice. Adam had idealized his father and uncle and was deeply disturbed when he learned of their problems. He couldn't understand their addictive needs or why they would throw away success and happiness.

Survivor Guilt Dreams

Adam tried many times to convince his father to straighten out his life. Although he knew intellectually that he wasn't responsible, Adam couldn't shake the feeling that he should rescue his father. As his efforts failed and his father's problems became known publicly, Adam felt as if he was failing the older man. When his father died of an accidental overdose, Adam was devastated. In the weeks following the death, Adam had a recurring Survivor Guilt dream that upset him greatly.

my father is sucked down a manhole

My father is being sucked into a manhole. I am desperately trying to pull him out, but the dark, seething sewage water is sucking him down lower and lower. I strain with all my might, but I'm losing my grip and he is sinking. Though I keep struggling for what seems like an eternity, he is finally drawn down into the darkness and swept away.

In the dream, Adam's desperate attempts to rescue his father fail. To Adam, the dark, raging sewer waters represent the drugs and depression that captured his father and pulled him down from a life of integrity into one of disgrace.

Adam knew that his feelings for his father were unresolved and that the dream was telling him something about his inability to recover from the death. As the months went by, he began to understand that he needed to get over the guilt that was haunting him about failing to rescue his father. Part of his desperation came from a need to deny his father's fall from grace. He came to accept that his idealization of his father had been crushed, just as his idealization of his ex-wife had been shattered earlier. (See his dream, "The Fallen Idol," in chapter 5.) He had harbored fears that he would meet the same fate as his father: succumbing to alcohol or drugs and seeing his success and connection with his family deteriorate.

Spiritual Beings Dreams

As Adam continued to resolve his guilt and ultimately his anger at his father for disappointing him, his dreams began to change. After his uncle's death three years later, Adam's manhole dreams ceased and the dreams of his father often had a more spiritual quality. One dream in particular was a signal to Adam that he had reached a new level of acceptance and resolution.

I am seeing my father and his brother walking down the street together arm in arm. They're young again—two beautiful young men. It seems like they are floating along like angels, their feet not touching the ground.

In this Spiritual Beings dream, his father and uncle are close again and peaceful in a world beyond. Adam felt that he had worked through his guilt and anger and restored earlier positive memories of his father. Adam's Angels Walking dream has elements that are often present in the dreams of people who have resolved their grief over a parent or other deceased relative. It usually takes one or more years before this kind of Spiritual Beings dream appears.

Resolving the Loss of a Spouse

It's very difficult for widows and widowers to shake loose the cloud of depression and grief that hovers over them. Sarah, who had been married to Harry for forty-nine years, knew that cancer would soon claim his life. During his illness, he prepared her for his departure, teaching her how to manage the family finances and maintain the house. All the practical preparations did not, however, prepare Sarah for the magnitude of the loss she experienced when Harry passed away.

In the months following his death, Sarah had frequent nightmares that Harry had returned to their living room and would move toward her, urgently trying to tell her something. She could never hear or understand what he was saying because he would vanish before he completed his important message. She would awaken from these dreams feeling desolate in the knowledge that he was no longer with her.

Two years after his death, Sarah still thought about Harry many times each day. During this period, a vivid dream helped her see that the acute period of grieving had subsided.

I'm dreaming again of Harry. His face, his look is so real that I think he's alive again. I can see him walking toward me with his big blue eyes and his arms outstretched to me. I'm standing up, and I say excitedly, "Where did you come from? I thought you were dead!" He hugs me and says, "I just want to make sure that all is well with you, my darling." It felt so good to see him and hear his voice again.

Sarah was shaken by the dream because of how real Harry appeared in it. She recalled that the previous night, she had stared for a long time at the picture of him in her bedroom. She had even kissed the picture before she went to sleep.

At first, she was saddened by the dream. But as the image of Harry in the dream came to her over and over again, she began to feel a sense of comfort. After two years, her husband's voice had become a concerned voice inside her. The sense of incompleteness and anguish about her husband's death was no longer so painful.

When grief begins to reach a stage of resolution or partial resolution, Reassurance from the Dead dreams give hope and help the grieving person build a cherished image of their lost loved one.

Twelve years later, at age eighty-five, Sarah reported that she still drew comfort in thinking about the dream and how real Harry had appeared in it. She never again had such a vivid dream of him.

Coping with an Accidental Death

Dina, an emergency room nurse, had been divorced for three years before she met Ricardo, a fellow nurse in her hospital. She had not dated much after her divorce and wanted to be more careful in choosing another partner. However, their relationship progressed quickly and passionately until they became engaged six months after meeting.

Soon after their engagement, Ricardo went on an overnight camping trip with a couple of old friends from college. On the night he was supposed to return, Dina came home from work and found a series of urgent messages on her answering machine from Ricardo's best friend. She knew something was wrong when the friend insisted that he come over to talk with her immediately. She never suspected, however, that her fiancé had died that day. Although he'd been wading in shallow water, he had mysteriously drowned while others were swimming not far away. Dina kept asking Ricardo's friend if he was telling the truth. The words just wouldn't sink in. That night she had the following dream.

RICARDO'S RETURN

I am at the emergency room. I am lying down feeling very depressed and unresponsive. One of the doctors comes into the room and asks what is going on. He says he got a horrible-sounding message on his answering machine. Someone takes him into another room to tell him Ricardo died. I see people that look like Ricardo, and then I see Ricardo. I am totally in love with him and in awe of him. He checks his mailbox and sees a note that I left him there (which I had done the day before he died). He looks at me, but no one else sees him. Suddenly he goes out the back door smiling and doing a dance.

When she awoke from this Reunion with the Dead dream, Dina called Ricardo's answering machine, which was still on, and told him how much she loved him. Even though she knew he wasn't there, she wanted to believe that he would get the message.

Dina felt that this first dream had to do with her inability to believe what had happened. She was feeling the full power of her love for Ricardo as if he were not dead but only entertaining her with a short visit, then leaving, as he would sometimes do in the hospital where they worked.

During the weeks following his death, Dina was wracked with grief. She wanted to deny the obvious. She imagined seeing him everywhere she went. She spent hours crying. Dina felt a terrible sense of loss; their love and the possibilities of their marriage would never develop. She felt desolate and abandoned, just when she thought she had found the love of her life.

Despite all her turmoil, Dina reached out to her friends, calling them in the middle of the night when she was crying, asking for help in a way she never had before. This was the first death of anyone close to her. Through her intense grief, she felt that she came to value her own life and her friends more. She was beginning to feel acutely alive. She had a new desire to live and to make the most of her precious time.

As she worked hard to overcome her denial, Dina had another dream two months after Ricardo's death.

SMELLING THE EMBALMING FLUID

I am out at the stables where Ricardo used to take me horseback riding. Ricardo moves toward me, and we start walking together. He is looking at me, but he doesn't say anything so I know he is dead. I ask him, "What were you doing in the water when you don't know how to swim?" I remember smelling the smell of the chemicals of embalming fluid (which I later realized I had smelled at the funeral).

The anger that Dina felt in this dream had not been accessible to her earlier. Not only was Ricardo unable to swim, but his mother had drowned when he was ten. How could he have been so stupid as to go into the water alone? How could he have left her when their love was still young?

Two months after Ricardo's death, Dina was still grieving, but she felt that she was beginning to recover from the terrible depression that had gripped her. Her embalming fluid dream helped her to see that her denial was beginning to subside. She was now able to express the full range of feelings she had about Ricardo's death.

Children's Grief Dreams

There are many stumbling blocks for children as they cope with losses of people and pets who are close to them. Younger children may not have the cognitive maturity to understand the finality of death nor the life experience to know that the emotional pain of bereavement does not last forever. They don't realize that with family support and the passage of time, grief slowly recedes, and the person they have lost continues to live on as a presence that is less painful and more cherished.

In addition to lacking the slowly acquired ability to understand the nature of death, children younger than eight have difficulty distinguishing dreaming from reality. And it is definitely not easy for adults, let alone young children, to cope with some of the common Grief dreams that may feature vampires, coffins, corpses, ghosts, and other very creepy characters. When kids encounter the haunting image of a recently deceased grandparent in a dream, they may be terrified within the dream and wake extremely confused and upset.

Grieving children are prone to nightmares and may even have night terrors, a terrifying form of sleep disorder that occurs in the early stages of sleep and is accompanied by rhythmic motions and panicked shouts for help. During night terrors, children appear to be awake but are actually in an odd state of semiconsciousness. These episodes last just a few minutes but frighten parents. They are generally harmless, and children usually forget them when they awaken.[7]

Complications may also result from an entire family being afflicted by grief. When Mom and Dad are in mourning, they may be less attentive to their child's emotional needs. A grieving child senses that his or her parents are extremely sad and may not want to bother them. Children may not even know why they are more tearful and moody or why they are getting tummy aches when they think about Grandma being gone. Our children are not likely to have the words to tell us about their grief.

Despite their upsetting nature, Grief dreams offer parents crucial clues to their child's response to a loss. Listening to a child's nightmare about their deceased grandparent or even their dead pet frog can provide parents with a vehicle for easing the grief process and helping children navigate the stages of recovery from the loss of a relative, friend, or pet.

One young child dreamed that a monster transported her up to heaven. The dream suggests some confusion about the boundaries between life and death. It may also indicate a wish to join her departed brother. Dreams of joining relatives in heaven or other forms of reunions are common in adults' Grief dreams as well.[8]

Five-year-old Ian began to have nightmares and night terrors when his favorite uncle, Matt, was tragically killed in a motorcycle accident. He became tearful and moody and began to occasionally wet his bed. His Uncle Matt was the youngest of his father's brothers and a freshman at a local university. Matt used to take Ian out frequently for ice cream, movies, and other activities. Ian had even ridden on his uncle's motorcycle and would brag to his friends about his favorite uncle's Harley.

At first, Ian was mum about his nightmares. He insisted that they were "too scary" and hoped they would go away. Gradually, his nightmares grew more frequent and more terrifying. His parents encouraged Ian to talk about his nightmares as a way to reduce his worries. With that gentle persuasion, he finally and reluctantly revealed a dream that was troubling him.

HOLDING ON to UNCLE matt

I'm riding on the back of Uncle Matt's Harley, and we're going faster and faster, and I am holding on as tight as I can. All of a sudden, we start to fly off a big bridge. I'm falling way, way, way down to the water. I scream, "Matt, Matt, help me!" I'm choking in the water. I can't find him anywhere! I'm screaming "Help! Help!" but nobody comes to get me out.[9]

Ian's tearful question after telling the dream was, "Is Uncle Matt really dead? I felt like I was holding on to him just the way we used to." Ian's parents, who were also sobbing as they listened, confirmed that Matt was, indeed, dead. They reminded Ian of the detail of what they had done on the day of the funeral a month earlier—how the whole family had come together. Ian persisted in his belief in the dream's reality: "But it seemed like he was *really* there in my dream." "I know Ian, I can't believe it either," Ian's father, Roger, said.

For children and adults, denial is an inevitable phase in responding to the death of someone close. For Ian, dream and reality were muddled. He was confused about whether his uncle was really gone. In the dream, he may have also unconsciously merged his experience of loss with his fantasy of his uncle's experience of death. He had always identified strongly with his uncle, and in the dream he was facing a similar mortal danger. He was unconsciously preoccupied with the fear: "Am I about to die like my uncle?" If Ian had not shared the dream with his parents, he may have harbored the irrational belief, which is common in children and adults, that he caused the accidental death, perhaps by hanging on too tightly during the dream.

In his Desperately Searching dream, Ian was choking and nearly drowning. Dreams may use the image of drowning to symbolize overwhelming emotions. Ian, like his parents, was indeed feeling overwhelmed—unable to express his needs or be rescued from the drowning pool in his nightmare.

Although Ian's parents had encouraged him to share the dream, they were not an objective audience. They too were devastated by the memories that the dream evoked and felt guilty that they had neglected to check in regularly with Ian in the weeks after Matt's death. In part due to Ian's dream, they decided to seek counseling to help the whole family deal with the loss.

Grief dreams evolve in stages that exaggerate the painful loss at first. Gradually the dreams suggest acceptance and the re-creation of special moments with the deceased loved one. A year after Matt's death, Ian's nightmares were rare, and he began to have occasional dreams of riding on bicycles with his dad and his uncle. These healing dreams marked a resolution of the acute phase of grief. Ian was beginning to focus on images that suggested cherished positive memories of his uncle. Ian's bicycle dreams unconsciously solved the "dilemma" of his deadly motorcycle nightmares. The bicycle images replaced the motorcycles with a more benign vehicle that Ian had associated with family outings and his relationship with his father and uncle.

Resolving the Loss of a Child

The loss of a child is surely one of the most shattering events within the realm of human experience. In one study of marital stability after the death of a newborn, over 60 percent of the couples who suffered such a loss experienced marital discord that ultimately led to separation or divorce.[10] Furthermore, the incidence of severe psychiatric problems in men and women who suffer such a loss has been measured at over 33 percent.[11]

The research of Jungian analyst Judith Savage has provided us with powerful insights into parents' reactions to miscarriage, perinatal death (during pregnancy and delivery), neonatal death (between birth and four weeks), and infant death, such as in sudden infant death syndrome. Her book

Mourning Unlived Lives: A Psychological Study of Childbearing Loss explores dreams, fantasies, and mythological parallels that illuminate the process of recovering from the death of a child.

Desperately searching for a lost child is a prominent theme in the dreams of parents who suffer the death of an infant. One such dream reported by Savage was that of Carol, a single mother whose relationship with the child's father ended early in the pregnancy. She decided to continue the pregnancy, but her baby died in the twentieth week of pregnancy. This was one of four similar dreams.

searching for my baby

The dreams all started in a hospital after the baby was born. A nurse comes to my room to tell me that I had a son, but she didn't have him. She'd leave the room but never return. Then I'd get out of bed and search the hospital, asking everyone whether they'd seen my baby. No one had. Some people helped me; others didn't. I never find him.[12]

According to Savage, Desperately Searching dreams are common immediately after the infant's death. They often continue for three or four months and only stop when the parents have accepted that the loss is real and that all illusions of having the child return are gone.

Another dream theme Savage observed is that of reviving or resurrecting a deceased or fragile child. One woman had recurring dreams of tiny babies on the verge of death. Using her own breast milk, she was able to save them from the brink of death and nourish them until they reached a normal size.

Renowned pediatricians John Kennell and Marshall Klaus have stressed the importance of parents seeing a dead child as visual proof that the baby has died. In the case of any fetal loss occurring after the infant had begun to move in the womb, they recommend that the baby be shown to the parents to counteract denial and help them speed the mourning process. A private viewing in the hospital or mortuary and a funeral service can make a tremendous difference in the parents' capacity to resolve this traumatic loss.[13]

After the death of a newborn, infant, or older child and after a miscarriage, the parents often experience a torturous series of dreams that almost always includes themes of guilt and self-reproach. Such a dream was described by Freud in the chapter on "The Psychology of the Dream Processes" in his monumental book *The Interpretation of Dreams*. The dream was that of a father on the night his young son died of a prolonged fever. When the father fell asleep, his son's body was laid out with tall candles surrounding it. An old man was in charge of praying for the boy and watching the candles.

_____ father, don't you see i am burning?

My child was standing beside my bed and caught me by the arm and whispered reproachfully, "Father, don't you see I am burning?"

When the father awoke, he saw a glare of light coming from his son's room and rushed next door to find that one of the ceremonial candles had burned some of the shroud when the old man had fallen asleep.[14] This simple but poignant dream was caused in part by the brain's ability to sense danger even in the dream state. The words spoken by the dead child, however, may have had many meanings. Freud suggested that they may actually have been spoken by the boy on his dying day as he pleaded for relief from his burning fever. It is likely that the child's pleading voice also was touched off by a condensation of other memories and feelings. Perhaps this father was experiencing remorse that he hadn't responded in the past to his son's emotional needs. Perhaps he was wracked with guilt that he was unable to prevent his son's illness or save him from its ravages. Perhaps the dream was a denial of his son's death in its portrayal of him as still alive and therefore capable of being saved by some heroic effort.

In one of my own cases, Randy and Caroline had been married for one year when Caroline experienced a miscarriage after eight weeks of pregnancy. She'd had an ectopic pregnancy (the fetus was in the fallopian tube) that was misdiagnosed, and she almost bled to death. It wasn't clear whether she would be able to conceive again. As Caroline recovered slowly over the next month, she mourned the loss of her child as well as the hope that she and Randy would have a child together. Caroline was increasingly upset when Randy seemed to express little emotion about the miscarriage. Randy, too, wondered why he was feeling numb.

Soon after the loss of the baby, Randy had two horrifying nightmares. The first was an image of a woman who was bleeding heavily from a deep gash. The second featured an old, dying woman who needed a hospital bed for which Randy was forced to pay.

Randy was overwhelmed with anguish and unable at first to think about the meaning of these two nightmares. When he did finally explore these dreams, he felt that they helped him to understand the core of what was troubling him. He felt that he should have been more upset about the miscarriage. On the surface, Randy was playing the role of the devoted husband. When Caroline accused him of not caring, he felt guilty and began to question whether he really was a callous person. He became preoccupied with self-doubt and wondered whether he could ever be an adequate husband, let alone father.

His dreams showed him that he was, indeed, upset about the loss of the pregnancy. Furthermore, he was even more upset about the fact that his wife had nearly died and was only slowly recovering from the physical trauma. He also felt that his wife's complaints were valid. His dreams helped him to see that he hadn't been able to express his feelings because he was trying to be the strong partner while his wife was physically and emotionally weakened.

As Randy began to face the fears of his initial nightmares, he had the following dream, which illustrates how troubled he still was by his wife's condition. This was the beginning of a series of dreams in which Randy began to resolve the feelings he had been avoiding.

THE GREAT SOCCER PLAYER IS NOW TIRED

An Hispanic woman is being helped to walk by others. She has recently had a baby. Before that, she was a great soccer player. Now she can barely remember what she was doing. She says that she is very tired now.

Randy quickly realized that the great soccer player represented his wife. Not only was she athletic, she was a star player at her job and in performing and caring for him. He had not realized how upset and disoriented he was at seeing her appear weak for the first time.

As he discussed his dreams, Randy began to feel some of the emotions he had unconsciously avoided. He felt fear and sadness about the potential loss of his wife and empathy for her slow recovery. Beyond that, he began to grasp his pattern of avoiding intimacy in relationships because of his fear of becoming too dependent and risking emotional abandonment. With this greater understanding, he felt he could begin to be more responsive to his wife's needs. As Caroline recovered physically, they began to discuss the idea of adopting a child if Caroline couldn't conceive. Six months later, she did conceive and ultimately gave birth to a healthy child.

Like Randy, many of us react with fear and shame at our deep emotional responses to a loss. We feel that we should have it all together; when we don't, we hide our true feelings. Through our dreams we can understand our vulnerability and appreciate our humanness. Dreams show us that our emotional wounds heal slowly.

When a parent has traversed the stages of grieving, they begin to have dreams that suggest that a resolution is taking root. Dream researcher Dr. Rosalind Cartwright experienced the tragic loss of her twenty-eight-year-old daughter, Christine, who had only recently received her Ph.D. In the middle of the night, Dr. Cartwright received a horrific call from the police informing her that her daughter had been killed by a speeding driver.

At first, she was unable to dream of her daughter. The images were blocked due to the overwhelming magnitude of loss. Gradually, she began to dream about Christine, and an amazing evolutionary process occurred. She witnessed her daughter growing up in a series of dreams. Her initial dreams portrayed Christine as a toddler in trouble who needed to be rescued by her mother. Cartwright pulled Christine out of the toilet, saved her from a car accident, and protected and comforted her in other ways. As time passed, Christine appeared older and older. After a number of months, Cartwright had a vivid dream that helped her break out of her grief and realize that she could not save her daughter and that the death was not her fault.

I THOUGHT YOU WERE DEAD

I was at a big convention waiting for an elevator with a crowd of people. Now an adult, Chris joined me there. "Christine," I said, "I am so glad to see you. I thought you were dead." "I am," she said. "I only came to be with you until you get used to the idea."

Cartwright found the Reassurance from the Dead dream extremely comforting. Her daughter's words and presence in the dream were not only reassuring but were similar to how she imagined her daughter would have reacted. This breakthrough dream was the last in her series of Grief dreams. "The Threat and Rescue dreams turned to acceptance and appreciation," and this transformation of her dreams about her daughter heralded the resolution of her grief.

Grieving the Loss of a Pet

The death of a cherished pet can be profoundly upsetting and may trigger a grieving process that closely resembles the grief we might feel for a close friend or relative. In fact, many of us form attachments to our pets that fill crucial emotional needs that are not adequately met by human relationships. This is especially true for people who are not in a primary relationship or those who have no children or whose children have left home. Pets are also precious to people who have suffered losses and wounds in earlier relationships. A loyal dog may last through many relationships and always be there for you when you want to play or take a walk. A cuddly cat may meet your needs for affection when your marriage is stressed or when you are feeling neglected in other ways.

A number of years ago, when I saw a sign in my veterinarian's office for a grief support group for pet owners, I chuckled and thought to myself,

"Only in California." But when both of our young cats were hit by a car, killing one and nearly crippling the other, I understood how disturbing the death of a pet can be. And when that surviving kitten had used its nine lives and died after being our family's companion for fourteen years, we experienced another painful period of grief.

These experiences helped me understand the dream of a woman who had recently suffered the loss of her fourteen-year-old dog. She had the dream on a Dream Quest wilderness backpacking workshop in the Big Sur region of California. We were camped on a ridge overlooking a mountain called Pico Blanco, which the Ohlone Indians considered to be a sacred site. According to legend, it was on that mountaintop that the mythical Coyote was said to have begun their tribe after surviving a great flood.

In the morning, Barbara, age forty, recorded this disturbing dream in her journal.

NURSING a coyote

There is a wild dog nearby, maybe a wolf or coyote. I lie still because I'm not sure if it will attack me. Somehow I fall back to sleep and wake up (still in the dream), and when I awaken the dog is lying asleep on my chest.

When we met as a group to explore her dream, she was initially confused by it, but she soon associated it with her fear of wild animals and with our discussion of the Coyote legend the previous evening. When I asked her to imagine that she was reexperiencing the dream, she began to describe the feeling of the coyote on her chest as heavy. She became tearful as she thought of her dog, Emily, who was a mixed breed but looked a little like a coyote.

Other group members remarked about the paradoxical quality of the dream image: the dangerous wild coyote sleeping peacefully on her breast. As Barbara talked further about the sadness she had experienced when Emily died, she realized that the dream also might have something to do with the fact that she'd just turned forty and was childless. The loss of her nurturing relationship with her dog underlined a painful struggle to accept that she did not have a child to nourish and was nearing the age when it would be difficult or impossible to conceive. Her poignant associations led others in the group to grieve over losses of parents, friends, and pets, some of which had occurred years earlier.

Reactions to death are downplayed in our society. Grief reactions to the loss of a pet are generally trivialized. Barbara had hidden her grief about Emily's death and in doing so had begun to experience the depression that often accompanies blocked grief.

For children and others who have an especially strong attachment to a special pet, focusing on dreams can help in the process of getting over their loss. This exploration helped Barbara to see that Emily's death was not a trivial matter and that she needed to mourn the loss of an important companion.

Death Symbolism in Dreams

We often have dreams that refer to death when there has been no actual death of anyone close to us. Direct and symbolic references to death are a universal theme in dreams. They are psychologically rich with meaning but often misunderstood or interpreted in an overly literal fashion.

We must be extremely cautious in using dreams to make concrete predictions of the future. This is especially true of dreams foretelling death. If most dreams that contain death symbolism were accurate predictions of doom, there would be few of us left on the planet.[15]

Dreams with death symbolism bear important psychological messages. When references to death or death symbolism appear in your dreams, you may want to consider a number of possible avenues for understanding them. Keep in mind that we're speaking generally, and your own dreams may relate to issues that are not mentioned here.

When you dream about the death of someone close to you, it may be related to angry or vengeful feelings toward that person. One dreamer who had unresolved resentment toward his father dreamed that his father died in an airplane crash.

It is important to remind ourselves that dreams exaggerate and distort our feelings and impulses. The appearance of hostile intentions or actions in a dream does not imply that the dreamer is on the verge of acting on such an impulse.[16]

Death dreams may serve as a kind of unconscious self-reproach when we feel that we have failed in our responsibilities to our children or other people for whom we provide care. Ann Faraday cites a dream that she had about her young daughter dying of syphilis. Her dream was frightening and puzzling to her until she reviewed her mental associations to the dream image. She remembered rolling around on the floor with her daughter the previous night. As she thought about this, she could imagine her mother's critical voice reprimanding her not to get her daughter so stimulated because she might die of a sexual disease. Although she was able to laugh at the critical voice, at the same time she knew that she had to be wary of its influence on her relationship with her daughter.[17]

Dreams of death that are not related to an actual death often indicate that a significant change or loss is occurring in a relationship or in some other aspect of your life. Viewing death dreams as related to a change in your relationship to yourself and to others will help you understand their meaning. These dreams are also helpful in understanding and working out earlier losses and deaths that may still be troubling.

Grief Dreams Inspire Creativity

Dante's love for Beatrice was immortalized in *The Divine Comedy*. When he gazed upon her in a white gown when they were both seventeen, he experienced rapture. That night he dreamed that he saw his beloved Beatrice.

DANTE'S DREAM OF BEATRICE

Love personified as a Lord, holding the sleeping Beatrice, naked but wrapped in a crimson mantle. In one hand, Love held Dante's burning heart. He awakened the woman and bade her eat the glowing heart. Then Love wept and gathered Beatrice up and ascended to heaven.[18]

This dream of her consuming his heart inspired Dante to write *La Vita Nuova,* a book of love sonnets and other poems inspired by his passion for Beatrice. When Beatrice died at the age of twenty-four, Dante was overwhelmed with grief and had many dreams and visions of Beatrice in paradise. These dreams and visions led to the creation of many more poems and ultimately to *The Divine Comedy.*

Other great authors and creative people have been inspired by dreams as they were emerging from their grieving. Following the death of his father in 1896, Sigmund Freud began to keep a journal of his dreams to help him deal with his loss. This journal was one source for his landmark work *The Interpretation of Dreams*. In that book, which Freud considered his greatest accomplishment, he set forth his theory that dreams disguise the wishes that would cause the dreamer intolerable anxiety if they were consciously acknowledged.

Novelist Isabelle Allende had a Grief Inspiration dream about her dead grandfather that directly inspired her choice of an ending for her book *The House of Spirits.* In the dream, her grandfather was dressed in black, and everything was black in the room except the white sheets. She was telling her grandfather that she had written the book and was explaining what it was about. This dream gave her the idea for an ending scene that portrayed the granddaughter sitting by her grandfather's bed, telling the story and waiting for the dawn to bury him.[19]

Dreams during periods of grief may be deeply troubling, but they can also be life changing. Although they may lead to depression, they can also lead to great inspiration, creative breakthroughs, and in some cases, turn the tide toward recovery from grief.

Dreams and Recovery from Loss

Dreams help us comprehend all the dimensions of human grieving. Through the window of our dreams, we can better understand our hidden feelings, bring them to the surface, and get the help we need to ease our suffering and get our lives back on track.

Exploring our dreams can also help us to clarify the symbolic losses that always go along with the death of someone close, such as the painful realization of our own mortality or the loss of the innocence and open-endedness of youth. These losses also may include enduring the death of long-held identities and roles, such as being a mother's daughter or a son's father.

In the midst of our sadness and desolation, dreams help us see the spiritual side of our grief, as in Doug's dream of crossing into the light or Adam's image of angels walking. Seeing spiritual elements in our dreams can help us find meaning and hope in a time of despair.

As at other turning points, dreams during grieving give us confirmation that we are resolving our losses. We can find meaning and sometimes even creative inspiration in the suffering that we endure during a period of grief, and our lives can be enriched by the memories that we carry with us.

11. perspectives on dream interpretation the benefits of an eclectic approach

Understanding Dream Symbolism

If you are puzzled about how to understand your own dreams, you're not alone. Most people are baffled by their dreams. They have no inkling of how to decipher the coded messages. Even the pioneers of dream interpretation, Freud and Jung, at first could not apply their theories to unravel the mysteries of their own dreams. Consequently, they developed practical techniques for exploring them. Over a period of years, each maintained a journal, observed patterns, and learned by trial and error to connect the feelings and themes in his dreams to important personal issues and turning points.[1, 2] In this chapter, you will follow in the footsteps of the great explorers of the inner world by learning how to appreciate and understand your own dreams.

To guide and inspire you to remember, explore, share, interpret, and benefit from your dreams, you will learn about a series of techniques and theories that will help you:

* understand the symbols, characters, content, and structure of your dreams

* learn the principles for sharing and exploring dreams with your friends, family members, and children

* understand the procedures for a collaborative dream-sharing group
* review core ideas from the principal models and schools of dream interpretation
* work on your dreams with a psychotherapist through the stages of a turning point

In chapter 12, you'll find a complete step-by-step program of techniques for keeping a dream wisdom journal, as well as dozens of do-it-yourself techniques for remembering, understanding, exploring, and resolving your dreams and nightmares.

Our dreams and the symbols in them do not have one specific meaning in the way that a riddle has one answer or a lock has one key. Rather they contain many levels of meaning, some of which may even be paradoxical. A useful approach is to view dream work as a process of discovery through which we encounter many ideas, theories, and hunches that make our dreams more meaningful and our feelings more understandable. Enjoying the journey can be as important as arriving at its endpoint.

Keep in mind what researcher and author Ann Faraday playfully called the tingle test. The tingle test is invoked when you receive an interpretation or reaction about your dream from another person. If you feel a physical reaction, it is likely that the interpretation is deeply relevant to you.[3]

The meaning of every dream symbol is unique to the dreamer and can only be understood within the context of a current life situation and current emotional concerns. *The most crucial step toward understanding the symbolism of our dreams is to explore our own associations with the dream images.* This emphasizes getting to know our feelings and fantasies more than just focusing on decoding a precise bottom-line interpretation. We can be guided by knowledge of common symbols and themes, but we must be careful to use our own feelings and intuition as the confirmation of any meaning we ascribe to a dream symbol.

In his book *The Dream and the Underworld,* Jungian analyst James Hillman suggests keeping dream images and symbols alive rather than reducing them to one bottom-line conclusion. In discussing a dream image of a black dog, Hillman states: "It is better to keep the dream's black dog before your inner sense all day than to 'know' its meaning (sexual impulses, mother complex, devilish aggression, guardian). A living dog is better than one stuffed with concepts or substituted by an interpretation."[4]

I do not favor the dream dictionary approach where you look up the meaning of a dream in a book of fixed symbolic interpretations. If we grasp for a cookbook method of looking up a dream's interpretation in a book on symbolism, we're likely to drift away from the dream's unique relevance to our life. For example, the meaning of a knife would be different if the dreamer had recently cut himself or been the victim of a knifing. And what if the dreamer was a knife salesman or a brain surgeon?

I encourage people to interpret dream symbols within the context of how they appear in the dream. Rather than looking at a dream symbol in isolation, *consider the entire image* and try to get the feel for what it is telling you about your life.[5] For example, many dream experts associate water symbolism with emotions or the unconscious. While those ideas may work for some dreams some of the time, we need to know much more about the qualities and feelings of the symbol and know about the dreamer's life experiences. Dreaming of water in a polluted puddle outside a chemical factory is very different from sweet cool water flowing gently from a mountain spring in a wilderness area. Also, the meaning of water to a gold-medal Olympic swimmer is certainly different than the nightmarish quality of a water dream to someone who had a near drowning experience.

Understanding Dream Characters

Analyzing the meaning of characters and relationships occurring in dreams can be tricky. Are the characters objective representations of a certain person? Are they telling you something about your current waking relationships? Or are they purely symbolic aspects of your own personality that are projected onto the stage of your dreams? I believe the answer is all of the above.

For example, in one of my own dreams, In the Orange Grove with My Grandfather (see the introduction), the encouraging advice from my grandfather was an aspect of our relationship before his death. But beyond symbolizing the resolution of my grief over his death, the dream also represented the grandfather part of me, that aspect of my own personality that experienced inner guidance and was fulfilled in my work of guiding others as a psychotherapist.

A valuable exercise that can be used in your dream sharing is to *pretend that each of the characters and elements in your dream represents a part of your own personality*. Begin with the character or object that was the most vivid or disturbing and ask yourself: How am I like this character? What part of me does this represent? We tend to identify with the perspective of the character who plays us in the dream, sometimes known as the dream ego.

It can be extremely revealing to assume the role of other characters in the dream, particularly those that are the most repulsive or threatening. Jung felt that these unacceptable or alien-feeling parts of our dreams are part of the *shadow* or negative aspect of our personality that remains concealed from the world and from oneself.[6] If you have a dream with a despicable character or infamous deed, imagine which part of you this dream element may represent. It can be a difficult but rewarding way to get to know the hidden, scorned, and upsetting aspects of your personality. Acknowledging and re-owning these denied parts of our personality is one of the goals of most forms of psychotherapy and one of the potential benefits of working with your dreams.

Another way to think about dream characters is inspired by the relational theories in contemporary psychoanalysis, which assume that the quality of a person's early relationships with their parents or caregivers shapes their personality and the quality of their later relationships and capacity for intimacy. Using this framework, you can focus not just on who the dream characters represent, but also on the nature of the interactive relationship between characters. To give an obvious example, a dreamer who suffered emotional and verbal abuse from their father as a child may observe frequent harsh interactions with problematic male or father figures in dreams. A dreamer who felt displaced by the birth of younger siblings may experience exclusion in dreams, and conversely a child who was well-loved may experience more warm and loving interactions in dreams. Therefore, the nature of the interpersonal dynamics in our dreams can give us insights into issues that carry over from our early relationships with our parents and family.

Objective versus Subjective Meanings

Although the bulk of our dream work involves an open-ended exploration of its subjective meanings, occasionally a dream will actually have an important literal or objective meaning. For example, in some cases a dream of a car losing its brakes and going out of control is related to a subjective experience of feeling out of control. As we saw in chapter 9, cars going out of control can even represent the growth of cancerous cells in the body. If you have a dream of a car going out of control, it may be worth considering whether your automobile's brakes are dangerously worn or whether something else is objectively wrong with your car; it can be important to look at the potential objective meaning of a dream. However, most of us tend to err on the side of looking too hard for objective meanings and neglecting subjective, symbolic possibilities. Although an occasional objective dream can be an eye-opener and startle us into dealing with some issue we have neglected, most dreams are more subtle and require us to patiently explore our associations to make connections beyond the dream's obvious, surface messages.

Classical Psychoanalytic Viewpoints

Freud emphasized how our dream images are linked to unresolved conflicts from early childhood that continue to haunt us each night. Freud's psychoanalytic theory was based on the principle of unconscious *wish fulfillment.* Using this frame of reference, unconscious wishes are taken to be sexual and aggressive needs that were blocked from full expression at key points in early development. Therefore, a classical Freudian analysis of a dream's symbols would tend to emphasize anxiety connected to unfulfilled erotic and aggressive desires that are released in the dream and camouflaged in the symbolism.[7, 8]

Freud distinguished between the manifest and latent content of a dream. The manifest content is what the dreamer remembers and describes as their dream. Freud viewed this as a disguise and defined the latent content as the concealed but more important underlying meaning usually linked to sexual and aggressive instincts that are consciously unacceptable and intolerable to the dreamer. Contemporary psychoanalyst Louis Breger has expanded the notion of latent content and asserted that latent content is a misnomer. Rather than hunting down the specific hidden, latent content, we should be open to discovering many levels of dynamic or even contradictory latent meanings.[9] So we are not looking for a twenty-five-words-or-less explanation that we can look up in a dream dictionary; we are seeking a set of hypotheses and descriptions that a psychotherapist and patient or a dreamer and listener explore collaboratively.

Object Relations and Self-Psychology Viewpoints

Some contemporary psychoanalysts see dreams (and the unconscious) as being shaped by images of our relationships with our parents and other caregivers in the first years of our life. From this point of view, dreams can reveal vital information about the nature of our present and past relationships with those who are closest to us.[10] Other theorists, following psychoanalyst Heinz Kohut, focus on how the Self is represented in dreams.[11] Does the dream depict a self-image that appears stable or fragmented? Do the images represent a capacity for initiative, or are the dream characters depleted of energy? Are the actors in the dream admired and valued, or are they disparaged and devalued?

Virtually all contemporary theorists view a dream's manifest content as more than disguise, having important meanings as well as camouflaging and distorting some aspects of the dream's underlying meanings. Sex and aggression are worthy areas to explore, but the underlying meanings of dreams may be linked to either past traumas or present conflicts in love or work, the quality and health of your past or present attachments to important family and friends, challenges to identity and self-esteem, reactions to life events and stages, both positive and negative.

Jungian Viewpoint

Jung shied away from establishing a uniform method of analyzing dreams. He preferred to treat each dream as unique and not necessarily fitting into patterns that we might impose.[12] He did, however, establish certain general principles for understanding dreams. A cornerstone of his approach to dream work was the idea that *nearly all dreams are compensatory.*[13] According to Jung, compensation is a psychological mechanism of balance that is inherent in all people and functions actively in our dreams.

A compensatory analysis of a dream may focus on different kinds of issues that have been neglected or exaggerated in our conscious awareness. For example, compensatory dreams may focus on unresolved grief, blocked assertiveness, unexpressed creativity, self-destructive thoughts and behaviors, or other issues.

In order to apply Jung's principle of compensation to understanding our own dream symbols, we must become aware of attitudes and relationships that may be out of balance. For example, if a dream portrays your father as having an angry outburst, you might ask yourself whether the anger expressed in the dream is compensating for some imbalance of anger or assertiveness in your life. Your father's anger may be exaggerating your own excessive anger or, conversely, might indicate that you are not aggressive enough to stand up for your own rights and needs.

Experiential and Existential or Humanistic Perspectives

Existential approaches developed by Medard Boss and expanded by Fritz Perls, Alvin Mahrer, and others have pointed us back to the importance of the dream experience.[14] They consider the process of exploring the emotional and the physical experiences of the dream in depth as being more crucial than goal-oriented analytic approaches that use explanation and interpretation. A key element is using discussion or waking fantasy to imagine or conjure reentering the dream and attempting to deepen the feelings and bodily sensations. Symbols are explored experientially and are considered to be either a disguise or a direct statement about the dreamer's life situation. There is an emphasis on collaboration between therapist and dreamer and using dreams to discover new directions in personal growth rather than on focusing only on past conflicts and psychopathology. Rather than just rehashing conflicts from the past, dreams and dream exploration are viewed as a unique and highly relevant route to creative solutions to life problems. Beyond that, dreams and dream work are viewed as having the potential to help integrate or make our personality whole and possibly as a route to mystical or spiritual awareness.

Cognitive and Dream Research Viewpoints

Most psychoanalytically based and Jungian approaches to dreams emphasize *complementary* interpretations and view dreams as containing symbolic information, which may exaggerate, distort, camouflage, and thus complement the manifest dream and contain issues of which the dreamer may be unaware. Cognitive and research-based approaches tend to focus on the *continuity* of the dream's manifest content with waking concerns and conflicts.[15] Therefore, someone who has experienced a recent loss will tend to have overt references to characters, settings, and interactions in their dreams that indicate preoccupations with loss and grief.

For those who want to explore the current state of research on dreams, a good starting point is the Association for the Study of Dreams' academic journal, *Dreaming*,[16] which is published by Human Science Press (see "Recommended Reading" for further suggestions).

Clara Hill developed a *cognitive experiential* approach in her book *Working with Dreams in Psychotherapy*. Professor Hill and her colleagues are the first to test a research method for dream interpretation. Hill's treatment model has three stages: exploration, insight, and action. In the exploration stage, the therapist guides the client to focus on feelings and thoughts evoked by dream images and to relate these to waking life. In the insight stage, the therapist helps orchestrate the raw material of the exploration stage and collaborates with the dreamer in gaining insights and formulating relevant meanings. In the action stage, therapists help clients come up with a plan for implementing life changes inspired by the experiences and insights they have gained.[17] Thus a dreamer who realized that her dream is about inappropriate partners for dating may decide to go about meeting men in a different way and to examine the influence of her relationship with her parents on her own poor choices of partners. Hill's exciting work may help to legitimize and reestablish the clinical use of dreams and will help us determine what aspects of dream interpretation are most effective and which individuals or conditions will benefit from dream exploration the most.

Cultural Viewpoint

Beliefs about what specific dreams symbols mean are embedded in many cultures. In some cultures, every dream is interpreted as a reversal—meaning the manifest dream always states the opposite of the dream's true significance.[18]

Some cultures view the color white in dreams as representing birth and purity; other cultures view white as representing death. Cultural differences in dream interpretation further discredit the use of dream dictionaries.

We must respect each dreamer's cultural beliefs and experiences if we are to help them understand and benefit from exploring their dreams. When you listen to a dream from someone who is from a different culture than you, find out about their cultural beliefs about dreams and their symbolism. This will help the dreamer feel more empowered and help the listener develop a richer understanding of both universal themes and cultural differences in the meaning of dreams.

An important aspect of the cultural approach is to use dreams to understand and help people who are experiencing acculturation or who are members of a minority group. Many dreams of immigrants and even second- and third-generation families reflect poignant themes of struggles with acculturation. A common recurrent dream for immigrants involves journeys back to their country of origin or place of birth. (See Elena's dream at the beginning of chapter 7.) Dreams of minority members of a culture also may contain important references to prejudice and struggles related to assimilation.

Developmental or Turning-Point Framework

During my graduate training, I had the opportunity to study with and present a detailed case to psychoanalyst Erik Erikson. His stages of development form part of the basis for the framework of this book. He emphasized that the growth of personality continues throughout the life cycle—even through late adulthood.[19] The maturing of the body and brain, early relationships with family, the cycle of adult relationships and friendships, and predictable passages and crises of maturing and aging all influence our personality and our dreams over our life span.

In *Dream Wisdom*, I have demonstrated how a life event and life stage perspective can greatly advance the understanding and therapeutic benefit we derive from dreams. Just as certain themes are universal—such as falling, flying, appearing naked, and losing your teeth—other themes are extremely common at specific life passages, such as expectant parents birthing furry mammals or grieving people dreaming of their deceased relative. When we understand the dream themes and key developmental issues connected to common passages and crises, we have access to a psychological map that can guide us in our dream work. When we explore associations with our turning-point dreams, we can understand the nature of how we face and cope with important life changes.

The Benefits of an Eclectic Approach

In my experience, restricting yourself to one school of interpretation limits the richness of what you can derive from a dream. When you approach a dream from many different angles, you are especially likely to develop your self-awareness and understanding. Consider the psychoanalytic emphasis on concealed references to sex and aggression, unresolved traumatic issues from your past, and images of your experience of self and close relationships with others. Examine the Jungian framework for universal and archetypal themes such as the great mother, the shadow, the wounded child, and the wise man or woman. Consider the cognitive and research perspective to see how your dream content reflects current conscious concerns and conflicts, your personality tendencies, and how your dreams compare to others with similar cultural backgrounds, medical conditions, psychological diagnoses, or even political beliefs. Keep the cultural perspective in mind to better understand a dreamer's unique beliefs about dreams and symbolism. Look through the experiential lens to savor a dream's pure emotional experience and to use it as a basis for personal growth and creative inspiration. And use the turning-point framework to see how you are resolving issues linked to current focal conflicts, life transitions, and traumatic events.

Sharing Dreams

Sharing our dreams with family or friends can make the dreams come alive. Even when there is no formal analysis, studies have shown that people who are trained to focus on remembering, exploring, and sharing dreams have pronounced therapeutic benefits: improved mood, fewer symptoms of psychopathology, and enhanced problem-solving abilities.[20, 21]

When you relate one of your dreams to a friend, he or she can offer you a fresh perspective and help you see it in a new way. Because the listener doesn't feel the terror of your nightmare, they can help you obtain more perspective, relieve your guilt if you are blaming yourself excessively, and see the universal dimension of it. An act as simple as retelling the dream once or twice may unleash hidden feelings and insights. I recommend that you *tell the dream in the present tense as if you were experiencing it for the first time.* Be aware of your feelings and body sensations as you tell it. Be open to any new parts you may remember and to any ideas or insights that may emerge as you retell it. Rather than reading it, tell it from memory, and then return to your journal and read it out loud again. The parts that you forgot to mention are likely to be significant.

When you listen to someone else's dream, I recommend that you "welcome the dream" before offering any kind of analysis or interpretation. Welcoming a dream means appreciating it as a special gift, a form of intimate sharing that is best received with sensitivity and respect for the person's feelings. Welcoming a dream rather than interpreting or analyzing it will make a friend feel understood, secure, and encouraged to go on with a deeper exploration of the dream. Your insights are likely to be colored by your own needs and concerns, and it is best to let others discover the essence of their dreams at a comfortable pace.

When someone shares a dream with you, listen carefully and empathize with the dreamer as if you were sharing the experience. If you use your imagination and pretend the dream is your own, you can be helpful by communicating your own experience. Because of the universal themes that often appear, you may be deeply affected by another person's dream just as you would by hearing a poem or seeing a movie.

Sharing your dreams regularly with friends or family members can deepen the emotional bonds in your relationships and help to work out conflicts when they arise. If you are in a long-term relationship, I recommend sharing dreams on a regular basis. In addition, when parents take an interest in their children's dreams and encourage family dream sharing, the children will grow up placing a high value on dreams.

Dream Groups

Dream-sharing groups have become increasingly popular in North America, Western Europe, Australia, and parts of Asia. Within hospitals, schools, churches and synagogues, support groups, and workshops, people have used dreams for therapeutic healing, problem solving, personal growth, and spiritual inspiration.[22, 23]

A group of people focusing on a dream energizes both the dreamer and the other participants. Each dream opens up a world of unexpected ideas. The combined life experience of all the members gives the dreamer access to the whole group's repertoire of insights. Those involved are often amazed by how easily they can be touched by another dreamer's feelings and conflicts.

My approach to dream sharing is closely aligned with the Experiential Dream Groups pioneered by Montague Ullman, M.D., a psychoanalyst and dream researcher and the world's most influential proponent of dream groups. The central procedure in Ullman's group dream exploration approach is for each member to refrain from directing interpretations at the dreamer and to preface every statement about another person's dream with the following prelude: "If this were my dream, I would feel..." This simple statement creates an arena of safety for the dreamer and allows all the group members to be emotionally open to the issues and images in the dream.[24]

Ullman stresses two key factors in dream groups: the safety factor and the discovery factor. The safety factor emphasizes the voluntary nature of sharing and gives authority to the dreamer as to when or how to curtail or expand the exploration of their dream.[25] Because of the intimate nature of dream sharing, the group members should try to provide an emotionally supportive and nonintrusive atmosphere and refrain from subjecting the dreamer to an onslaught of armchair analysis. The members can offer their own emotional responses and should remain open to discovering new truths about themselves. They must be careful not to impose their experiences or ideas on the dreamer. Rather, they can offer their responses as possible meanings that may or may not strike a chord with the person.

Ullman's discovery factor emphasizes an atmosphere of playful experimentation with images and feelings that invite the dreamer to respond with new perspectives. Discoveries may occur in the retelling of the dream. They may be sparked by the group's enthusiastic sharing of their emotional response. Or discoveries may occur in an extended discussion and ensuing dialogue. Frequently, discoveries continue after the group meeting or in follow-up discussions.

Ullman has referred to his approach as *dream appreciation.* His model is clearly distinguishable from psychotherapeutic or research approaches that attempt to explain, interpret, or categorize a dream or dream series. In contrast to interpretation, Ullman emphasizes a process-oriented approach that involves the emotional responses of the whole group and focuses on the emotional and creative experience of exploring the many levels of a dream's meaning.

Dreams and Psychotherapy

Although we have emphasized ways to work with dreams without the guidance of a psychotherapist, many people will seek the services of a mental health professional at some point in their life. As we've seen, our dreams can help us realize when we've reached a turning-point impasse that calls for professional help. This section seeks to demystify some of the ways that psychotherapists work with dreams and offers guidelines to enhance the benefits you can receive from your work with a therapist.

The use of dreams in psychotherapy is currently waning. The causes for this evolution are diverse. In part, the dominant influence of behavioral and empirical approaches ignored dreams because they are hard to quantify and measure. In part, the advent of managed care and limitations on the duration of psychotherapy has created the false notion that there is not enough time to focus on dreams. An additional powerful influence on the increasing neglect of dream work in psychotherapy is the failure of graduate schools to offer courses on the clinical use of dreams. Most graduate students and professional practitioners I have trained had absolutely no previous formal training in working with dreams.

When you begin therapy, be sure to pay special attention to the dreams you have after deciding to enter therapy and after the first few sessions. These initial dreams often contain valuable information about the nature of the impasse that you're facing in your life, your attitudes and response to therapy and the therapist, and your hopes for receiving help.

The way your therapist responds to your dreams will influence your inclination to explore them. If the therapist pays them little attention, your motivation and your recall will drop drastically. If, on the other hand, the therapist perks up, takes out a notepad, and welcomes your dream, you will tend to respond with a wealth of dreams and associations.

I recommend that therapists do not approach dreams as an expert or guru who offers a specific and firm interpretation. More helpful metaphors for dream work include that of a guide or midwife who helps you through the labors of free associating, exploring, and giving birth to a set of ideas and meanings that make sense to you and leave you feeling empowered about the discovery process. Therapists who encourage or incorporate the dreamer's ideas or associations into an open-ended discussion are usually the most helpful.

Another helpful metaphor for clinical work with dreams is that of testing a hypothesis. Although working with dreams is more of an art than a science, when I interpret dreams, I formulate various hypotheses about a dream's meanings. Then, in collaboration with the dreamer, we test the hypotheses to see whether they make sense and resonate emotionally with the dreamer.

When psychotherapists have received supervision or psychotherapy emphasizing dreams, they are most likely to use dream work in their own practice.[26] Psychotherapists who have been trained to work with dreams will look carefully at the dreams in each stage of psychotherapy, the dreams that appear to relate directly to the progress of the treatment, and the relationship between therapist and patient. In addition, psychotherapists may seek outside consultation and even use their own dreams about their feelings toward their patients to better understand and incorporate strong reactions they are having in the psychotherapy.

Many dreams during the course of psychotherapy depict transference feelings; that is, they depict your responses to the therapist and reveal feelings from important past relationships that you may transfer and project onto the therapist. Dreams about the therapist, the process of therapy, or even settings that seem to relate to the therapy experience can help therapist and patient understand how the therapy is progressing. Early in my own training as a psychotherapist, I was taking copious notes as my patient revealed a disturbing history of abuse. In the next session, he dreamed that a police officer was giving him a ticket. The officer wrote endlessly and ultimately continued writing on the dreamer's car, which enraged him. This dream helped me understand that I had to put the notepad away and pay more attention to his urgent need for emotional contact as well as to his rage and sense of deprivation. Therefore, therapists must be open to seeing a dream as reflecting both breakthroughs and impasses in the treatment's progress. In addition, therapists have to be flexible in the way they respond to the dream and the dreamer's needs.

It's important to remember that your dreams are a jumping-off point for expanding self-awareness and solving important life problems. Therefore, some dreams that are only discussed briefly may spark an extended exploration of a hidden feeling, forgotten memory, or relationship impasse. Other dreams may be discussed thoroughly over a number of sessions, comparing similar symbols and themes.

In chapter 8, we saw abundant evidence of how traumatic events continue to live on in people's dreams and nightmares. In many cases, people who have been abused in childhood will continue to have dreams with symbolic references to the unresolved emotional wounds that linger from the abuse. Although exploring these dreams can lead to breakthroughs, significant caution needs to be exercised. It is very important to thoroughly explore and not dismiss individual or recurring dreams that portray abusive dynamics including violent attacks, emotional abuse, or even sexual assaults. They can provide powerful insights and catharsis to the dreamer and may give therapists diagnostic information and direction that can lead to productive discussions of unresolved events from the past and present. However, having a distressing nightmare with violent or abusive interactions is by no means proof that early abuse or other traumas occurred. In fact, most dreams are more symbolic than literal, and abuse should not be assumed unless there is objective, corroborating evidence from the dreamer's life. Because of the memory's susceptibility to outside influence, therapists working with dreams should not overemphasize or push an agenda of seeking out recovered memories. They should weave a balance between taking upsetting dreams and their possible connection to past trauma very seriously and being cautious about taking dream symbols too literally. Working with posttraumatic nightmares can open doors that lead to healing old trauma, but psychotherapists must be cautious about inadvertently influencing their patients and creating or confirming false memories.[27, 28]

The American Psychological Association has established guidelines for the ethical handling of possible recovered memories in psychotherapy and has made them available on their website at www.apa.org/pubinfo/mem.html. They have also sponsored publications that cover this vital but very thorny subject, including the 1997 volume *Treating Patients with Memories of Abuse,* by Samuel Knapp and Leon VandeCreek.

It's better to explore your dreams at your own pace and come up with your own insights, with your therapist's guidance, than to have them spoon-fed to you. If your therapist does give you an interpretation that feels off track, be sure to question it. Ask for further explanation and make sure it jibes with your own feelings.

Carl Jung was emphatic on this point. He felt that the analyst should refrain from insisting on an interpretation if it did not ring true for the dreamer. According to Jung, dream work was a collaboration between therapist and patient, not an expert dispensing interpretations.[29]

When I offer explanations and interpretations for a dream, it is usually in a tentative form, as a working hypothesis or a series of possibilities. If I say too much or too little or get too excited about my view, I can take the sense of discovery away from the dreamer. After working collaboratively with the dreamer to formulate hypotheses about a dream, we test our formulations to see whether they make sense and resonate emotionally with the dreamer.

Dreams also can help you decide when to end your therapy. In general, when you are contemplating leaving therapy, you'll want to consider whether you've made progress or whether you're running away from an issue or a feeling that's too painful to face at this point in your life. Looking at your termination dreams can help you and your therapist understand the nature of your decision to leave therapy.[30]

In psychotherapy, working with a series of dreams can help reveal hidden and repressed feelings and conflicts. It can also help both the therapist and the dreamer understand the impact and progress of therapy. Dreams provide a metaphoric vehicle for discussing issues that may be harder to understand or talk about directly. This is especially true for children who may reveal dreams about issues that they don't have words or concepts to describe. Dream sharing can also provide a forum for revealing and exploring the agonies of such issues as abuse or grief and the ecstasy of such issues as romantic love, creative inspiration, and spiritual and mystical experiences.

12. a practical guide to exploring your dreams and nightmares
the dream wisdom journal, glossary, and other creative techniques

In this chapter you'll find everything you need to keep a dream wisdom journal and create a permanent personal dream theme glossary. Within your journal and glossary, you can document exercises, experiments, projects, and insights about your own dream symbols, characters, and settings. Also included are detailed explanations for the following experiential techniques for working with your own dreams:

1. Enhancing your ability to *Remember Your Dreams* and minimize obstacles to dream recall

2. Learning a *Dream Wisdom Journal* format to record dreams and to decode the meanings of characters, emotions, settings, and themes that recur in your dreams

3. Using the *Experiential Dream Work Menu* to dream your dreams onward using self-expressive techniques such as creative writing, waking-fantasy exercises, and artistic and dramatic expression techniques to create new endings and alter the course of unresolved dreams

4. Completing a *Dream and Nightmare History* that surveys your life history of memorable dreams including early dreams, recurrent dreams and nightmares, and dreams from specific turning points and crises

5. Creating a *Universal Dream Inventory* that catalogs your common dream symbols and themes and helps you identify universal and turning-point symbols in your dreams

6. Setting up an ongoing *Personal Dream Theme Glossary* that will be a compendium of your dream history, common personal symbols, and themes, and a portfolio of your favorite insights and projects inspired by your dreams

7. Implementing *Nightmare Remedies* that will help you to convert upsetting dreams into meaningful experiences that provide you with vital information about your inner needs and conflicts

8. Using *Dream Incubation*—or asking your dreams to answer a general question—for personal and creative problem solving

9. Maintaining a *Two-Week Dream Journal* to enhance your recall of dreams and look carefully at your inner changes

10. Using the *Turning-Point Life Review* to guide you through a life passage or crisis

11. Learning *Dream Catching* guidelines for parents, educators, and psychotherapists on how to help children explore dreams, resolve nightmares, and use dreams for expressive arts projects

Remembering Your Dreams

Remembering dreams does not require complicated procedures or high-tech gadgets. Your attitude and receptivity are all it takes. If you approach your dreams with curiosity and interest, you are likely to succeed no matter what procedures you use.[1]

The right way to remember and document your dreams is whatever way works best for you. Most people prefer to record their dreams in a journal first thing in the morning. Others use a tape recorder or a sketch pad, or simply tell their dreams to a partner or supportive friend.

Probably the single most important thing we can do to enhance our recall of dreams is to *keep pen and paper by the bedside.* A special notebook or journal that is aesthetically pleasing can become a treasure chest of your inner life stories. This is your dream wisdom journal. Both children and adults enjoy decorating their dream wisdom journal with illustrations of their dream symbols, photos of recurrent dream characters, or collages of different aspects of their dreams.

Another helpful technique for improving your memory of dreams is to *review the day's events in the evening before going to sleep.* You can write your review in your journal or share it with your partner. Focus on interactions and events that provoked strong feelings. This can make you more sensitive to the issues that you're most likely to dream about and heighten the probability that you'll remember a dream. At the same time as your evening review, you may also want to picture the faces of the people who are most important to you and about whom you are most likely to dream. Visualizing them will raise the issues and feelings that are dominant in those relationships. This process will help you establish linkages between your dreams and the challenging aspects of your close relationships.

If you are having difficulty remembering your dreams, try to relax in the evening by listening to music, taking a bath, or practicing relaxation or meditation exercises. Avoid alcohol, drugs, and medications, and limit your caffeine intake, as these suppress dreaming. *As you are falling asleep, give yourself a simple suggestion that you will remember your dreams in the morning.* This suggestion strengthens your intention and reminds you to remain alert and ready to receive dreams when you awaken.

Each night of our lives, we enter four to six phases of rapid eye movement sleep (REM), which is highly correlated with vivid dreams. The first REM dreaming cycle of the night may only last ten minutes, but each subsequent phase, occurring at about ninety-minute intervals, gets longer. Because the last dream period of the night is the longest, you have the greatest chance for recalling a dream in the morning. To maximize your chances for remembering a dream, plan to wake up naturally or set a (nonmusic) alarm about fifteen minutes earlier than your usual wake-up time. If you do awake during the night with a dream, make sure to jot down key phrases or you'll tend to forget them by morning. A word or image stored in short-term memory requires ten minutes of wakefulness for our brain to transfer it into our long-term memory banks; a written reminder can help provide that conscious connection.

When you awaken, reserve a few quiet moments and lie still with your eyes closed or unfocused. Some people find it helpful to stay in the same position in which they awoke and to avoid turning. You can linger in a half-dream state, and your dream will often stay with you as you make a gentle transition from sleeping to waking. In the half-dream state of waking up or falling asleep, you may also see vivid images that are akin to dreams. The imagery can be enjoyable to witness and meaningful in much the same way as your dreams.

The technical term for the half-dream state of waking up is the *hypnopompic state* and images seen while falling asleep are called *hypnogogic*.[2]

Always record a dream, no matter how fragmentary, frightening, or unimportant it may seem. During the night or when you awaken, *begin by jotting down key words and phrases* even if they are not in a logical order. Often, one word or phrase will later trigger the recall of many more details from a dream.

For children, encouragement, parent modeling, and night and morning rituals can enhance dream recall. Children who are encouraged to remember and value their dreams will develop heightened recall that will often last a lifetime. When children perceive that their parents or older siblings find dreams interesting, they will want to get in on the action. If they witness family dream discussions, they will be eager to participate. A nightly ritual that refers to the value and enjoyment of dreams and conveys parental interest will act as a suggestion to the child. Morning dream checks, breakfast discussions, emotional and even physical reassurances to ease nightmares, and praise for the originality of each dream will also lead to frequent recall meaningful discussions.[3]

Obstacles to Dream Recall

Many people have difficulty remembering their dreams. They get tripped up by assumptions and attitudes that cause them to dismiss dreams as unworthy of further consideration. Obstacles to dream recall include the beliefs that a dream is:

* fragmentary and therefore useless
* too trivial or just a repeat of daily events
* illogical, nonsensical, or confusing
* bewildering, morally repulsive, or terrifying
* inadequate in some way, for example, lacking universal symbols or an appealing coherent story line

If you occasionally dismiss your dreams as worthless for any of the reasons above, you increase the likelihood of having difficulty remembering dreams. It's important to value every dream as a potential source of insight and change. If you find yourself tempted to minimize the importance of a particular dream or of your dreams in general, keep in mind that even the tiniest, most confusing, mundane dream fragment can have profound meaning.

Creating a Dream Wisdom Journal

The most valuable book on dreams that you'll ever read is the one that you write yourself: your personal dream wisdom journal. Writing down dreams reinforces your ability to remember them and activates feelings, associations, memories, and insights that might otherwise be neglected.

The type of journal you select is not a crucial factor. A spiral notebook, three-ring binder, sketch pad, or clipboard will work just as well as a specially purchased journal. A night light or flashlight can be valuable for writing down dreams during the night if you don't want to disturb your spouse or partner.

Don't become so obsessive about writing your dreams and organizing your journal that it becomes a chore. Quality is more important than quantity. One dream explored in depth is more valuable than a month's worth of dreams that remain untouched in your journal.

Keeping a journal gives you the opportunity to review a series of dreams. *A dream series presents a more complete view of your inner life than does one dream.* In your journal you can observe recurring characters, emotional themes, and situations that may not have been initially apparent. Often a repetitive theme or character alerts you to a situation or relationship that is unresolved or undergoing transition.

There are many techniques for structuring a dream wisdom journal. Most people who maintain an ongoing journal devise their own method of organization. In my dream seminars, I recommend using the following phrase as a mnemonic device for beginning your associations and organizing your journal: *review key dream facets.*

1. Review: Go over emotionally charged events of the previous day or two. Picture people's faces and your recent interactions with them. Make notes in your dream wisdom journal in the evening.

2. Key: Jot down key words and phrases that come to mind just as you wake. Use these keys to unlock the rest of your dream. With the keys, you can reconstruct a dream later in the day if your time is limited in the morning.

3. Dream: Use the keys as a framework for reconstructing your dream. Write as quickly as you can to avoid the temptation to censor or compose your dream. By faithfully recording all the dream's elements, even those that seem disorganized, you can later harvest the richer nuances of meaning.

4. Facets: This acronym stands for *feelings, associations, characters, ending, title, summary.* This sequence provides a guide for organizing and cataloging your responses to a dream.

F—Feelings. Note positive and negative emotions that arise in a dream, such as sadness, sexual desire, guilt, anger, joy, or love. Also note the quality of your mood when you awoke.

A—Associations. Write down ideas, insights, memories, and hunches that come to mind as you contemplate the dream. It is best to brainstorm and not worry about whether your ideas seem relevant to the dream.

C—Characters. Identify the characters in the dream. Who do they remind you of? How did you relate with them in the dream? Keep in mind that dreams often merge attributes of different people or portray a character as a disguised reference to someone else.

E—Ending. How does the dream conclude? Is the ending resolved, partially resolved, or unresolved? The degree of resolution correlates with the stage you have reached in resolving the dilemmas that the dream is addressing.

T—Title. Create a title for your dream that describes a crucial element and will help you remember it when you're rereading your journal or analyzing a dream series.

S—Summary. Summarize the main themes of your dream and try to link them with important issues that you're facing in a current turning point or in situations and relationships in your life. Based on your summary of this dream, what ideas or strategies for change can you think of?

Experiential Dream Work Menu: Creative Techniques for Exploring Your Dreams

Once you've remembered or written down a dream, there are many avenues for further exploration. Creating a relaxed, receptive, and dreamy state of mind is an important first step. I call this the dream space. The dream space is akin to daydreaming. You can enter it by closing your eyes and letting the dream's images and characters come back to life. Let your feelings and ideas flow freely without trying to direct or control them.

Freud used a form of the dream space when he encouraged his patients to lie on the couch, tell their dreams, and free-associate, communicating their thoughts and feelings without censorship. Jung felt that the therapeutic process was enhanced when his patients were able to "dream their dreams onward," or engage in a focused exploration of their dreams.

To help people enter the dream space, I invoke the advice of the Story Lady who used to visit my elementary school each week. Before launching into a fanciful story, she would implore all the children to "stretch your imagination" to accommodate the poetic license she was about to take. In a similar fashion we must suspend our desire to analyze and instead enter the storylike world of our dreams.

This approach involves reexperiencing our dreams—marveling at the visual imagery, being awed by the emotional intensity, and being humbled by the monsters and gangsters that pursue us. When we've reexperienced the dream in this exploratory way, our eventual analysis will be more on target when making connections between our nocturnal images and our waking concerns. The dream space exercise provides a springboard for deeper exploration of dreams.

Dream Space

1. Choose a dream that you want to focus on.

2. Find a comfortable, relaxed location where you will not be distracted.

3. From your journal, read the dream silently and/or review the events and feelings of the dream.

4. Close your eyes and pretend you are reentering and reliving your dream.

5. Imagine that you are experiencing the events and feelings of the dream as if they were actually happening.

6. Open your eyes and jot down spontaneous notes on the feelings, associations, and insights that you became aware of during the dream space exercise.

7. (Optional) Share your feelings and ideas with a trusted friend or family member.

From the dream space exercise, you can branch out in many directions. The following journal exercises have been found to be highly effective when used for individual dream work, in dream groups, and in workshops. If you are not oriented toward writing, each exercise can be adapted for verbal sharing. Younger children may need a parent's help when dictating their thoughts or selecting a dream and organizing an experiential project. Choose a dream and try one or more of the following exercises combined with the dream space exercise.

Automatic Writing

You'll need your dream wisdom journal and a timer. Set the timer for between two and ten minutes, and complete the dream space exercise. For the last part of the exercise, write as fast as you can without stopping to think or worry about whether you are making sense until your time is up.

Dream Dialogue

Choose two characters or two objects in a dream and write a dialogue in the form of a play script. Again, write as fast as you can without censoring or putting your pen down. Take a minimum of five minutes or as long as you need.[4]

Dreaming the Dream Onward

Reenter your dream using the dream space exercise. Continue your dream beyond its ending. You can use a silent fantasy, tell another person as you make it up, or write a new ending in your journal. If the new ending is unresolved, try to imagine a more positive resolution to the dream.

The Art of Dreaming

Using a variety of expressive arts techniques is an ideal way to begin or expand your exploration of a dream. Both children and adults will find these enjoyable techniques valuable for understanding dreams. You can draw pictures of a recent dream or nightmare or a childhood or recurring dream. You do not have to be an artist to try this. Nonartists sometimes have an easier time if they set aside any concerns about artistic talents. Don't worry about being realistic or drawing every part of the dream. Concentrate on color and emotions in your drawings as well as characters and events.

These "nothing fancy" art projects could include drawing or painting a dream with your favorite media, such as pencils, markers, watercolors, or chalk. Making a collage from magazines and photos is a surprisingly powerful way to express a dream for both children and grown-ups. You can also sculpt images from a dream or use your camera to take snapshots that evoke images from your dreams.

There are some fun and enlightening group art exercises for working with dreams. These include having a group of people listen to a dream, and having everyone draw it as if it were their own dream. Alternatively, each member can take a turn drawing their own dream and sharing their drawing and their dream. For families, groups, or in educational settings, try making a gallery or album of dream art.

Telling and Retelling Your Dream

Tell your dream in the present tense once or twice. Be aware of your feelings, associations, and body sensations. Tell your dream again from the perspectives of various dream characters. Note your feelings and how they change as you tell and retell your dream. Tell a dream you have written in your journal without looking at your notes, and then read it aloud from your journal. Note what you have left out, embellished, or changed.

Dramatizing Your Dream

A variety of dramatic and theatric techniques can generate insights into the meaning of dreams. In Gestalt therapy, the dreamer dramatizes dialogues spinning off from the dream. In this approach, the dreamer talks to an empty chair that represents another character or switches chairs to alternate roles. Group variations on this theme include having additional people play and then switch roles. Both the dreamer and the other participants try to get the feel of each dream role and then discuss their reactions afterward. Another option is to have the dreamer cast members of a dream group or workshop into the various roles in the dream. Dream dialogues and dramatizations can use objects or even settings as "characters." The classical example of this is from Gestalt therapist Fritz Perls, who surprised a dreamer and invited her into having a dialogue with a rug that was in her dream. Guess what? The dreamer soon realized that she felt "stepped on" in various relationships in her life!

Past, Present, Future, and Connections

Past: Reenter your dream using the dream space exercise, and allow your imagination to drift back in time. Jot down the first three memories from the past that come to mind; leave some space after each. Jot down the names of the first three people that come to mind; again leave some space after each.

Present: Experience your dream again, and note three events of the last two days that were significant to you. Note the names of two or three people in your present life that come to mind as you think about your dream. They may or may not appear in the dream. Leave some space after each entry.

Future: Once again reenter your dream using the dream space exercise. Write down two or three events that you'll be facing in the near future. Also write down the names of three people with whom you'll be having important interactions in the near future. Leave some space after each entry.

Connections: In the spaces that you left, jot down notes and phrases describing the memories and people you have noted. Do any of your notes generate ideas or insights about how your dream is connected to your past, present, and future?

After each of the above exercises, jot down further ideas or insights that may have occurred to you. Discuss them with someone you trust. Do your associations produce links between your dream and any important relationships, stressful events, or turning points in your life?

Dream and Nightmare History

At the beginning of my courses and workshops, I ask participants to complete a history of their memorable dreams and nightmares. Then I start a class discussion, and at first there is hesitation. As soon as someone tells a childhood dream or a recurrent nightmare, the floodgates open. The excitement of sharing and hearing both the variations and the common themes of dreams tends to jog everyone's memory and leads to a discussion.

Between the first and second meeting of ongoing courses, I have each participant complete a dream and nightmare history, which we discuss the next week. To complete your history, use your dream wisdom journal or a computer file and write out answers to each of the dream and nightmare history's categories. For those who are less inclined toward writing, you can have a group discussion. For children, encourage drawings or other projects.

1. First dreams and early dreams: Describe your first remembered and/or early childhood dreams with as much detail as you can. Write or discuss any significant life events connected to these dreams such as moving, the death of a relative or pet, parents' divorce, accident or illness in the family, or traumatic event or loss.

2. Recurrent dreams: Describe any recurrent themes, characters, or settings that have occurred in your dreams. Note any significant life events connected to these dreams.

3. Nightmares: Describe any memorable nightmares, recent or past. Have you experienced common nightmare themes such as being chased, threatened, abandoned, or injured or themes involving natural disasters, terrorism, loss, or severe illness? Note any significant life events connected to these dreams.

4. Big dreams and memorable dreams: Describe your most memorable dream(s). Note any significant life events connected to these dreams.

5. Dreams during life transitions: Describe any memorable dreams connected to relationship formations or breakups, graduation, leaving home, career crises and turning points, having a child, traumatic events, grief, or aging. Note the significant life events connected to these dreams.

Universal Dream Inventory

In *Dream Wisdom,* we have emphasized the dream themes common to life passages. It is also valuable to be familiar with the most common universal themes that occur across cultures and across time.[5] Dream researchers Calvin Hall, G. William Domhoff, and others have explored the nature of repetitive dreams and recurrent themes and elements in dreams[6] and have demonstrated that some dream themes recur over years and even decades in people who have kept extended journals.[7] I have found this to be true for myself and for my patients and friends and colleagues. It is easy to see the potential importance of identifying recurrent dreams and themes and working to connect them with persistent emotional issues and conflicts.

When people learn about the common dreams of flying, falling, appearing naked, and being chased, they frequently recognize a number of their own dreams on the list. This knee-jerk reaction represents a desire to have an expert reveal the true meaning of their dreams. Rather than giving dictionary meanings, I suggest that my students and patients use the following list to identify patterns in their own dreams. Then I encourage them to explore which dreams they have had and what those dreams mean to them. Once you have determined which of the universal themes have occurred in your dreams, a next step is to list all the repetitive symbols in your dreams and in your family or culture. You can collect and catalog both your personal and universal dreams in the dream theme glossary (see the next section).

To determine which universal dreams you tend to have, use the following list of twenty of the most common dream themes that I have encountered over the years. In addition, you may want to consult the larger list in the dream theme index (page 284).

1. Flying on your own or in a plane (also plane crashes)

2. Failing or forgetting to study for an exam in high school or college or forgetting your lines for a presentation, speech, or play

3. Appearing naked or partially clad in public

4. Falling

5. Being paralyzed or partially or totally restricted in movement, like trying to run away but being unable to move fast enough

6. Getting chased or kidnapped

7. Having sexual adventures, including overt references to heterosexual or homosexual acts

8. Suffering natural disasters such as earthquakes, tidal waves, fire tornadoes, floods, or volcanoes or out-of-control natural forces

9. Experiencing technological disasters such as explosions, terrorist acts, nuclear war, chemical contamination, or plane crashes

10. Losing your teeth, often with the teeth seeming to crumble

11. Experiencing violent or mortal threats, attacks, or injuries to self or others

12. Being rejected, abandoned, betrayed, or humiliated

13. Driving or being in cars (also crashing a car, brakes locking, or going out of control)

14. Missing a bus, train, or plane (also arriving late or missing an appointment)

15. Discovering new rooms in a house or building

16. Finding or losing money, a wallet, a purse, or valuables

17. Having people appear from your past

18. Returning to a home, school, or setting from childhood

19. Experiencing pregnancy and birth (also seeing yourself or another person pregnant or birthing)

20. Encountering dead persons either known or unknown to you who may be currently living or dead

If your most common dream themes are not on this list, don't fret. The fact that your dreams branch out in other directions does not mean that you are deficient or bizarre. Although there are universal dreams and recurrent turning-point dreams, there are infinite variations and forms that arise from the creativity of our dreaming mind. In addition, just because you have a repetitive dream or theme, don't assume that the meaning is fixed or stable. Dreams that appear very similar on the surface may have many variations of meaning at different times in your life and in response to different events and passages. One of my most recurrent dreams involves returning to my high school where I have forgotten to take a class or an exam that would allow me to graduate. Another variation is that I decide to return to high school to complete an unfinished course even though I already have my Ph.D. and am quite a bit older than the other students! This dream usually occurs when I am completing a project or preparing for a task that is stressful, and it often represents an inner rehearsal, such as completing a high school course. As I was completing this book, I had a Return to High School Dream that started with a sense of incompletion and anxiety, but ended with my preparing to graduate. Thus my anxiety about completing the book was beginning to be superseded by the sense of completion that goes with graduating from a school or, in this case, a book.

Creating a Personal Dream Theme Glossary

When you have explored your dream history and compiled your most common universal and turning-point themes, you are ready to create you own personal dream theme glossary. A dream theme glossary is a compendium of the recurring themes, symbols, titles, and universal themes of your dreams and a catalog of your lifetime dream history. You can develop your dream theme glossary in a journal, notebook, or album. A good approach for an expandable dream theme glossary is to use a three-ring binder or a computer file so you can add to it over the course of your lifetime. Your dream theme glossary is where you will keep your dream and nightmare history, common universal and personal dream symbols, dream FACETS exercises, and dream-inspired writing and artwork.

Your dream theme glossary will be a kind of encyclopedia and portfolio of your dream life. Parents may want to help or guide their children in designing a dream theme glossary. Like a childhood photo album or baby book, it will last a lifetime.

Nightmare Remedies: Rescripting Bad Dreams

During a crisis or after a traumatic event, it is important to know that nightmares are more common and upsetting. We experience each nightmare as a traumatic event, and for those who have experienced violence, a natural disaster, accident, or other trauma, posttraumatic nightmares rub salt in our emotional wounds. Keep in mind that moderately upsetting nightmares may actually be a positive sign of normal coping, but very graphic nightmares that are repetitive and unchanging may signal an emotional impasse.

Nightmare remedies are self-help techniques that can help adults and children break the spell of their bad dreams and use them for personal growth and creative inspiration. A simple method for transforming nightmares is to use the 4 R's of nightmare relief: reassurance, rescripting, rehearsal, and resolution.[8]

Reassurance is the first and most important step in relieving nightmares. This breaks the nightmare's spell. For family members or children, physical as well as emotional comforting may help. Once you feel reassured and the nightmare's reign of terror has been overthrown, you can relax, become curious about the nightmare's meaning and message, and begin to approach the dream in a more playful manner.

Knowing that occasional nightmares are normal and their frequency and intensity may increase during crises may also be reassuring. A key factor, especially for children, is not to dismiss or ignore the nightmare with a message that "it's just a dream" or that you should just ignore it. Nightmares, especially during a life crisis, are very hard to ignore.

Rescripting a dream can follow reassurance.[9] Rescripting uses discussion, fantasy, writing, art, or drama to reexperience and revise different parts of the dream narrative with the goal of opening up new endings and directions. You can use techniques from the Experiential Dream Work Menu to transform and tame a nightmare's most threatening interactions and moments. This can be as simple as rewriting one or more new endings for the dream or may involve free associations to link the conflicts in the nightmare with unresolved life issues.

Rosalind Cartwright has developed what she calls the RISC method for rescripting and detoxifying bad dreams. RISC is an acronym for Recognizing, Identifying, Stopping, and Changing bad dreams. She recommends "changing negative dream directions into their opposite" by creating new conclusions for dreams. By rehearsing these new endings consciously, they eventually begin to change the threatening nature of the dreams.[10]

Rehearsal is the third R needed to implement a nightmare remedy. This parallels Cartwright's model and involves multiple forays and trials of rewriting and reenacting the dream. If you are having nightmares about an auto accident or a serious physical injury, imagining one new ending may only be the beginning. Depending on your creative inclinations, you may need to write out several new endings, sketch or paint the dream's threatening elements, or role-play with a friend, psychotherapist, or dream group. Creating new endings does not have to involve killing your dream adversary. The terrorist or robber or wild animal can be frozen or shackled. Walls, cages, force fields, or even magic wands can be used as you rehearse dream solutions. Adults may need to loosen up their imagination, but children take to this easily, especially with adult guidance. Nonviolent strategies for subduing dream villains can model creative problem-solving strategies for children.

Rehearsal is similar to a phase of psychotherapy called "working through," which involves taking breakthrough insights and testing them out in a variety of ways with different people and situations. When nightmares are extremely painful or repetitive or are related to a profound trauma, rescripting and rehearsing dream solutions may need to be repeated before the nightmares subside. It is important to understand that conjuring up one new fantasy ending for a dream is not going to solve a deep problem that may be causing the nightmares. However, even if dream rehearsals must be repeated for people who are suffering more severe trauma, the initial efforts at rescripting may dramatically reduce the incidence of post-traumatic nightmares.

Resolution is the final nightmare remedy. Discussion and various trials of rescripting and rehearsing solutions usually trigger insights about what life issues are causing the nightmares. At this point, the dreamer is ready to resolve the nightmare, alone or with help. Resolution occurs when the dreamer brainstorms and identifies behaviors that they can further examine or try to change. In Clara Hill's three-stage model, this is called the action stage.[11] Examples of resolution would be Lisa's work-related nightmare series in chapter 6, which included the dream, "Too Many Chefs Spoil the Stew." After rescripting the dream, she realized that she had denied her assertive side and was being taken advantage of by the employees in her restaurant. After rehearsing various dream-assertiveness strategies for rescripting the attacks by her wayward employees, she made a series of real-life changes that led to exerting more clear authority at work and being more aware of her tendency to deny her assertive side.

We do not have to suffer nightmares in silence. Using the suggestions in this book, you can detoxify your nightmares and use them as a source of insight and personal growth. In more acute situations, resolving nightmares can create a breakthrough in dealing with the aftermath of a traumatic situation.

Using Dream Incubation for Personal Problem Solving

Psychologist Henry Reed, Ph.D., developed a contemporary adaptation of an ancient technique for healing and problem solving. He drew heavily upon the incubation ritual that the ancient Greek physician Hippocrates frequently prescribed. Seekers would journey to hundreds of different temples dedicated to the god Asklepios, where they would pray for a dream that would heal their body or their soul.[12]

The core of Reed's dream incubation technique is to select a crucial life issue that you want to resolve or understand more deeply. The issue might be an impasse in a relationship, a turning point at work, or a serious physical illness. A period of preparation involves focusing on that issue and exploring all consciously conceivable avenues for resolving it. This exploration process involves working with a guide, therapist, or even a trusted friend. Journal writing is also an effective tool for reviewing and integrating your conscious preparations for dream incubation.[13]

It's best to form a question to ask yourself and write it in your journal. Open-ended incubation questions are preferable; they allow you to learn something new and unexpected. Examples of questions that might be used include: "How do I feel about this career change I am about to embark on?" or "Why do I feel stuck in grief about my husband's death?"

Narrowly focused questions that call for a yes or no answer are less valuable. They make you search for fixed answers rather than being open to new perspectives on your question. In fact, the manifest content of an incubated dream doesn't always relate directly to the question you ask. You may discover answers to questions you hadn't thought to ask that are more pressing than the one you selected consciously.

After preparation, an incubation ceremony is conducted for one or more nights. The dreamer concentrates on the incubation question and makes a suggestion to himself that he will try to have a dream that will respond to the issues that need resolution. When a dream is received, it is discussed thoroughly, and the dreamer is encouraged to translate the exploration into a written summary of the incubation experience.

Just as artists and writers often have inspiring dreams when they are deeply absorbed in a creative project, we increase the likelihood of dreaming about a pressing dilemma in a new and enlightening way when we concentrate on that issue.[14] Keep in mind that incubation and dream questions do *not* involve controlling our dreams. When we try to control our dreams, we overlook the essence of what they offer: a glimpse into the unconscious and an encounter with unknown parts of ourselves.

Two-Week Dream Journal Program

A two-week period for collecting dreams has been used as both a research technique and a vehicle for dream exploration and interpretation. The dreams can be viewed individually or as a series with its own evolving themes and symbols. The appeal of this concentrated period of attention is that it's neither intimidating nor time-consuming, and it usually brings fruitful results, even for people who have never before kept a journal or focused on remembering their dreams.

The two-week dream journal has been used as a dream collection technique in dozens of studies that have analyzed dreams to understand the patterns in the dreams of different groups of people. When I conducted research on the Oakland Firestorm survivors and on the dreams of expectant fathers,

I used a two-week collection period with instructions similar to those given here. Among the forty-eight expectant fathers in my study, the average number of dreams recalled was more than seven. Few of the men had ever remembered as many dreams in such a short period of time prior to that.[15]

The two-week period can of course be extended in further two-week increments or indefinitely if you enjoy keeping a dream wisdom journal. It can be extremely helpful to do the two-week dream journal program with a friend or as part of a dream group or class. If you are currently involved in individual or group psychotherapy, sharing the results of this program can be a valuable addition to working with your therapist.

Here are the instructions for preparing and carrying out a two-week dream journal program for recalling and exploring your dreams.

PART I *Before the two-week period:*

1. Select or create a journal or notebook, and keep it by the side of your bed.

2. Decide on a two-week period to carry out the program. Mark your calendar.

3. Arrange with a partner to share and exchange dreams if desired.

PART II *During the two-week period:*

1. Write down every dream you have during the two-week period, no matter how fragmentary or unimportant it may seem at the time.

2. For each dream you recall, use the *review key dream facets* procedure described earlier.

3. For each dream, complete one of the techniques described in the Experiential Dream Work Menu such as dream space, automatic writing, dream dialogue, or one of the dream-inspired art exercises.

4. For each dream that you remember, use some of the suggestions for understanding symbolism presented in "Understanding Dream Symbolism" in chapter 11.

PART III *After the two-week period:*

1. Read everything that you have written—all the dreams, dream facets and other exercises, journal entries, and the insights you gained from discussions with others during this period.

2. Summarize in your journal and/or discuss with someone the patterns, ideas, and insights that occur to you.

3. Finally, at the end of your two-week period, make one final written or oral statement summarizing what you have learned, and try to develop specific strategies for making life changes based on your insights from the two-week dream journal program.

Turning-Point Life Review: Changing the Way You Change

History repeats itself. Not infrequently, we repeat mistakes and self-defeating patterns from past relationships and career situations. The turning-point life review exercise is designed for people who are undergoing a life transition or who want to understand and enhance their pattern of coping with major life stresses. It reviews your history of facing change and helps you to identify both effective and dysfunctional coping mechanisms in how you navigate life's passages. By understanding your successful coping strategies, you can play your strong suit, and by identifying self-defeating patterns, you can learn from history and avoid impasses in coping with life crises.

PART I *Past turning-points review:*

1. List the major turning points that have occurred in your life as a child and an adult; for example, marriage, divorce, moving, leaving home, having children, injuries, illnesses, deaths, career decisions and changes, traumatic events, or financial or legal problems. In writing the list, leave about a quarter of a page after each turning point.

2. Think about what happened during each turning point. What were your immediate reactions? What stages did you go through? What kind of support did you get from family or friends? In the blank space after each turning point, or with your discussion partner, summarize the answers to these questions.

3. Review what you wrote or discussed about each turning point. Summarize any patterns in the impasses and ways that you found to begin to resolve the emotional challenges. Do you see any patterns in the ways you reacted to or resolved past turning points that may apply to the present turning point you are experiencing?

PART II *Turning point emotional inventory:*

Use your journal and/or discussions with someone else to complete these questions.

1. *Stresses:* What current stresses are you facing? What are the emotional challenges of this turning point?

2. *Physical symptoms:* Are you having problematic physical symptoms (for example, headaches, stomach distress, or sleep disturbance)?

3. *Psychological symptoms:* Are you experiencing disturbing psychological symptoms (for example, depression, anxiety, or phobias)?

4. *Behavior problems:* Are you experiencing behavior problems (for example, substance abuse, difficulty with anger, antisocial behavior, or impasses in relationships)?

5. *Role changes:* How are you handling role and identity changes?

6. *Stage and resolution:* At what stage of the turning point are you? Are you experiencing any degree of resolution of symptoms, impasses, or conflicts?

PART III *Life review—summary and strategies for change:*

Reviewing your responses to parts I and II, summarize the patterns you observed in how you have reacted to and resolved past and present turning points. From the patterns you discern, is there anything you might do to alter your unproductive ways of facing change and to enhance coping strategies that have worked well? Successful strategies might include:

* reaching out for emotional support or professional help when necessary

* limiting self-defeating behaviors

* overcoming denial of powerful emotions such as grief, anger, and guilt

* learning lessons from past mistakes

* trying to heal wounds from the past

* experimenting with new attitudes, activities, and relationships

* searching for new sources of happiness

Write notes on your summary and strategies for change and/or set aside time to share your experiences and insights from this exercise with a trusted friend or professional.

Dream Catching for Kids: A Guide for Parents, Educators, and Therapists

Most adults have learned to forget their dreams. Children are very receptive to remembering and believing in the importance of their dreams. With encouragement from parents, family, teachers, and psychotherapists, children will recall dreams fairly easily. They will also be more likely than adults to share their nightmares rather than suffer in silence.[16]

When children reveal a dream, parents have an opportunity to communicate with them about a powerful emotional experience. This enhances parent-child communication and alerts parents to possible emotional conflicts that their child is experiencing (see "The Menacing Unicorn—A Kindergartner's Nightmare" in chapter 2). In addition, when parents lend a loving ear to their child's nightmares, a sense of relief is generated, and fears linked to the nightmare will melt away and lead to discussions about issues that may be triggering the bad dreams.

Parents, educators, and psychotherapists can help children unlock both the emotional healing and the communication potential of dream exploration with some simple guidelines and exercises. Many of the exercises in this chapter, especially those in the experiential dream work menu, can easily be adapted for children of all ages.

Children are especially receptive to art-oriented projects that spin off from discussions of dreams and dreaming. For preschoolers and elementary age children, craft-oriented projects like making dream catchers, dream pillows with aromatic herbs, and artistically decorated dream journals will open up conversation and exploration. Group sharing of dream-inspired projects works well in classrooms as well as in Scout troops, religious schools, and after-school programs. Creating a gallery, museum, or individual portfolio of dream art can be an ongoing or periodic source of inspiration and activity.

For children below the age of ten or eleven (depending on their skill and motivation for writing), I encourage parents to have the children dictate their dreams and have the parents transcribe them. For middle and high schoolers, creating and keeping a dream wisdom journal is a very exciting and engaging project that can lead to discussion, research, science projects, and dream-inspired art projects. Information on dream-oriented projects for students and teachers can obtained at the Association for the Study of Dreams website at www.asdreams.org.

For psychotherapists or school counselors, encouraging the sharing of dreams and nightmares can enhance rapport and open up topics for conversation that might not easily arise through direct discussion. The focus should be on the process of sharing rather than on trying to satisfy the need for a quick interpretation. Providing reassurance for nightmares and suggestions or guided exercises with art, creative writing, or drama will make the experience both enjoyable and safe and often will lead to a deepening trust in the counseling relationship. Dreams and nightmares that parents or children report can help psychotherapists diagnose painful conflicts.

Children of all ages appreciate an opportunity to learn about universal dreams, nightmare remedies, enhancing dream recall, cultural beliefs about dreams, lucid dreams, repetitive themes and symbols, and how experts approach dreams.

From the womb nearly to the tomb, we dream every single night. During difficult times when we undergo life passages, our dreams become more vivid and give us access to crucial information about how we are coping and where we are blocked. These turning-point dreams are a source of insight, creative inspiration, and inner wisdom that can guide us through all of the ages and stages of our lives.

recommended reading

Career Transitions

Bolles, Richard. *What Color Is Your Parachute?* Berkeley, CA: Ten Speed Press, 2002. (This book is updated annually and has an excellent bibliography.)

Lore, Nicholas. *The Pathfinder: How to Choose or Change Your Career for a Lifetime of Satisfaction and Success.* New York: Fireside, 1998.

Children's Dreams and Sleep

Schaeffer, Charles. *Clinical Handbook of Sleep Disorders in Children.* New York: Aronson, 1995.

Siegel, Alan, and Kelly Bulkeley. *Dreamcatching: Every Parents' Guide to Exploring and Understanding Children's Dreams and Nightmares.* New York: Three Rivers Press, 1998.

Creativity and Dreaming

Barrett, Deirdre. *The Committee of Sleep: How Artists, Scientists and Athletes Use Their Dreams for Creative Problem-Solving and How You Can Too.* New York: Crown Publishers, 2001.

Epel, Naomi. *Writers Dreaming.* New York: Carol Southern Books, 1993.

Mellick, Jill, and Marion Woodman. *The Art of Dreaming: A Creativity Toolbox for Dreamwork.* Berkeley: Conari Press, 2001.

Cross-Cultural Approaches to Dreamwork

Bulkeley, Kelly. *Spiritual Dreaming: A Cross-Cultural and Historical Journey.* Mahwah, NJ: Paulist Press, 1995.

Tedlock, Barbara, ed. *Dreaming: Anthropological and Psychological Interpretations.* Santa Fe, NM: SAR Press, 1992.

Divorce and Separation

Ahrons, Constance. *The Good Divorce: Keeping Your Family Together When Your Marriage Falls Apart.* New York: HarperPerennial, 1996.

Hetherington, Mavis, and John Kelly. *For Better or For Worse: Divorce Reconsidered.* New York: Norton, 2002.

Wallerstein, Judith, Julia Lewis, and Sandra Blakslee. *The Unexpected Legacy of Divorce: The 25 Year Landmark Study.* New York: Hyperion, 2000.

Exploring Your Dreams

DreamTime—The Magazine of the Association for the Study of Dreams. www.asdreams.org/dreamtime.

Jung, C. G. *Man and His Symbols.* New York: Dell, 1964.

Krippner, Stanley, and Mark Waldman, eds. *Dreamscaping: New and Creative Ways to Work with Your Dreams.* Los Angeles: Lowell House, 1999.

Taylor, Jeremy. *Where People Fly and Water Runs Uphill: Using Dreams to Tap the Wisdom of the Unconscious.* New York: Warner Books, 1992.

Ullman, Montague, and Claire Limmer. *The Variety of Dream Experience: Expanding Our Ways of Working with Dreams.* New York: Continuum, 1979.

Grief, Mourning, Death, and Dying

Coryell, Deborah Morris. *Good Grief: Healing through the Shadow of Loss.* Santa Fe, NM: Shiva Foundation, 1997.

Garfield, Patricia. *The Dream Messenger: How Dreams of the Departed Bring Healing Gifts.* New York: Simon and Shuster, 1997.

Noel, Brook, and Pamela Blair. *I Wasn't Ready to Say Goodbye: Surviving, Coping and Healing after the Sudden Death of a Loved One.* New York: Champion, 2000.

von Franz, Marie-Louise. *On Dreams and Death.* Boston: Shambala, 1987.

Illness and Dreams

Garfield, Patricia. *The Healing Power of Dreams.* New York: Fireside, 1991.

Siegel, Bernie. *Peace, Love and Healing: Bodymind Communication and the Path to Self-Healing.* New York: Harper and Row, 1989.

Life Passages and Midlife

Brehony, Kathleen. *Awakening at Midlife.* New York: Riverhead Books, 1996.

Bridges, William. *Transitions: Making Sense of Life's Changes.* New York: Addison-Wesley, 1980.

Garfield, Patricia. *Women's Bodies, Women's Dreams.* New York: Ballantine, 1988.

Levinson, Daniel, et al. *The Seasons of a Man's Life.* New York: Ballantine, 1978.

Viorst, Judith. *Necessary Losses.* New York: Simon and Schuster, 1986.

Marriage and Relationships

Gottman, John, and Nan Silver. *The Seven Principles for Making Marriages Work.* New York: Three Rivers Press, 2000.

Wile, Daniel. *What to Do after the Honeymoon.* New York: John Wiley, 1988.

Novels with Dream-Oriented Themes

Lagerkvist, Par. *The Sybil.* New York: Vintage Books, 1958. (Nobel Prize-winning author's story about the ancient Greek dream incubation temples.)

LeGuin, Ursula. *The Lathe of Heaven.* New York: Avon, 1973. (Great science fiction book about a dream therapist working with a dreamer whose dreams change history. A popular PBS movie version is available on DVD.)

Nightmares

Hartmann, Ernest. *Dreams and Nightmare: A New Theory of Dreams.* New York: Basic Books, 1998.

Kellerman, Henry, ed. *The Nightmare: Psychological and Biological Foundations.* New York: Columbia University Press, 1987.

Pregnancy

Colman, Libby, and Arthur Colman. *Pregnancy: The Psychological Experience.* New York: Noonday, 1990.

Kitzinger, Sheila. *The Complete Book of Pregnancy and Childbirth.* New York: Knopf, 1996.

Shapiro, Jerrold. *When Men Are Pregnant.* San Luis Obispo, CA: Impact Publishers, 1987.

Siegel, Alan. *Pregnant Dreams: Developmental Processes in the Manifest Dreams of Expectant Fathers.* Ann Arbor, MI: University Microfilms International, 1983.

Psychotherapy and Dreams

Delaney, Gayle, ed. *New Directions in Dream Interpretation.* Albany, NY: SUNY Press, 1993.

Fosshage, James, and Clemens Loew. *Dream Interpretation: A Comparative Study, Revised Edition.* New York: PMA Publishing, 1987.

Hill, Clara. *Dream Work: The Royal Road to Self Discovery.* Washington, D.C.: American Psychological Association Press, 2003.

Jung, C. G. *Dreams.* Princeton, NJ: Bollingen, 1974.

Lansky, Melvin. *Essential Papers on Dreams*. New York: New York University Press, 1992.

Schwartz-Salant, Nathan, and Murray Stein. *Dreams in Analysis*. Wilmette, IL: Chiron, 1990.

Research and Theories of Dreams and Dreaming

Domhoff, G. William. *The Scientific Study of Dreams*. Washington: American Psychological Association Press, 2003.

Jones, Richard. *The New Psychology of Dreaming*. New York: Grune and Stratton, 1970.

Moffitt, Alan, Milton Kramer, and Robert Hoffman, eds. *The Functions of Dreaming*. Albany, NY: SUNY Press, 1993.

Shafton, Anthony. *The Dream Reader: Contemporary Approaches to the Understanding of Dreams*. Albany, NY: SUNY Press, 1993.

Trauma and Dreams

Barrett, Deirdre. *Trauma and Dreams*. Cambridge, MA: Harvard University Press, 1996.

Cartwright, Rosalind, and Lynne Lamberg. *Crisis Dreaming: Using Your Dreams to Solve Your Problems*. New York: HarperCollins, 1992.

Herman, Judith. *Trauma and Recovery: The Aftermath of Violence—From Domestic Abuse to Political Terror*. New York: Basic Books, 1992.

Terr, Lenore. *Too Scared to Cry: How Trauma Affects Children and Ultimately Us All*. New York: Basic Books, 1990.

notes

Introduction

1. Alan Siegel, "Incubating My Inner Voice," *Sundance Community Dream Journal* 2, no. 1 (winter 1978).

2. Patricia Garfield, *Your Child's Dreams* (New York: Ballantine, 1984).

3. C. G. Jung, "On the Nature of Dreams," in *Dreams* (Princeton, NJ: Bollingen, 1974).

4. Joseph Campbell, *The Power of Myth* (New York: Doubleday, 1988).

5. Mircea Eliade, *Myths, Dreams, and Mysteries* (New York: Harper and Row, 1967).

6. Raymond de Becker, *The Understanding of Dreams* (New York: Bell, 1968).

7. Stephen Larsen, *The Shaman's Doorway: Opening the Mythic Imagination to Contemporary Consciousness* (New York: Harper and Row, 1976).

8. Carl O'Nell. *Dreams, Culture, and the Individual* (Novato, CA: Chandler and Sharp, 1976).

9. Siegel, "Incubating My Inner Voice," 1978.

10. Alan Siegel, "Dreaming Together," *Sundance Community Dream Journal* 1, no. 2 (spring, 1977).

11. Montague Ullman and Claire Limmer, *The Variety of Dream Experience: Expanding Our Ways of Working with Dreams* (New York: Continuum, 1987).

12. Alan Siegel, "Dream Quest: A Wilderness Ritual," *Association for the Study of Dreams Newsletter* 2, no. 3 (September 1985): 1–5.

13. Alan Siegel, "Dreams of Firestorm Survivors," in *Trauma and Dreams,* ed. Deirdre Barrett (Cambridge, MA: Harvard University Press, 1996).

14. Alan Siegel and Kelly Bulkeley, *Dreamcatching: Every Parent's Guide to Exploring and Understanding Children's Dreams and Nightmares* (New York: Three Rivers Press, 1998).

15. Association for the Study of Dreams Website, www.asdreams.org/2002.

16. Richard Jones, *The New Psychology of Dreaming* (New York: Penguin, 1970).

17. Louis Breger, "The Manifest Dream and Its Latent Meanings," in *The Dream in Clinical Practice,* ed. Joseph Natterson (New York: Jason Aronson, 1980).

18. Patricia Garfield, *Creative Dreaming: Plan and Control Your Dreams to Develop Creativity, Overcome Fears, Solve Problems, and Create a Better Self* (New York: Fireside, 1995).

19. Ann Faraday, *The Dream Game* (New York: Harper and Row, 1975).

20. Deirdre Barrett, *The Committee of Sleep: How Artists, Scientists and Athletes Use Their Dreams for Creative Problem Solving* (New York: Crown Publishers, 2001).

1. The Wisdom of Dreams at Life's Transitions

1. Anthony Shafton, "REM, etc" in *Dream Reader: Contemporary Approaches to the Understanding of Dreams* (Albany, NY: SUNY Press, 1995).

2. Rosalind Cartwright, Howard Kravitz, Charmane Eastman, and Ellen Wood, "REM Latency and the Recovery from Depression: Getting Over Divorce," *American Journal of Psychiatry* 148 (1991): 1530–1535.

3. Milton Kramer, "The Selective Mood Regulatory Function of Dreaming: An Update and Revision" in *The Functions of Dreaming,* eds. Alan Moffitt, Milton Kramer, and Robert Hoffman (Albany NY: SUNY Press, 1993).

4. William Dement, M.D., interview. *The Power of Dreams,* Discovery Channel, 1994.

5. Erik Erikson, *Childhood and Society* (New York: Norton, 1950).

6. Daniel Levinson, "Toward a Conception of the Adult Life Course," in *Themes of Work and Love in Adulthood,* ed. Neil Smelser and Erik Erikson (Cambridge, MA: Harvard University Press, 1980).

7. Gail Sheehy, *Passages* (New York: Bantam, 1976).

8. Gail Sheehy, *New Passages: Mapping Your Life across Time* (New York: Ballantine, 1996).

9. Daniel Levinson, *The Seasons of a Man's Life* (New York: Ballantine, 1979).

10. William Bridges, *Transitions: Making Sense of Life's Changes* (New York: Addison-Wesley, 1980).

11. Judith Viorst, *Necessary Losses: The Loves, Illusions, Dependencies, and Impossible Expectations That All of Us Have to Give Up in Order to Grow* (New York: Simon and Schuster, 1986).

12. Alan Siegel, *Pregnant Dreams: Developmental Processes in the Manifest Dreams of Expectant Fathers* (Ann Arbor: Dissertation Abstracts International, 1983).

13. Robert Bosnak, *Dreaming with an AIDS Patient* (Boston: Shambala, 1989).

14. Marie-Louise von Franz, *On Dreams and Death* (Boston: Shambala, 1987).

15. Robert Littman, "The Dream in the Suicidal Situation," in *The Dream in Clinical Practice*, ed. Joseph Natterson (New York: Jason Aronson, 1980).

16. Deirdre Barrett, *Trauma and Dreams* (Cambridge, MA: Harvard University Press, 1995).

17. Siegel, *Pregnant Dreams* (1983).

18. Alan Siegel, "Pregnant Dreams: The Secret Life of the Expectant Father," in *The New Holistic Health Handbook,* ed. Shepherd Bliss (New York: Viking Penguin, 1985).

19. Siegel, *Pregnant Dreams* (1983).

20. Ernest Hartmann, *The Nightmare: The Psychology and Biology of Terrifying Dreams* (New York: Basic Books, 1984).

21. Robert Coles, "A Taste of Fears," introduction to *Nightmares and Human Conflict,* John Mack (Boston: Houghton, 1970).

22. Carolyn Winget and Frederic Kapp, "The Relationship of the Manifest Content of Dreams to the Duration of Childbirth in Primiparae," *Psychosomatic Medicine* 34, no. 2 (July/August 1972).

23. Cartwright, Kravitz, Eastman, and Wood, "REM Latency" (1991).

24. Louis Breger, et al., "The Effects of Stress on Dreams," *Psychological Issues* 7, no. 3, monograph 27 (1971): 106–123.

25. Ernest Hartman, *Dreams and Nightmares: The New Theory on the Origin and Meaning of Dreams* (New York: Plenum, 1998), 4–13.

26. Breger, et al., "The Effects of Stress on Dreams" (1971): 184–191.

27. Kramer, "The Selective Mood Regulatory Function of Dreaming" (1993), 187.

28. Ernest Hartmann, *Dreams and Nightmares* (1998), 15.

29. Anthony Shafton, *The Dream Reader: Contemporary Approaches to the Understanding of Dreams* (Albany, NY: SUNY, 1995): 11–48.

2. First Dreams

1. Anthony Shafton, *The Dream Reader: Contemporary Approaches to the Understanding of Dreams* (Albany, NY: SUNY, 1995), 15.

2. Harry Fiss, "The Royal Road to the Unconscious Revisited: A Signal Detection Model of Dream Function" in *The Functions of Dreaming,* eds. Alan Moffitt, et al. (Albany, NY: SUNY Press, 1993).

3. Sigmund Freud, *The Interpretation of Dreams* (New York: Avon, 1965).

4. Alan Siegel and Kelly Bulkeley, *Dreamcatching: Every Parent's Guide to Exploring and Understanding Children's Dreams and Nightmares* (New York: Three Rivers Press, 1998).

5. Ibid.

6. Ibid.

7. Ibid.

8. C. G. Jung, *Memories, Dreams, Reflections* (New York: Random House, 1961).

9. Naomi Epel, *Writers Dreaming* (New York: Carol Southern Books, 1993).

3. Relationship Dreams

1. Dale Westbrook, *Dreams and First Marriages at Midlife Transition* (Ann Arbor: University Microfilms International, 1989), 159.

2. Keith Bradsher, "Ditching Your Betrothed May Cost You," *The New York Times*, 20 March 1990.

3. Westbrook, *Dreams and First Marriages* (1989), 150.

4. Ibid., 145.

5. Patricia Garfield, *Women's Bodies, Women's Dreams* (New York: Ballantine, 1988), 140–141.

6. C. G. Jung, *Dreams* (Princeton, NJ: Bollingen, 1974), 72.

7. Edward Whitmont and Sylvia Perera, *Dreams: A Portal to the Source* (London: Routledge, 1989), 25.

8. Westbrook, *Dreams and First Marriages* (1989), 130.

9. Ibid., 131.

10. Ibid., 132.

11. Ibid., 126.

12. Ibid., 142.

4. From Conception to Birth

1. Sigmund Freud, *The Interpretation of Dreams* (New York: Avon, 1965), 437.

2. Ibid.

3. Alan Siegel, "Pregnant Dreams: The Secret Life of the Expectant Father," in *The New Holistic Health Handbook,* ed. Shepherd Bliss (Lexington, Massachusetts: Stephen Green Press, 1985).

4. Carolyn Winget and Frederic Kapp, "The Relationship of the Manifest Content of Dreams to the Duration of Childbirth in Primiparae," *Psychosomatic Medicine* 34, no. 2 (July/August 1972).

5. Siegel, "Pregnant Dreams: The Secret Life of the Expectant Father" (1985).

6. Myra Leifer, *The Psychological Effects of Motherhood: A Study of First Pregnancy* (New York: Praeger, 1980), 78.

7. Libby Lee Colman and Arthur D. Colman, *Pregnancy: The Psychological Experience* (New York: Noonday, 1990).

8. Robert Gillman, "The Dreams of Pregnant Women and Maternal Adaptation," *American Journal of Orthopsychiatry* 38 (1968): 688–692.

9. Alan Siegel, *Pregnant Dreams: Developmental Processes in the Manifest Dreams of Expectant Fathers* (Ann Arbor: Dissertation Abstracts International, 1983).

10. Patricia Maybruck, "An Exploratory Study of the Dreams of Pregnant Women," (Ph.D. diss., Saybrook Institute, San Francisco, 1986.)

11. Eileen Stukane, *The Dream Worlds of Pregnancy* (New York: Quill, 1985), 47–49.

12. Colman and Colman, *Pregnancy: The Psychological Experience* (1990).

13. Gillman, "The Dreams of Pregnant Women" (1968).

14. Eileen Stukane, *The Dream Worlds of Pregnancy* (1985), 74–78.

15. Patricia Garfield, *Women's Bodies, Women's Dreams* (New York: Ballantine, 1988), 192.

16. Gillman, "The Dreams of Pregnant Women" (1968).

17. Colman and Colman, *Pregnancy: The Psychological Experience* (1990).

18. Siegel, *Pregnant Dreams: Developmental Processes* (1983).

19. Ray Lacoursiere, "Fatherhood and Mental Illness: A Review and New Material," *Psychiatric Quarterly* 46, no. 1 (1972): 109–124.

20. Joy Lewis, "Fathers-to-Be Show Signs of Pregnancy," *The New York Times,* 2 April 1985.

21. Jacqueline Clinton, "Expectant Fathers at Risk for Couvade," *Nursing Research* 35, no. 5 (September/October 1986): 290–295.

22. W. Trethowan, "The Couvade Syndrome," in *Modern Perspectives in Psycho-Obstetrics,* ed. J. Howells (New York: Bruner/Mazel, 1972).

23. Sam Bittman and Sue Zalk, *Expectant Fathers* (New York: Ballantine, 1980), 10–14.

24. James Herzog, "Patterns of Expectant Fatherhood," *Dialogue: A Journal of Psychoanalytic Perspectives* (Summer 1979).

25. Elizabeth Bing and Libby Colman, *Making Love during Pregnancy* (New York: Noonday, 1989). See also Jerold Shapiro, *When Men Are Pregnant: Needs and Concerns of Expectant Fathers* (San Luis Obispo, CA: Impact, 1987).

5. Separation and Divorce Dreams

1. Mavis Hetherington and John Kelly, *For Better or For Worse: Divorce Reconsidered* (New York: Norton, 2002), 273.

2. Joy Rice and David Rice, *Living through Divorce: A Developmental Approach to Divorce Therapy* (New York: Guilford, 1986), 21.

3. Ibid.

4. Judith Wallerstein and Sandra Blakeslee, *Second Chances: Men, Women and Children a Decade after Divorce* (New York: Ticknor and Fields, 1989).

5. Mavis Hetherington and John Kelly, *For Better or For Worse: Divorce Reconsidered* (New York: Norton, 2002), 274.

6. Rice and Rice, *Living through Divorce* (1986), 22.

7. Rosalind Cartwright, "Who Needs Their Dreams? The Usefulness of Dreams in Psychotherapy," *American Journal of Psychoanalysis* 21, no. 4 (1993): 539–547.

8. Rosalind Cartwright, "Dreams and Adaptation to Divorce," in *Trauma and Dreams,* ed. Deirdre Barrett (Cambridge: Harvard University Press, 1996).

9. Rosalind Cartwright, "Dreams and Divorce" (paper presented at the Association for the Study of Dreams Conference, London, June 1989).

10. Rosalind Cartwright, "Who Needs Their Dreams?" (1993).

11. Rosalind Cartwright, "Role of REM Sleep and Dream Variables in the Remission from Depression," *American Journal of Psychiatry* 148, no. 11 (1991): 1530–1535.

12. Michael Bears, Rosalind Cartwright, and Patricia Mercer, "Masochistic Dreams: A Gender-Related Diathesis for Depression Revisited," *Dreaming: Journal of the Association of the Study of Dreams* 10, no. 4 (2000): 211–220.

13. Irene Trenholme, Rosalind Cartwright, and Glen Greenberg, "Dream Dimension Differences during a Life Change," *Psychiatry Research* 12 (1976): 35–45.

14. Rice and Rice, *Living through Divorce* (1986), 66.

15. Judith Wallerstein, Julia Lewis, and Sandra Blakeslee, *The Unexpected Legacy of Divorce: The 25 Year Landmark Study* (New York: Hyperion, 2000).

16. Mavis Hetherington and John Kelly, *For Better or For Worse: Divorce Reconsidered* (New York: Norton, 2002).

17. Alan Siegel and Kelly Bulkeley, *Dreamcatching: Every Parent's Guide to Exploring and Understanding Children's Dreams and Nightmares* (New York: Three Rivers Press, 1998).

18. Ibid.

19. Ibid.

20. Ibid.

6. Work Dreams

1. Samuel Osipow, "Career Issues through the Life Span," in *Psychology and Work: Productivity, Change and Employment,* eds. M. Pallak and R. Perloff (Washington, D.C.: American Psychological Association, 1986).

2. Lisa Grunwald, "Is It Time to Get Out?" *Esquire* (April 1990), 130–141.

3. Susan Knapp, "Teaching the Use of the Dream in Clinical Practice," in *The Variety of Dream Experience: Expanding Our Ways of Working with Dreams,* eds. Montague Ullman and Claire Limmer (New York: Continuum, 1987).

4. Joseph Campbell, *The Power of Myth* (New York: Doubleday, 1988), 229.

7. Midlife Dreams

1. Daniel Levinson, et al., *The Seasons of Man's Life* (New York: Ballantine, 1978).

2. Janet Giele, "Adulthood As Transcendence of Age and Sex," in *Themes of Work and Love in Adulthood,* eds. Neil Smelser and Erik Erikson (Cambridge, MA: Harvard University Press, 1980).

3. C. G. Jung, *Memories, Dreams, Reflections* (New York: Random House, 1961), 195.

4. Murray Stein, *In Midlife* (Dallas: Spring Publications, 1983), 7–22.

5. Levinson, *The Seasons of Man's Life* (1978), 191–259

6. Samuel Osherson, *Finding Our Fathers: How a Man's Life Is Shaped by His Relationship with His Father* (New York: Ballantine, 1986).

7. Levinson, *The Seasons of Man's Life* (1978), 197.

8. Christine Downing, *Journey through Menopause: A Personal Rite of Passage* (New York: Crossroad, 1989).

9. Ann Mankowitz, *Change of Life: A Psychological Study of Dreams and the Menopause* (Toronto: Inner City, 1984).

10. Downing, *Journey through Menopause* (1989), 21–54.

11. Ibid., 21–54.

12. Mankowitz, *Change of Life* (1984), 34.

13. Jung, *Memories, Dreams, Reflections* (1961), 223–224.

8. Posttraumatic Nightmares

1. Ernest Hartmann, *The Nightmare: The Psychology and Biology of Terrifying Dreams* (New York: Basic Books, 1984), 214–219.

2. *DSM-IV. Diagnostic and Statistical Manual of Mental Disorders,* rev. 4th ed. (Washington, D.C.: American Psychiatric Association, 1994), 424–429.

3. Lewis Engel and Tom Ferguson, *Imaginary Crimes: Why We Punish Ourselves and How to Stop* (Boston: Houghton-Mifflin, 1990).

4. Patricia Adler, *Fire in the Hills: A Collective Remembrance* (Berkeley: Patricia Adler, 1992).

5. Alan Siegel, "Dreams of Firestorm Survivors," in *Trauma and Dreams,* ed. Deirdre Barrett (Cambridge, MA: Harvard University Press, 1996).

6. Robin Gihvan, "Studying Dreams from the East Bay Inferno," *San Francisco Chronicle,* 1 July 1992.

7. Laura Myers and Associated Press, "Nightmares Still Plague Survivors," *Oakland Tribune,* 25 June 2002

8. "Firestorm Survivors Still Have Nightmares" *CNN Headline News,* 25 June 1992.

9. Anneli Rufus, "Interpreting Dreams of Fire," *East Bay (California) Express,* 26 June 1992.

10. G. William Domhoff, *Finding Meaning in Dreams: A Quantitative Approach* (New York: Plenum, 1996).

11. To control for the length and quantity of dreams, the first five dreams containing between 25 and 300 words were used for quantitative content analysis measurements. The content analysis compared 215 fire survivors' dreams with 70 fire evacuees' dreams and 90 dreams of the control group.

12. For the fire evacuees, five other dream themes showed trends toward significance. These included separation anxiety, damaged body parts, events out of control, father, and familiar persons.

13. Brooks Brenneis, "Theoretical Notes on the Manifest Dream," *International Journal of Psychoanalysis* 56, no. 197 (1975): 197–206.

14. Alan Siegel, "Dreams of Firestorm Survivors". The "Fire Seed" dream was unusually clear in its manifest representation of survivor guilt and punishment. Other subjects judged as suffering from survivor guilt did not have easily identifiable guilt and punishment themes in their manifest content.

15. Ibid.

16. Ibid.

17. Ibid.

18. Ibid.

19. Ibid.

20. Hartmann, *The Nightmare* (1984), 192.

21. Will Lester, "New Yorkers Affected by September 11," *Associated Press,* 18 May 2002.

22. Matt Lauer, "Traumatic Dreams Due to World Trade Center Attacks. Is It Normal? What Can We Do to Assuage These Traumatic Nighttime Episodes?" interview by Alan Siegel, *NBC Today Show,* 9 October 2001.

23. Judith Herman, *Trauma and Recovery: The Aftermath of Violence—From Domestic Abuse to Political Terror* (New York: Basic Books, 1992), 155.

24. Ibid., 62.

25. Barry Krakow, "An Open-Label Trial of Evidence-Based Cognitive Behavior Therapy for Nightmares and Insomnia in Crime Victims with PTSD," *American Journal of Psychiatry* 158, (2001): 2043–2047.

26. Karen Hagerman Muller, "Jasmine: Dreams in the Psychotherapy of a Rape Survivor," in *Trauma and Dreams,* ed. Deirdre Barrett (Cambridge, MA: Harvard University Press, 1996).

27. Marquis Wallace and Howard Parad, "The Dream in Brief Psychotherapy," in *The Dream in Clinical Practice,* ed. Joseph Natterson (New York: Jason Aronson, 1980).

28. Ibid., 418–419.

29. Ibid., 422.

30. Mardi Horowitz, *Stress Response Syndromes* (New York: Jason Aronson, 1976).

31. Harry Wilmer, "Combat Nightmares: Toward a Theory of Violence," *Spring Journal* (1986), 122.

32. Ibid., 126.

33. Ibid.

34. Hartmann, *The Nightmare* (1984), 192–195.

35. Wilmer, "Combat Nightmares" (1986), 131.

36. Adrianne Aron, "The Collective Nightmare of Salvadoran Refugees," in *Trauma and Dreams,* ed. Deirdre Barrett (Cambridge, MA: Harvard University Press, 1996), 140.

37. Ibid.

38. Adrianne Aron, personal communication with author, July 1990.

9. Healing Dreams

1. Meredith Sabini, "Dreams As an Aid in Determining Diagnosis, Prognosis, and Attitude towards Treatment," *Psychotherapy and Psychosomatics* 36 (1981): 24–36.

2. Robert Bosnak, *Dreaming with an AIDS Patient* (Boston: Shambala, 1989).

3. Jane Hawes, Ph.D., personal communication with author, July 1990.

4. *Webster's New Twentieth Century Dictionary of the English Language Unabridged.*

5. Eileen Stukane, *The Dream Worlds of Pregnancy* (New York: Quill, 1985), 37.

6. Robert Smith, "Do Dreams Reflect a Biological State?" *Journal of Nervous and Mental Disease* 175, no. 4 (1987).

7. Sabini, "Dreams As an Aid," (1981): 26.

8. Bernie Siegel, *Peace, Love and Healing: Bodymind Communication and the Path to Self-Healing; An Exploration* (New York: Harper and Row, 1990), 64–73.

9. C. G. Jung, "The Practical Use of Dream Analysis," in *Dreams* (Princeton, NJ: Bollingen, 1974), 106–109.

10. Marie-Louise von Franz, *On Dreams and Death* (Boston: Shambala, 1987), 19–20.

11. Jackson Lincoln, *The Dream in Primitive Cultures* (Baltimore, MD: Williams and Watkins, 1935).

12. John Spaulding, "The Dream in Other Cultures: Anthropological Studies of Dreams and Dreaming," *Dream Works* 1, no. 4 (summer 1981).

13. Carl O'Nell, *Dreams, Culture, and the Individual* (Novato, CA: Chandler and Sharp, 1976).

14. James Kirsch, "The Role of Instinct in Psychosomatic Medicine," *American Journal of Psychotherapy* 3 (1949): 253.

15. Meredith Sabini and Valerie Maffly, "An Inner View of Illness," *Journal of Analytic Psychology* 26 (1981): 123.

16. Harold Levitan, "The Dream in Psychosomatic States," in *The Dream in Clinical Practice,* ed. Joseph Natterson (New York: Jason Aronson, 1980).

17. Harold Levitan, "The Functions of Dreaming," Audio Digest Psychiatry Tapes (Glendale, CA: Audio-Digest Foundation, vol. 11, no. 24, 1982).

18. John Prendergast, *Dreams by People with Life-Threatening Illness* (Ann Arbor, MI: University Microfilms International, 1986).

19. Selma Hyman, "Death-in-Life—Life-in-Death: Spontaneous Process in a Cancer Patient," *Spring Journal* (1978): 27–41.

20. Marie-Louise von Franz, *C. G. Jung: His Myth in Our Time* (New York: Putnam), 287.

21. Prendergast, *Dreams by People with Life-Threatening Illness* (1986).

22. John Sanford, *Dreams: God's Forgotten Language* (New York: Lippincott, 1968), 60.

23. von Franz, *On Dreams and Death* (1987), 146.

24. Prendergast, *Dreams by People with Life-Threatening Illness* (1986).

10. Grief Dreams

1. Carl O'Nell, *Dreams, Culture, and the Individual* (Novato, CA: Chandler and Sharp, 1976).

2. Srisakul Kliks, Ph.D., personal communication with author, June 1990.

3. Hans Mauksch, "The Organizational Context of Dying," in *Death: The Final Stage of Growth,* ed. Elisabeth Kübler-Ross (Englewood Cliffs, NJ: Prentice Hall, 1975).

4. Joy Rice and David Rice, *Living through Divorce: A Developmental Approach to Divorce Therapy* (New York: Guilford, 1986).

5. Patricia Garfield, *The Dream Messenger: How Dreams of the Departed Bring Healing Gifts* (New York: Simon and Shuster, 1997).

6. Ibid.

7. Alan Siegel and Kelly Bulkeley, *Dreamcatching: Every Parent's Guide to Exploring and Understanding Children's Dreams and Nightmares* (New York: Three Rivers Press, 1998).

8. Garfield, *The Dream Messenger* (1997).

9. Siegel and Bulkeley, *Dreamcatching* (1998).

10. Judith Savage, *Mourning Unlived Lives: A Psychological Study of Childbearing Loss* (Wilmette, IL: Chiron, 1989).

11. Marshall Klaus and John Kennell, "Caring for Parents of an Infant Who Dies," in *Maternal Infant Bonding: The Impact of Early Separation or Loss on Family Development* (St. Louis: C. V. Mosby, 1976).

12. Savage, *Mourning Unlived Lives* (1989).

13. Klaus and Kennell, "Caring for Parents" (1976).

14. Sigmund Freud, *The Interpretation of Dreams* (New York: Avon, 1965).

15. Ann Faraday, "Death and the Dreamer," in *The Dream Game* (New York: Harper and Row, 1974).

16. Calvin Hall, *The Meaning of Dreams* (New York: McGraw-Hill, 1966).

17. Faraday, "Death and the Dreamer" (1974).

18. Garfield, *The Dream Messenger* (1997), 215–216

19. Naomi Epel, *Writers Dreaming* (New York: Carol Southern Books, 1993).

11. Perspectives on Dream Interpretation

1. Sigmund Freud, *The Interpretation of Dreams* (New York: Avon, 1965).

2. C.G. Jung, *Memories, Dreams, Reflections* (New York: Random House, 1961).

3. Ann Faraday, *The Dream Game* (New York: Harper and Row, 1974).

4. James Hillman, *The Dream and the Underworld* (New York: Harper and Row, 1975), 122–123.

5. James Hillman, "An Inquiry into Image," *Spring Journal* (1978): 62–88.

6. Mary Ann Mattoon, *Understanding Dreams* (Dallas: Spring Publishing, 1984).

7. Richard Jones, *The New Psychology of Dreams* (New York: Grune and Stratton, 1970).

8. Melvin Lansky, ed., *Essential Papers on Dreams* (New York: New York University Press, 1992).

9. Louis Breger, "The Manifest Dream and Its Latent Meanings," in *The Dream in Clinical Practice,* ed. Joseph Natterson (New York: Aronson, 1980).

10. James Fosshage and Clemens Loew, *Dream Interpretation: A Comparative Study,* rev. ed. (New York: PMA, 1987).

11. Harry Fiss, "The Royal Road to the Unconscious Revisited: A Signal Detection Model of Dream Function," in *The Function of Dreams* (Albany, NY: SUNY Press, 1995).

12. Jolande Jacobi, ed., *C. G. Jung: Psychological Reflections* (New York: Harper, 1961).

13. Mary Ann Mattoon, *Understanding Dreams* (Dallas: Spring, 1984).

14. Alvin Maher, *Dreamwork in Psychotherapy and Self-Change* (New York: Norton, 1989).

15. G. William Domhoff, *Finding Meaning in Dreams: A Quantitative Approach* (New York: Plenum, 1996).

16. *Dreaming: Journal of the Association for the Study of Dreams.*

17. Clara Hill, *Working with Dreams in Psychotherapy* (New York: Guilford, 1996).

18. Shafton, *The Dream Reader* (1995).

19. Levinson, Daniel, "Toward a Conception of the Adult Life Cycle," in *Themes of Work and Love in Adulthood,* ed. Neil Smelser and Erik Erikson (Cambridge, MA: Harvard University Press, 1980).

20. Harry Fiss, "Current Dream Research: A Psychobiological Perspective," in *Handbook of Dreams: Research, Theories, and Applications,* ed. Benjamin Wolman (New York: Van Nostrand Rheinhold, 1979).

21. Rosalind Cartwright, et al., "Focusing on Dreams: A Preparation Program for Psychotherapy," *Archives of General Psychiatry* 37 (March 1980): 275–277.

22. Stanley Krippner, *Dreamscaping: New and Creative Ways to Work with Your Dreams* (Los Angeles: Roxbury Park, 1999).

23. Montague Ullman and Claire Limmer, *The Variety of Dream Experience: Expanding Our Ways of Working with Dreams* (New York: Continuum, 1988).

24. Ibid.

25. Ibid.

26. Douglas Armstrong, "Factors Affecting the Use of Dreams in Psychotherapy: Professional and Personal Factors," *Dream Time: Magazine of the Association for the Study of Dreams* 13, no. 4 (winter 1997).

27. "Questions and Answers about Memories of Abuse," *American Psychological Association Website,* www.apa.org/pubinfo/mem.html.

28. Samuel Knapp and Leon VandeCreek, *Treating Patients with Memories of Abuse* (Washington: American Psychological Association Press, 1997).

29. Mattoon, *Understanding Dreams* (1984), 173.

30. Roy Whitman, "Termination Dreams," in *The Dream in Clinical Practice* (New York: Aronson, 1980).

12. A Practical Guide to Exploring Your Dreams and Nightmares

1. Alan Siegel, "Dreams: The Mystery That Heals," in *The New Holistic Health Handbook: Living Well in a New Age,* ed. Shepherd Bliss (Lexington, MA: Stephen Greene Press, 1985), 95–101.

2. Anthony Shafton, *The Dream Reader: Contemporary Approaches to the Understanding of Dreams* (Albany, NY: SUNY Press, 1998), 15.

3. Alan Siegel and Kelly Bulkeley, *Dreamcatching: Every Parent's Guide to Exploring and Understanding Children's Dreams and Nightmares* (New York: Three Rivers Press, 1998).

4. Alan Siegel, "Dreams: The Mystery That Heals," in *The New Holistic Health Handbook: Living Well in a New Age,* ed. Shepherd Bliss (Lexington, MA: Stephen Greene Press, 1985).

5. Patricia Garfield, *The Universal Dream Key: The 12 Most Common Dream Themes around the World* (New York: Harper Perennial, 2001).

6. G. William Domhoff, "Personal Dream Histories: Their Theoretical and Practical Relevance" (Unpublished paper, Department of Psychology, University of California, Santa Cruz, 1993).

7. G. William Domhoff, "The Repetition of Dreams and Dream Elements: A Possible Clue to the Function of Dreams," in *The Functions of Dreaming,* ed. Alan Moffitt, et al. (Albany, NY: SUNY, 1993).

8. Alan Siegel and Kelly Bulkeley, *Dreamcatching: Every Parent's Guide to Exploring and Understanding Children's Dreams and Nightmares* (New York: Three Rivers Press, 1998), 80–91.

9. Gordon Halliday, "Treating Nightmares in Children," in *Clinical Handbook of Sleep Disorders in Children,* ed. Charles Schaeffer (New York: Aronson, 1995).

10. Rosalind Cartwright and Lynne Lamberg, *Crisis Dreaming: Using Dreams to Solve Your Problems* (New York: Harper Collins, 1992).

11. Clara Hill, *Working with Dreams in Psychotherapy* (New York: Guilford, 1996).

12. Henry Reed, "Dream Incubation: A Reconstruction of a Ritual in Contemporary Form," *Journal of Humanistic Psychology* 16, no. 4 (1976): 53–70.

13. Henry Reed, *Getting Help from Your Dreams* (Virginia Beach, VA: Inner Vision, 1985).

14. Deirdre Barrett, *The Committee of Sleep: How Artists, Scientists and Athletes Use Their Dreams for Creative Problem-Solving—And How You Can Too* (New York: Crown Publishers, 2001).

15. Alan Siegel, *Pregnant Dreams: Developmental Processes in the Manifest Dreams of Expectant Fathers* (Ann Arbor: University Microfilms International, 1983).

16. Siegel and Bulkeley, *Dreamcatching* (1998).

reader feedback

You are invited to visit the *Dream Wisdom* website, www.dreamwisdom.info. On the website, you can:

- give me feedback on your responses to this book
- participate online in research that I am conducting on memorable dreams, universal dreams, and dreams and nightmares during life's crises and turning points
- receive updates for the dream wisdom journal and workbook that will help you organize your personal dream wisdom journal, dream and nightmare history, dream glossary, and two-week dream journal program
- learn about links to other online articles, resources, events, and websites related to dreams and nightmares
- connect to the Association for the Study of Dreams educational website and their bulletin board, conferences, and publications
- purchase additional copies of *Dream Wisdom* and other dream-related publications

You can reach me at
Alan Siegel, Ph.D., P.O. Box 9332, Berkeley, CA 94709-0332
or log on to my website, www.dreamwisdom.info
or email me at feedback@dreamwisdom.info.

DReam tHeme INDeX

INDeX

Kaislestown (Frau Laternback Imolady)
Germany 1969
Judge manlstrate
Married 9 Am + 1:00 pm

Father
William W. Williams

Johnny White 5-29-75

Vicki White · 7/22/71

John White Jr. 5/21/48

Barbara passed Ap 75 - 3/5/196
2017 ← Emans Ga

Mom passed 1996

Dad passed 1971
3 month pregnant
with Vicki

Michael Reda   melbourne
Michael Louis Reda
Titusville fl. · Pittsburg florida
                          PA-